I THOUGHT IT WAS JUST ME

I THOUGHT IT WAS JUST ME

Women Reclaiming
Power and Courage in a
Culture of Shame

Brené Brown

GOTHAM BOOKS

GOTHAM BOOKS
Published by Penguin Group (USA) Inc.
375 Hudson Street, New York, New York 10014, U.S.A.
Penguin Group (Canada), 90 Eglinton Avenue East, Suite 700, Toronto, Ontario M4P
2Y3, Canada (a division of Pearson Penguin Canada Inc.); Penguin Books Ltd, 80 Strand,
London WC2R 0RL, England; Penguin Ireland, 25 St Stephen's Green, Dublin 2, Ireland
(a division of Penguin Books Ltd); Penguin Group (Australia), 250 Camberwell Road,
Camberwell, Victoria 3124, Australia (a division of Pearson Australia Group Pty Ltd);
Penguin Books India Pvt Ltd, 11 Community Centre, Panchsheel Park, New Delhi–110 017,
India; Penguin Group (NZ), cnr Airborne and Rosedale Roads, Albany, Auckland 1310,
New Zealand (a division of Pearson New Zealand Ltd); Penguin Books (South Africa)
(Pty) Ltd, 24 Sturdee Avenue, Rosebank, Johannesburg 2196, South Africa

Penguin Books Ltd, Registered Offices: 80 Strand, London WC2R 0RL, England

Published by Gotham Books, a division of Penguin Group (USA) Inc.

First printing, February 2007
10 9 8 7 6 5 4 3 2 1

LIBRARY OF CONGRESS CATALOGING-IN-PUBLICATION DATA
Brown, C. Brené
    I thought it was just me : women reclaiming power and courage in a culture of shame /
Brené Brown.
    p. cm.
    ISBN-13: 978-1-592-40263-2 (hardcover)
    1. Women—Psychology.   2. Shame.   I. Title.
HQ1206.B765 2007
152.4'4082—dc22   2006026945

Printed in the United States of America
Set in Janson • Designed by Elke Sigal

FOR THE WOMEN WHO INSPIRE ME

my mom
my sisters
my daughter
my friends
my teachers
my students
my sister social workers
the artists and activists
the researchers and writers
the women who shared their stories to make this work possible

CONTENTS

ACKNOWLEDGMENTS

Writing this book has fundamentally changed my life. Every time it became too hard, I thought about the research participants who contributed to this book and to my understanding of shame. They courageously shared their experiences based only on their faith in my promise to be honest and accurate with their stories. Each and every one willingly embraced their fears in order for us to learn. I cannot thank them enough. I sincerely hope they find that this book honors the spirit of their contributions, their work and their wisdom.

In addition to the women who shared their stories with me, I owe an extraordinary debt to the people who both personally and professionally supported me through this process and helped me bring this work to life. Personally, I could not have done this without the love, support and courage of my husband, Steve. I was absolutely sustained by his faith in my ability, his respect for my work and his commitment to our family. I'm equally grateful for what a wonderful father he is and for his ability to make me laugh.

My children, Ellen and Charlie, fill my life with love and

laughter. They inspire me, keep me grounded and make it very difficult for me to take myself too seriously.

In many different ways, this work would not be possible without my parents. Their greatest gifts have been what they have taught me and continue to teach me. From my mother, Deanne Rogers, I've learned about courage, strength and perseverance. Chuck Brown, my father, gave me the gifts of critical thinking, debate and activism. These lessons helped me realize my dream of finishing my Ph.D. and writing this book. To my mother's partner David and my dad's partner Molly, I thank you for your willingness to embrace our family and share your lives with us. I also want to acknowledge my grandmother, Ellen, who was also an inspiration to me. I try to carry her spirit and kindness with me.

To my brother, Jason, and my sisters, Ashley and Barrett, we are on a special journey together and I'm so grateful to be sharing it with you. Our history, love and laughter are important forces in my life. To Mike, Ashley's husband, and Amaya, my beautiful niece, thank you for bringing so much joy to our family. To Audrey, Jason's wife, we're glad you're here—you've always felt like family.

When I married Steve I inherited a wonderful family. To Corky and Jack, Bill and Jacobina, Memo, Bebo and David, it is impossible for me to think of my life without you—you are my family.

I have had the extraordinary fortune of working with people who are both colleagues and good friends. I am forever indebted to my dear friend, Charles Kiley, who has generously walked every step of this journey with me. I couldn't have done it without him. I also owe special thanks to my friends, colleagues and sister social workers, Dawn Fey Hedgepeth, Cheryl Dunn and Beverly McPhail. Their willingness to share their expertise and experiences contributed greatly to this book. I want to thank illustrator David Robinson and graphic designer Doni Hieronymus, for their artistic contributions. I also want to acknowledge Cole Schweikhardt of Squidz Ink Design and Daniel Levine and Marian Mankin of DMLCo for their support and help with my Web site.

I am so lucky to be surrounded by wonderful friends and mentors. I wish there was some way, beyond a simple thank you, to let the following women know how much they've touched my life: Angela Blanchard, Margarita Flores, Karen Holmes, Jean Latting, Ann McFarland, Barb Nowak, Susan Robbins, Ruth Rubio, Karen Stout, Susan Turell, Jody Williams and Laura Williams.

I am also fortunate to be affiliated with two outstanding organizations. First, I want to thank the faculty, staff and students at the University of Houston Graduate College of Social Work. It is a true privilege to be a social worker and part of this learning community. Second, I want to acknowledge the Nobel Women's Initiative. I am grateful for the opportunity to work with such wise and wonderful activists, scholars and peace-builders.

There is a third group of activists and scholars I'd like to thank—a group of women who have changed the way I look at myself and at the world. My mother gave me a copy of Harriet Lerner's book, *The Dance of Anger*, when I was in my early twenties. It was my first nonfiction psychology book. I remember reading it and thinking, "I'm not alone!" By the third chapter, I had fallen in love with the power of books. When I started teaching, I carried bell hooks's book, *Teaching to Transgress*, with me at all times. Jean Kilbourne's book, *Can't Buy My Love*, forever changed the way I watch TV, read magazines and listen to music. I turned to the Stone Center at Wellesley to better understand who I wanted to be in the context of my social work career. I still buy Mary Pipher's book *Reviving Ophelia* for all of my friends with daughters, and her new book, *Writing to Change the World*, is required reading for my students. The list of authors who have changed my life is endless; however, these powerful women have certainly made the greatest impression. I thank them for making this a better world and for forging the path for what has now become my career.

Last, I want to thank the people who believed enough in this work to turn it into a book—something I don't take for granted. I extend a heartfelt thanks to my agent, Stephanie von Hirschberg, for lending her wisdom, integrity and sense of balance to this process. To my editor, Erin Moore, I feel so fortunate to work with a woman who embodies the authenticity, courage and compassion I write about in my book—thank you. I also want to recognize the other team members at Gotham Books—Bill Shinker, Jessica Sindler, Lisa Johnson, Ashwini Ramaswamy and the great folks behind the scenes who turned my dangling modifiers into coherent sentences and my crumpled pages into a beautiful book.

INTRODUCTION

When people hear the word *shame*, they often have one of two responses: "I'm not sure what you mean by shame, but I know that I don't want to talk about it," or "Oh, shame. I know it well, but I don't want to talk about it." As a shame researcher, I understand our reluctance to talk about it—shame is so powerful that we sometimes feel shame just talking about shame. But after spending six years interviewing hundreds of women about their lives, here's what I've learned: We all experience shame. It is an absolutely universal emotion.

The less we understand shame and how it affects our feelings, thoughts and behaviors, the more power it exerts over our lives. However, if we can find the courage to talk about shame and the compassion to listen, we can change the way we live, love, parent, work and build relationships.

People often want to believe that shame is reserved for the unfortunate few who have survived terrible traumas, but this is not true. Shame is something we all experience. And, while it feels like shame hides in our darkest corners, it actually tends to lurk in all of the familiar places, including appearance and body image, motherhood, family, parenting, money and work, mental and physical health, addiction, sex, aging and religion.

This book offers information, insight and specific strategies for understanding shame and building "shame resilience." We can never become completely *resistant* to shame; however, we can develop the *resilience* we need to recognize shame, move through it constructively and grow from our experiences. Across the interviews, women with high levels of shame resilience shared four things in common. I refer to these factors as the four elements of shame resilience. The four elements of shame resilience are the heart of this book. As we learn more about shame resilience and start to put the elements into practice, we can start to move through the by-products of shame—fear, blame and disconnection—and move toward the courage, compassion and connection we need to live our best, authentic lives.

I've dedicated my career to studying shame and its impact on women, men and children. In my study with women, I've had the opportunity to interview over three hundred participants of all ages, races, ethnicities and life situations. I've also gone back and reinterviewed sixty women who have applied some of the strategies in this book to learn what strategies have been effective and what barriers they've faced.

If you're not sure of shame's impact on our own life, it may help to read some quotes from my interviews. In these quotes, you can start to see the complex weaving of shame, fear and cultural expectations.

"Sex is such a big issue between me and my husband. Sometimes it's great. Other times, I'll start thinking about my body and how much it has changed in the past ten years. I start to feel panicked. I imagine him judging me against these ideals I have in my head. In these moments, I lose it. I'll pick a fight or do anything to escape and get my clothes back on."

"One day I was driving down the street in our neighborhood and I stopped next to a car full of young men at a light. They were looking over and smiling. I smiled back and even blushed a bit. Then out of nowhere, my fifteen-year-old daughter, who was sitting in the backseat with her best friend, snapped, 'Geeez, Mom, stop looking at them. What do you think—they're flirting with you? Get real!' I could barely hold the tears back. How could I have been so stupid?"

"When I look at myself in the mirror, sometimes I'm OK. But other times I just see fat and ugly. I get totally overwhelmed—like I can barely breathe. I get sick to my stomach and disgusted. I just want to hide in the house so no one sees me."

"I'm forty-one and I just went back to school to get my degree. Half of the time I don't know what they're talking about—I just sit there and nod my head like an idiot. I feel like a phony—like I'm not smart enough to be there. When these feelings come over me I want to just slip away . . . really, just grab my purse, slip out the back and never go back."

"My life looks pretty good on the outside. Nice husband, nice house, cute kids—the whole package. On the inside it's another story. If we didn't care so much about what other people think, we'd get a divorce. We barely talk to each other. Both of our kids struggle in school. We have to make these outrageous contributions to the school just to make sure they don't get kicked out. It's getting harder and harder to keep it all together. Every now and then I know my friends see glimpses of the truth—they have to. It literally makes me sick when I feel like they can see through it all."

"I constantly feel judged as a mother; like nothing I do is right or good enough. The worst is when other mothers put you down. One disapproving look from another mother can cut me to the core."

"I don't tell anyone about the things I've gone through—I don't want them to feel sorry for me or think differently about me. It's easier to keep my past to myself. Just thinking about being blamed or judged for my past causes me to lose my breath."

"No one knows how bad things are with my husband—they'd think less of him and less of me for staying with him. I'm constantly lying and making up stories to cover up. When I lie, I feel sneaky and ashamed."

Sound familiar? For most of us, the answer is yes. Shame is universal. To varying degrees, we all know the struggle to feel comfortable with who we are in a society that puts so much importance on being perfect and fitting in. We also know the painful wave of emotion that washes over us when we feel judged or ridiculed about the way we look, our work, our parenting, how we spend our money, our families or even the life experiences over which we had no control. And it's not always someone else putting us down or judging us; the most painful shaming experiences are often self-inflicted.

The constant struggle to feel accepted and worthy is unrelenting. We put so much of our time and energy into making sure that we meet everyone's expectations and into caring about what other people think of us, that we are often left feeling angry, resentful and fearful. Sometimes we turn these emotions inward and convince ourselves that we are bad and that maybe we deserve the rejection that we so desperately fear. Other times we lash out—we scream at our partners and children for no apparent reason, or we make a cutting comment to a friend or colleague. Either way, in the end, we are left feeling exhausted, overwhelmed and alone.

We spend an extraordinary amount of time and energy tackling the surface issues, which rarely results in meaningful, lasting change. When we dig past the surface, we find that shame is often what drives us to hate our bodies, fear rejection, stop taking risks or hide the experiences and parts of our lives that we fear others might judge. This same dynamic applies to feeling attacked as a mother or feeling too stupid or uneducated to voice our opinions.

Until we start addressing the role shame plays, we may temporarily fix some of the surface problems, but we can't silence the old tape in our head that suddenly blares some version of "something is wrong with me." For example, that imposter or phony feeling at work or school rarely has anything to do with our abilities, but has more to do with that fearful voice inside of us that scolds and asks, "Who do you think you are?" Shame forces us to put so much value on what other people think that we lose ourselves in the process of trying to meet everyone else's expectations.

Shame: The Silent Epidemic

When you spend years studying a topic like shame, it is easy to forget how much people dislike and fear the topic. My husband constantly reminds me not to take it personally when people make the "I just smelled something bad" face after I tell them I'm a shame researcher. A couple of years ago, I had a personal experience that taught me a lot about shame and why courage and compassion are so critical to shame resilience.

I was flying to Cleveland to give a lecture at Case Western Reserve University. As I settled into my window seat, a very energetic woman plunked down in the aisle seat on my row. I had seen her in the airport chatting up a storm with other waiting passengers and airline employees. After holding up aisle traffic for the better part of five minutes, she got her bags stuffed under the seat in front of her, turned toward me and introduced herself. We talked for a minute about the Houston weather before she asked, "So what do you do and why are you going to Cleveland?" As the plane took off, I raised my voice a bit and said, "I'm a researcher and I'm going to give a lecture at Case." "How wonderful," she responded. "What do you study?" Still fighting against the roar of the engines, I leaned toward her and said, "Women and shame."

Her eyes widened and she let out an enthusiastic "Oh, wow." She leaned so far toward me that her entire upper body was perched over the empty seat between us. "Women in chains! That's so interesting. Tell me more about it." By this time the airplane was quiet again. I smiled and said, "Not women in chains . . . women and shame." "Shame?" she asked, in a shocked and disappointed voice. "Yes," I replied. "I study shame and the various ways it affects women's lives."

With that, the conversation was over. She averted her eyes, then told me that she needed to get some rest. For three hours we sat silent in our seats. Every now and then I could feel her looking at me and perusing my laptop screen out of the corner of her eye. The first couple of times, I turned toward her to smile and acknowledge her, but immediately she would pretend to be sleeping. One time she even threw in a little snore, which I knew was fake because she was wiggling her feet the entire time.

When I returned to Houston I had dinner with a colleague who is a violence researcher. I was anxious to tell my "women in chains" story to someone who could relate to the pitfalls of researching a less-than-popular topic. After we laughed about "women in chains" being preferable to women and shame, she confessed that most people are quite interested in her research and she's normally the one who fakes being asleep on the plane. "I don't understand," I said. "These are both serious epidemics. Do people actually think shame is worse than violence?" She thought for a minute then said, "Well, no. They are both serious epidemics, but shame is a silent epidemic. People understand violence and can talk about it. We're still afraid of shame. Even the word is uncomfortable. You're studying a topic that people have been taught and socialized not to discuss. It's as dangerous as violence— but we just keep pretending that it's not happening."

I believe my colleague was right—shame is a silent epidemic. It's a problem of epidemic proportions because it has an impact on all of us. What makes it "silent" is our inability or unwillingness to talk openly about shame and explore the ways in which it affects our individual lives, our families, our communities and society. Our silence has actually forced shame underground, where it now permeates our personal and public lives in destructive and insidious ways. Shame was once largely misunderstood and discounted by social scientists, but now a growing number of researchers and practitioners are examining shame and its role in a wide range of mental and public health issues, including depression, anxiety disorders, addiction, eating disorders, bullying, suicide, sexual assault and all types of violence, including family violence.

Like the growing epidemic of violence, for many, shame has strangely become both a form of self-protection and a popular source of entertainment. Name calling and character assassinations have replaced national discussions about religion, politics and culture. We use shame as a tool to parent, teach and discipline our children. Television shows promising cutthroat alliances, backstabbing, hostile confrontations, exclusion and public humiliation consistently grab the top ratings. And at the same time we use shame to defend and entertain ourselves, we struggle to understand why the world feels so scary, why politics have turned into blood sport, why children are suffering higher levels of stress and anxiety, why popular culture appears to be sinking to all-time lows and why a growing number of us feel alone and disconnected.

As is the case with many epidemics, it seems that we are so mired in our own struggle to take care of ourselves and our families, we just don't see the connections that allow us to make sense of it and begin to address it as a large-scale problem. We can't see the enormity of it—we think it's a personal problem or a self-esteem issue rather than a serious social problem.

To better understand the shame experience, I want you to meet Susan, Kayla, Theresa and Sondra. I had the opportunity to interview them early in my research and again several years later, after they had started putting the shame resilience strategies into practice. Throughout the book, their unfolding stories will serve as important examples of how powerful, and sometimes difficult, it can be to practice courage, compassion and connection.

Susan was in her late twenties when we met. She had been married for three years and had a daughter who had just celebrated her first birthday. Susan had loved her career as a physical therapist but had spent the previous year at home with her baby. As family finances grew tighter, she had decided to return to work part-time. In our interview, she recalled the day when she thought the right job had landed in her lap. She remembered being absolutely ecstatic. Not only had she been offered a perfect part-time physical therapist position, but her church had an open slot for her daughter in their Mother's Day Out program. Anxious to share her good news, she called her older sister. Rather than congratulating Susan, her sister responded to the news by saying, "I'm not sure why you even had a child if you're not interested in raising her." Susan remembers feeling like she had been punched in the stomach. She said, "I could hardly breathe. It was devastating. My first thought was 'I'm a bad mother.' By that evening, I was reconsidering the job offer."

When I interviewed Kayla, she was in her mid-forties and had built a successful career in advertising. She lived alone in large city on the East Coast. Kayla's father had recently been diagnosed with Alzheimer's and she was struggling to balance the pressures of her career with her new role as her father's primary caregiver. She explained that the most difficult issue was dealing with her boss, Nancy. Kayla described Nancy as "the kind of person you never share personal information with." When I asked her to explain what she meant, she said that Nancy had perfected the art of the personal attack—the more Nancy knew about your life, the more ammunition she had for her arsenal. When Kayla's mother died two years prior, Kayla struggled with depression. She had confided in Nancy about the depression, only to have Nancy bring it up in front of other colleagues. Kayla said that, despite her fear of Nancy's attacks, she knew she might miss some work while she looked for a long-term care facility, so she explained her father's situation to Nancy. Kayla still looked shocked as she described the very first staff meeting she attended after she told her boss. During the meeting, Nancy announced that Kayla was going to be pulled off her current project. Kayla said, "She looked right at me and said to the group, 'You know Kayla. There's always some kind of drama.'" Kayla describes that moment as "pure paralysis." "I froze. I felt so small and sliced open. Was Nancy right? Am I a flake? How could I have been so stupid to trust Nancy?"

When I met Theresa she was thirty-five, and had three children ranging from age three to eleven. She described an experience that probably lasted no more than five minutes but, for her, represented one of her greatest struggles. She remembered standing in front of her mirror and feeling extreme anxiety and hatred about her body. She said, "It was one of those days when nothing fit—I had tried on every pair of jeans that I could find." She said she found herself grabbing at the inside of her thighs and pinching the fat that hung over the side of her bra and chanting, "This is disgusting. I'm disgusting." She said the entire episode was more stressful because she could hear her kids fighting over the television in the other room while the phone rang off the hook. She started screaming at her kids, "Will someone get the damn phone? I know I'm not the only one who hears it. Damn it!" She finally buried her head in her hands and started sobbing. When she raised her head up she saw her toddler standing a few feet away. He told her in a frightened voice, "I'm sorry Mommy's sad." As she stared at him, she was flooded with feelings of shame and self-blame. Theresa told me she would never forget that day and explained, "Sometimes I just get sick of it all—my body, my kids, my house— my entire life. I have these pictures in my head of what I want everything to look like, and it's never that perfect. I just can't ever pull it all together. On top of it, I feel so ashamed when I take it out on my kids."

Sondra, a high school teacher in her mid-fifties, seemed both angry and sad when she told me, "I used to love to debate politics with my brother-in-law. We did it for years. One night when my husband and I were driving home from Sunday dinner, he told me that he hated when I argued with his brother. He told me he had always hated it. He said, 'Donald is a smart guy. He's got a master's degree. I wish you wouldn't get into it with him.' Then he told me that I sounded uneducated and stupid and it made him look bad. I became totally withdrawn around his family."

Are Susan, Kayla, Theresa and Sondra simply struggling from low self-esteem? No. Shame and self-esteem are very different issues. We *feel* shame. We *think* self-esteem. Our self-esteem is based on how we see ourselves—our strengths and limitations—over time. It is how and what we think of ourselves. Shame is an emotion. It is how we feel when we have certain experiences. When we are in shame, we don't see the big picture; we don't accurately think about our strengths and limitations. We just feel alone, exposed and deeply flawed. My friend and colleague Marian Mankin described the difference between shame and self-esteem this way: "When I think about my self-esteem, I think about who I am in relation to who I want to be, where I come from, what I've overcome and what I've accomplished. When I feel shame, I'm taken back to this place of smallness where I lose that sense of context. I'm returned to a small place—I can't see everything else. It's just a small, lonely place."

If these stories aren't about self-esteem, could they simply be about the company we keep? Does Susan just have a mean sister? Is Kayla simply the victim of an insensitive remark? Is Theresa's struggle with perfection an isolated case? Is Sondra's husband the only problem? The answer to all these questions is no. If you look at all four of the examples concerning motherhood, work, perfectionism and speaking out, you'll see that shame is the primary weapon used in these cultural wars.

We are constantly threatening mothers with the shame of "not doing what's best for their children" or "making selfish or ignorant choices." Similarly, Kayla's experience points to the shame culture that has taken over many workplaces. We are expected to produce and keep our professional and personal lives artificially compartmentalized in order to succeed. Her boss's comment is a product of that culture. Although we're told (and want to believe), "You are not your job," the messages from employers, colleagues and the media counter that well-intentioned adage with "You are exactly what you do, how well you do it and what you earn."

When it comes to Theresa's struggle, we need to understand that shame is the voice of perfectionism. Whether we're talking about appearance, work, motherhood, health or family, it's not the quest for perfection that is so painful; it's failing to meet the unattainable expectations that lead to the painful wash of shame. Last, Sondra's story speaks to the power of shame as a social tool that's often used to keep us quiet. Nothing silences us more effectively than shame.

As you can see, shame is much more than insensitive communicating or a self-esteem issue; it is a basic human experience that is becoming an increasingly divisive and destructive part of our culture. During certain times and in certain situations, we all struggle with feelings of not being good enough, not having enough and not belonging enough. I have found that the most effective way to overcome these feelings of inadequacy is to share our experiences. Of course, in this culture, telling our stories takes courage.

Courage, Compassion and Connection

Courage is a heart word. The root of the word *courage* is *cor*—the Latin word for heart. In one of its earliest forms, the word *courage* meant "To speak one's mind by telling all one's heart." Over time, this definition has changed, and today, we typically associate courage with heroic and brave deeds. But in my opinion, this definition fails to recognize the inner strength and level of commitment required for us to actually speak honestly and openly about who we are and about our experiences—good and bad. Speaking from our hearts is what I think of as "ordinary courage."

I'm not sure where the term *ordinary courage* first appeared, but I discovered it in an article on women and girls by researcher Annie Rogers. I think the idea of ordinary courage speaks to the importance of telling our stories. It is especially difficult to practice ordinary courage in today's culture of shame—a culture full of fear, blame and disconnection. However, practicing the strategies in this book will help all of us reclaim our courage and power; and even start to change the culture.

To understand how shame is influenced by culture, we need to think back to when we were children or young adults, and we first learned how important it is to be liked, to fit in, and to please others. The lessons were often taught by shame; sometimes overtly, other times covertly. Regardless of how they happened, we can all recall experiences of feeling rejected, diminished and ridiculed. Eventually, we learned to fear these feelings. We learned how to change our behaviors, thinking and feelings to avoid feeling shame. In the process, we changed who we were and, in many instances, who we are now.

Our culture teaches us about shame—it dictates what is acceptable and what is not. We weren't born craving perfect bodies. We weren't born afraid to tell our stories. We weren't born with a fear of getting too old to feel valuable. We weren't born with a Pottery Barn catalog in one hand and heartbreaking debt in the other. Shame comes from outside of us—from the messages and expectations of our culture. What comes from the inside of us is a very human need to belong, to relate.

We are wired for connection. It's in our biology. As infants, our need for connection is about survival. As we grow older, connection means thriving—emotionally, physically, spiritually and intellectually. Connection is critical because we all have the basic need to feel accepted and to believe that we belong and are valued for who we are.

Shame unravels our connection to others. In fact, I often refer to shame as the fear of disconnection—the fear of being perceived as flawed and unworthy of acceptance or belonging. Shame keeps us from telling our own stories and prevents us from listening to others tell their stories. We silence our voices and keep our secrets out of the fear of disconnection. When we hear others talk about their shame, we often blame them as a way to protect ourselves from feeling uncomfortable. Hearing someone talk about a shaming experience can sometimes be as painful as actually experiencing it for ourselves.

Like courage, empathy and compassion are critical components of shame resilience. Practicing compassion allows us to hear shame. Empathy, the most powerful tool of compassion, is an emotional skill that allows us to respond to others in a meaningful, caring way. Empathy is the ability to put ourselves in someone else's shoes—to understand what someone is experiencing and to reflect back that understanding. When we share a difficult experience with someone, and that person responds in an open, deeply connected way—that's empathy. Developing empathy can enrich the relationships we have with our partners, colleagues, family members and children. In Chapter 2, I'll discuss the concept of empathy in great detail. You'll learn how it works, how we can learn to be empathic and why the opposite of experiencing shame is experiencing empathy.

The prerequisite for empathy is compassion. We can only respond empathically if we are willing to hear someone's pain. We sometimes think of compassion as a saintlike virtue. It's not. In fact, compassion is possible for anyone who can accept the struggles that make us human—our fears, imperfections, losses and shame. We can only respond compassionately to someone telling her story if we have embraced our own story—shame and all. Compassion is not a virtue—it is a commitment. It's not something we have or don't have—it's something we choose to practice. Can we be with someone who is in shame and open ourselves up enough to listen to her story and share her pain?

An Overview of the Book

This book is divided into eleven chapters, including this introduction. In Chapter 1, I'll share stories and examples in order to build a definition of shame and differentiate shame from other emotions like guilt, humiliation and embarrassment. In Chapter 2, we'll explore the basics of resilience—empathy, courage, compassion and connection.

Chapters 3–6 will focus on the four elements of shame resilience. In my research I found that women with high levels of shame resilience had four things in common. When practiced together, these four elements move us toward resilience. In each of these four chapters, I'll share specific strategies that we can use to help us develop shame resilience and information on how we can overcome some of the common barriers women face as they begin to put these strategies into practice.

The culture of shame is driven by fear, blame and disconnection, and it is often a powerful incubator for issues like perfectionism, stereotyping, gossiping and addiction. In Chapters 7–9, I'll explore these issues and others in the context of developing and maintaining our shame resilience. The final chapter will present ideas for actually changing the culture: What does shame resilience mean for our children, the men in our lives, our spiritual lives, our workplaces and our families?

Shame is a difficult topic. However, as painful as some of the stories may be, the raw honesty of their truths confirms that the information and ideas in this book are tremendous sources of hope and promise for women. *I believe that we are all capable of developing resilience to shame.* We are all capable of turning the pain caused by shame into courage, compassion and connection. Equally important, we are all capable of helping others do the same.

However, it is vitally important to recognize the complexity of this work. This is not "four easy steps" to shame resilience or some other simple recipe for overcoming shame. Cookbook answers don't work when it comes to addressing an issue like shame, or, for that matter, any other complex human issue. In fact, it can even be shaming when we believe that there are easy remedies for complicated problems—we tend to blame ourselves for not being able to "get it."

It has been said that real freedom is about setting others free. In the spirit of that powerful definition, my greatest hope is that we will reach out across our differences and through our shame to share our stories and to connect with those who need to hear, "You are not alone."

I THOUGHT IT WAS JUST ME

ONE

Understanding Shame

W hen people ask me how I became a shame researcher, I tell them that my career was built around one sentence: "You cannot shame or belittle people into changing their behaviors." When I was in my twenties, I worked in a residential treatment facility for children. One day during a staff meeting, the clinical director, who oversees the therapeutic work done with the children, spoke to us about helping the kids make better choices. He said, "I know you want to help these kids, but you must understand this: You cannot shame or belittle people into changing their behaviors."

He went on to explain that, regardless of our intentions, we can't force people to make positive changes by putting them down, threatening them with rejection, humiliating them in front of others or belittling them. From the moment the words were spoken, I was absolutely overwhelmed by this idea. For weeks, I thought of little else. Yet, no matter how long and hard I thought about it or how many times I repeated the statement out loud, I couldn't get my head around it. There were minutes when I thought it was, at best, pie-in-the-sky, wishful thinking, and then there were brief seconds when I believed it was the truest thing I'd ever heard. But, despite my confusion, I recognized that there was something incredibly important about understanding shame. As it turned out, I spent the next ten years of my life researching shame and its impact on our lives.

I eventually left my job at the residential treatment facility to attend graduate school. Over the next seven years, I earned master's and doctoral degrees in social work. My entire education was driven by that powerful proposition—"You CANNOT shame or belittle people into changing their behaviors." I wanted to understand how and why we use shame. I also wanted to understand the consequences of attempting to use shame to change people. It's not that I publicly "studied shame"—I just listened, learned and tested every piece of new information against that proposition. Here's what I have learned:

- Can you use shame or humiliation to change people or behavior? *Yes and no. Yes, you can try. In fact, if you really zero in on an exposed vulnerability, you could actually see a very swift behavior change.*
- Will the change last? *No.*
- Will it hurt? *Yes, it's excruciating.*
- Will it do any damage? *Yes, it has the potential to scar both the person using shame and the person being shamed.*
- Is shame used very often as a way to try to change people? *Yes, every minute of every day.*

I also learned that most of us, if not all, have built significant parts of our lives around shame. Individuals, families and communities use shame as a tool to change others and to protect themselves. In doing this, we create a society that fails to recognize how much damage shame does to our spirit and to the soul of our families and our communities.

One reason we don't see the connections between our personal struggles and larger cultural issues goes back to the "silent" part of "silent epidemic." We do not talk about shame. We experience it, we feel it, we sometimes live with it for an entire lifetime, but we don't talk about it. When was the last time you had a meaningful conversation about shame? If you're like most people, the answer is never. Despite our society's relatively new openness to discussing other emotions like fear and anger, shame remains taboo.

I think it's important to understand that it's not just "plain folk" who avoid the topic of shame. It's also mental health professionals, researchers, physicians and other professionals who are often the ones we depend on to identify and spark the first discussions about social epidemics. After I completed the first component of my research, I spent seven months traveling across the nation, presenting my work to helping professionals. For many of them, even those who had been in medical or psychotherapy practices for decades, it was their first time attending a workshop on shame. On their feedback forms, many of the participants wrote that it was one of the most personally difficult workshops they had attended. And for many of the attendees, it was their first exposure to shame research.

Unlike many of the other topics that professionals study, there is no "us and them" when it comes to shame. As professionals, we don't have the luxury of thinking, "Let me learn about this topic that affects my patients so I can help them." Shame is universal— no one is exempt. If we can't talk about shame and examine the impact it has in our own lives, we certainly can't be helpful to others.

Of course, there are some researchers and practitioners doing very important work on women and shame—June Tangney and Ronda Dearing, researchers and clinicians at the Stone Center at Wellesley; Harriet Lerner; and Claudia Black to name just a few. However, it's been my experience that the topic remains as silenced in the mental health community as it is in the community at large.

This "professional silence" is important to understand because there are studies that identify shame as the dominant emotion experienced by mental health clients, exceeding anger, fear, grief and anxiety. So, if the mental and public health communities aren't talking about shame or providing enough safe spaces for people to get help with shame issues, how do we ever begin to talk about it? How do we confront a feeling or experience that, by its very nature, is something we don't want to talk about?

Defining Shame

These questions point to the absolute power of shame. Shame is an emotion that we have all felt, yet when we try describe it, when we try to make it accessible for other people to understand, we struggle to find the words. Even when we find the words, it is rare that people will want to listen. Experiencing shame is painful. Just listening to someone share a shaming experience can be almost as painful.

I quickly came to believe that the first step in understanding shame is developing a shared vocabulary to communicate our experiences; therefore, my first goal was to develop a definition of shame. When I asked the research participants to define shame for me, they either gave me their personal definition or they shared an experience as an example. Here are some of their definitions:

- Shame is that feeling in the pit of your stomach that is dark and hurts like hell. You can't talk about it and can't articulate how bad it feels because then everyone would know your "dirty little secret."
- Shame is being rejected.
- You work hard to show the world what it wants to see. Shame happens when your mask is pulled off and the unlikable parts of you are seen. It feels unbearable to be seen.
- Shame is feeling like an outsider—not belonging.
- Shame is hating yourself and understanding why other people hate you too.
- I think it's about self-loathing.
- Shame is like a prison. But a prison that you deserve to be in because something's wrong with you.

- Shame is being exposed—the flawed parts of yourself that you want to hide from everyone are revealed. You want to hide or die.

You can see by these examples that it's virtually impossible to explain shame without evoking the incredibly powerful and overwhelming feelings associated with it. When I asked how shame feels, women used words like *devastating, noxious, consuming, excruciating, filleted, small, stained, incredibly lonely, rejected* and *the worst feeling ever.* I often refer to shame as a "full-contact" emotion. When we experience it or even listen to a friend's story about a shaming experience, we often have a visceral and physical response. It's emotionally overwhelming, but we also feel it in our bodies.

After hearing so many diverse, yet related, definitions, I realized that it would be helpful to have a simple definition that captures the emotion and meaning that I heard in the interviews. So I compiled the definitions, analyzed them and developed this conceptual definition:

> *Shame is the intensely painful feeling or experience of believing we are flawed and therefore unworthy of acceptance and belonging.*

While the definition gives us a starting point, what really breathes life into our understanding of shame are the examples that women shared as they struggled to put words around the concept.

- Shame is my mom still being hateful about my weight. Every time I go home to visit with my husband and kids the first thing she says is "My God, you're still fat!" and the last thing she says when I walk out the door is "Hopefully you can lose some weight." She's screwed me up so bad already you think she'd be over it by now, but no, she just keeps going.

- I don't hate having sex. I don't really enjoy it, but I don't totally hate it. I have three kids and now that I have them, I don't even see the point in sex anymore. If I never had sex again, I'd be fine and I know that's totally not normal and it makes me feel very ashamed. Like something is really wrong with me. I hate those articles that say the average married couple has sex three times a week. I'm thinking, "Geez, that's not me," and I feel a lot of shame about that because I really wouldn't care if I never had it again. It's bad because I know my husband doesn't feel like that. He could be one of those people having it three or four times a week.

- When I was in high school my mom committed suicide. She hung herself in her bedroom in our house. The neighborhood constable found her. From that day forward I was "the girl whose mom hung herself." It was the worst imaginable thing in my life. My dad forced me to finish high school there, but I've never gone back. My dad died a couple of years ago, and in some ways I was relieved, because I never wanted to see or go back to that neighborhood again. It's funny because I think if my mom would have died of cancer or something else, people would have been more understanding; people wouldn't have been so cruel. But when it's suicide, it's completely different. My mother was the crazy lady who hung herself, so that means I must be crazy too. I even think some of my friends' parents were scared of me and my dad. That's shame.

- My oldest son is a drug addict. His younger brother and sister just despise him. When he comes home to stay for the weekend or visit, it's just always a horrible situation. My daughter always says, "Mom, hide all your nice stuff; don't leave your purse on the table." Good God, they're talking about their brother. I guess I know they're right but I don't know what I did, I don't know why this is happening and I'm so ashamed of him and I'm so ashamed of how we treat him. It's the hardest thing, I think, in our family right now.

- When I was in middle school, my aunt's boyfriend molested me. I told my older sister and she told my parents. I don't remember exactly what they said, but they called me and my sister into the living room and told us that we shouldn't talk about it with any-one. My mom told me that she would deal with my aunt. I don't know what happened, but I never saw him again. My aunt never said anything about it to me. My sister was so pissed. She stayed mad at my parents for years. I just became a quiet person. Ashamed and quiet.

- I think all of the body stuff is shaming. It's like you never get to see normal bodies or you never get to read about what normal bodies do. I think you're always thinking, "Do other people's breasts look like this?" "Do other people get hair here and no hair there?" "Do other people smell like this?" "Does this look like this?" "Do you get pimples there?" I think everything about your body that you don't see on the perfect people on TV or in the magazines, you wonder if you're the only person and you gross yourself out and that's what shame is. Shame is when you're grossed out by yourself—it's when your very own body makes you sick. I'd like to see a book that has all the in-formation, like this is twenty ways this can smell, or this is a picture of fifty "normal women's" breasts and here's what they can look like. Then you can be like "Oh, OK, I'm normal." But you have to ask, "Who would pose for that?" Probably not nor-mal people. Then you'd be comparing yourself to crazy people. It's just ridiculous that no one is ever going to talk about the weird stuff out of the fear that they're actually the one person that has that. Then it's like "Uh-oh." Then it's double worse because then you're ashamed and you think you're supposed to be ashamed.

- Five years ago, I quit my job and my husband and I took out a second mortgage so I could start my own business. After two years I had to shut down my online clothing store. It was devastating. You always hear about the people who give up everything to follow their dreams and they are always very successful and happy. I'm in debt, in a terrible new job and ashamed that I couldn't make it work. I got everyone around me excited and involved, then I failed. I'm ashamed of being a failure.

- When we were growing up, my sister and I used to fight all the time about which one of us was closest to my mom, and now we fight about who has to take care of my mom or whose house she's going to stay in. . . . It's like you look at yourself and you look at your children and you think, "God, one day my kids are going to be fighting about who has to take care of me?" And then you think, "Oh, it's gonna be different for me—this is not gonna happen to me," but you know, I remember my mom saying that too. And then you think, "Oh, my God, what if she knew that we were arguing about who had to take her?" I mean that, I don't know if my sister is ashamed, but I'm certainly ashamed about my struggle to deal with my mom.

- Infertility was shaming for me because it was a lonely feeling. I felt as if no one else could understand my pain, especially all those around me with children. You feel as if something is wrong with you or that you are somehow being punished for something you've done wrong. You wonder in the back of your mind if this is somehow in the "plan" because you are unfit to be a mother.

- My husband is a very successful business owner, a leader in our church and a good husband and father. I know there's nothing seriously wrong with him, but I think he is addicted to adult Web sites. We've never talked about it and I certainly haven't told anyone but my sister. Her advice is to not worry about it. I just know he's on the computer very late at night and we get lots of charges from the Web sites on our credit card. I didn't even know until I was checking our e-mail for someone's address and I saw e-mails from the porn sites. It was so disgusting. That's when I checked the credit card. If anyone found out, I would die. Not only would people think that he's a pervert, they'd think something is wrong with me. That somehow I'm to blame because he had to go to the Internet for sex. I can't even talk to him about it—I would die of shame if anyone else found out.

The pain in these stories is palpable. At the exact time that our society embraces shaming, blaming, judgment and rejection, it also holds acceptance and belonging as immensely important. In other words, it's never been more impossible to "fit in," yet "fitting in" has never been more important and valued.

An Early Call for Compassion

If this book is going to serve as a helpful tool on our journey to shame resilience, I think it's critical to acknowledge, right from the start, how difficult it is to read some of the stories in this book—how very painful it can be to just hear "shame." When a friend or family member shares her or his shame story, or even when we read about a stranger's shame experience in a book, we often have one of two reactions.

If we can relate to the story because it's an issue that we face, the experience is often both painful and strangely comforting. The pain stems from being forced to think about an issue that we probably try to keep under the surface. The comfort comes from recognizing that we are not alone in our struggles; we aren't the only one.

One reason shame is so powerful is its ability to make us feel alone. Like we are the only one or somehow we're different from everyone else. When we hear stories that mirror our own shame experiences, it helps us know we aren't alone. Of course, if the story hits too close to home, we can actually find *ourselves* in the grip of shame. Rather than just listening and responding to someone else's experience, we become overwhelmed with our own feelings of shame.

When we hear stories about shame that don't fit with our experiences, our first reaction is often to distance ourselves from the experiences—"My mother would never say that" or "I don't get women who don't enjoy sex" or "She's so naïve—her husband's a wacko." The distancing turns very quickly into blame, judgment and separation. This fuels the shame epidemic. Let me give you an example of my own struggle to practice compassion.

When I interviewed Allison, the young woman whose mother had committed suicide, I was appalled by the reaction of her friends, neighbors and even teachers. During the months following her mother's death, she couldn't go anywhere without hearing whispers, experiencing the isolation of people intentionally avoiding her or being confronted with inappropriate questions about the details of her mother's suicide. At first Allison felt that the rejection was undeserved—she knew it wasn't her fault and that her mother's mental illness was not a reflection on her. But as the whispering continued, she began to believe that somehow her mother's suicide meant she was also "defective" (her own word). This is when the shame started and left her feeling completely ostracized and alone.

I stewed over this interview for a couple of weeks. I felt great compassion and empathy for Allison; however, I was mired in feelings of anger, judgment and blame. I felt self-righteous anger toward those people who had lacked any sensitivity and treated her so unfairly. I spent days thinking about my reaction to her story, until, finally, I was confronted by some hard truths.

First of all, if we are going to understand shame, we must not only seek to understand Allison's experiences, but the reactions of those around her. We can't simply "shift shame" from Allison to her "insensitive neighbors." Shaming her neighbors and friends would be equally destructive. Second, we have to dig deep and be honest about how we might react as a neighbor or friend.

If I came home from work and saw an ambulance and police cars surrounding a neighbor's house, I'd immediately patch into the neighborhood phone tree to find out what happened. I might not walk over and stand around gawking, because I'd like to believe I'm above that—or at least I'd want my neighbors to think I'm above it. Instead, I'd call someone who had walked over, which is probably worse. Unless I was extremely aware of what I was doing and I was consciously working not to gossip, I would probably be equally guilty of talking about it, speculating why, wondering about the details and drawing false conclusions. I can just hear conversations where we're saying things like "I knew something wasn't right over there" or "You know, one day I saw her . . ." I might even make assumptions about the mental stability of Allison's father or about Allison herself following such a traumatic event. I might become uncomfortable letting my daughter play at her house.

In other words, I might become exactly what I hated and, at first, refused to understand. Why? Because I'm a terrible person like Allison's teachers, neighbors and friends? No—it's because I'm human and situations like that can throw us into our own fear, anxiety, grief and, sometimes, even into our own shame. And to alleviate those overwhelming feelings, we seek connection with others—sometimes in incredibly hurtful and destructive ways, like gossiping and excluding others.

If we really want to get at the heart of the beast, we have to understand more than what it feels like to experience shame. We need to understand when and why we are the most likely to engage in shaming behaviors toward others, how we can develop our resilience to shame and how we can consciously make the effort not to shame others. Not all of the stories presented here will mirror our own experiences, but I suspect many will feel uncomfortably familiar. Our level of resilience to shame is not dependent solely on our ability to recognize these behaviors and emotions in ourselves, but also on our ability to build connections with others. These connections require us to understand what we share in common when it comes to shame.

Shame 101

What do we need to know and understand in order to build resilience to shame? How do we connect with our authentic selves and build meaningful connections with others? Why, when it comes to the isolating emotion of shame, is there so much power and freedom in simply understanding the deep connections among all of our experiences?

These are complex questions, and before we can answer them we need to address some of the basics of shame. In this section we will start to build an understanding of shame, including how it is different from guilt, humiliation or embarrassment, and how shame operates in our lives. Once we have built this foundational understanding of shame, many of the connections that have been so elusive will begin to emerge and make sense in the context of our lives.

Embarrassment, Guilt, Humiliation and Shame

One of the simpler reasons shame is so difficult to talk about is vocabulary. We often use the terms *embarrassment, guilt, humiliation* and *shame* interchangeably. Without much thought, we whisper, "That was so humiliating!" when we walk out of a restroom with toilet paper stuck to our shoe or shout, "Shame on you!" to a child who has unfortunately (but age-appropriately) colored on the table rather than in the coloring book.

It might seem overly sensitive to stress the importance of using the appropriate term to describe an experience or emotion; however, it is much more than just semantics. "Speaking shame," or being able to identify and label these emotions, is one of the four elements of shame resilience.

Within the research community, there are interesting debates about the relationships between embarrassment, guilt, humiliation and shame. Although there is a small group of researchers who believe that all four of these emotions are related and represent varying degrees of the same core emotion, the vast majority of researchers believe that the four are separate, distinct experiences. Like most of the studies on shame, my research strongly supports the argument that embarrassment, guilt, humiliation and shame are four different emotional responses.

Embarrassment is the least powerful of these emotions. Women described "embarrassing situations" as much less serious than either guilt or shame. Embarrassment is, by definition, something that is fleeting, often eventually funny and very normal (e.g., tripping, misspeaking, etc.). Regardless of how embarrassing a situation might be, we know (or at least have heard) that it happens to other people and we know it will go away. I don't want to walk out of the bathroom with toilet paper on my shoe, but if I do, I'll know I'm not the first or only one to have done it.

Guilt is probably the term most often confused with shame. And unfortunately, the effects of this confusion transcend semantics and "term confusion." Often, when we try to shame others or ourselves into changing a behavior, we do so **without** understanding the differences between shame and guilt. This is important because guilt can often be a positive motivator of change, while shame typically leads to worse behavior or paralysis. Here's why.

Guilt and shame are both emotions of self-evaluation; however, that is where the similarities end. The majority of shame researchers agree that the difference between shame and guilt is best understood as the differences between "I am bad" (shame) and "I did something bad" (guilt). Shame is about who we are and guilt is about our behaviors. If I feel guilty for cheating on a test, my self-talk might sound something like "I should not have done that.

That was really stupid. Cheating is not something I believe in or want to do." If I feel shame about cheating on a test, my self-talk is more likely to sound like "I'm a liar and a cheat. I'm so stupid. I'm a bad person."

Guilt is holding an action or behavior up against our ethics, values and beliefs. We evaluate that behavior (like cheating) and feel guilt when the behavior is inconsistent with who we want to be. Shame is focusing on who we are rather than what we've done. The danger of telling ourselves that we are bad, a cheat, and no good, is that we eventually start to believe it and own it. The person who believes she is "no good" is much more likely to continue to cheat and fulfill that label than the person who feels guilt.

Along with many other shame researchers, I've come to the conclusion that shame is much more likely to be the source of destructive behaviors than it is to be the solution. It is human nature to want to feel affirmed and valued. When we experience shame we feel disconnected and desperate for belonging and recognition. It's when we feel shame or the fear of shame that we are more likely to engage in self-destructive behaviors, to attack or humiliate others or to stay quiet when we see someone who needs our help.

On the other hand, when we apologize for something we've done, make amends to others or change a behavior that we don't feel good about, guilt is most often the motivator. Recognizing we've *made a mistake* is far different than believing we *are a mistake*. Of course, you can shame someone into saying, "I'm sorry," but it's rarely authentic.

I'm often asked if the same experience can cause shame for one person and guilt or embarrassment for someone else. The answer is yes. This is why we need to be careful not to make assumptions about what causes people to feel shame. To illustrate, I'll use a fairly innocuous example: remembering someone's birthday. There have been times in my life when forgetting someone's birthday, especially that of a family member or a close friend, has really made me feel embarrassed—"I can't believe I forgot to do that." I recovered quickly with a simple phone call. "I'm so embarrassed I forgot your birthday—I hope you had a great one."

There have been other times in my life where I have felt very guilty about forgetting someone's birthday, because it wasn't simply an oversight or a slipup; it reflected a lack of priorities—priorities that I didn't feel good about and wanted to change.

However, following my return to work after I had my daughter, Ellen, small things, like forgetting to send a birthday card or to call to RSVP for a party, would elicit very strong feelings of shame in me. I would sometimes find myself fabricating huge lies about why I had forgotten to call or send a gift. During that time in my life, I felt like everything I did was half-assed. I felt like I was a mediocre faculty member, a mediocre mother and partner, a mediocre friend and a mediocre sister and daughter. So when I did do something like forget a birthday, I wouldn't feel like "Oh, man, I can't believe I forgot to do that." I would say, "God, I am so stupid, I can't do anything right."

Ellen is now seven and I've recently returned to work after spending several months at home with my second baby, Charlie. I still struggle with remembering birthdays and feeling overwhelmed and mediocre at times, but I've worked my way back to guilt. I've decided that remembering birthdays is important to me; however, I've also acknowledged that balancing work and parenting requires lots of flexibility and advanced planning. Now I stock up on belated birthday cards as well as the regular kind. So, as you can see, we can experience embarrassment, guilt or shame over the same situations. It just depends on where we are in our lives.

Humiliation is another word that we often confuse with *shame*. Donald Klein captures the differences between shame and humiliation when he writes, "People believe they deserve their shame; they do not believe they deserve their humiliation." If you go back to the initial definitions given by the research participants, you can see that one of the themes that runs through several of the definitions is this concept of "deserving." One woman said, "Shame is hating yourself and understanding why other people hate you too." Another woman actually used the term *deserve* and said, "Shame is like a prison. But a prison that you deserve to be in because something's wrong with you."

Let me give you an example of the difference between shame and humiliation from my recent research on how shame is used to parent and teach. If a teacher announces a child's failing grade in front of the class and calls him "stupid," the child is likely to experience shame or humiliation. If the child believes the teacher's announcement and name-calling is unfair and undeserved, the child will most likely feel humiliated rather than ashamed. If, on the other hand, the child buys into the message that he is stupid and deserves to be called out in front of his peers, that leads to shame.

Based on the research I'm conducting on the impact of using shame to parent and discipline in schools, I think shame is often more destructive than humiliation for two reasons. First, it's bad enough to have a child labeled "stupid" at school, but it's far more detrimental if the child actually believes she is stupid. If a child is shamed into believing that he or she is stupid, the child is potentially being set up for a lifetime of struggle.

Second, I'm finding that the child who experiences humiliation rather than shame is much more likely to come home and tell a parent or caregiver about her experience than the child who experiences shame. In this case, if our child tells us about her humiliating experience, we have the opportunity to help her feel her way through it and address it with teachers and school administrators. The child who feels shame internalizes the messages and often starts to act out or shut down.

Of course, we need to understand that repeated humiliation can often turn into shame. If someone a child looks up to, like a teacher or a parent, repeatedly calls that child stupid, chances are that he will eventually believe it. In fact, all of us are very susceptible to having our humiliating experiences turn to shame, especially when the person who is putting us down is someone with whom we have a valued relationship or someone whom we perceive to have more power than we do, like a boss, a doctor or a member of the clergy.

Once we can distinguish among embarrassment, guilt, shame and humiliation, we can begin to look at why we experience shame and how it affects us. Understanding the "how and why" of shame is critically important because there is far more to shame resilience than surviving a shaming moment. If we want to successfully deal with the shame in our lives, we have to understand why we feel it and how it affects our lives, including the behaviors, thoughts and feelings we deal with every day.

The Shame Web

In the years I have spent immersed in this research, one of the most difficult questions to answer has been "What is the connection among all of these women's shame experiences?" The women who participated in the study were very diverse in terms of race, ethnicity, age, sexual orientation, religion/faith affiliations, physical and mental health characteristics and family roles. Approximately forty-one percent of the women identified themselves as Caucasian, twenty-six percent of the women as African-American, twenty-five percent as Latina and eight percent as Asian-American. The participants' ages ranged from eighteen to eighty-two, and the average age was approximately forty.

As I read through the interviews, analyzing all of their stories and experiences, I searched for connections. Clearly, what triggers shame in some of us has no impact on others. What some of us experience as devastating may feel mildly upsetting for others. Yet, when you read the descriptions and hear the stories of hundreds of women, it's very clear that there is something central in everyone's experience of shame.

Here is what I found:

Women most often experience shame as a web of layered,

conflicting and competing social-community expectations. These expectations dictate:

- who we should be
- what we should be
- how we should be

Once entangled in this web, women feel flooded with feelings of fear, blame and disconnection. I think it's safe to say that each of these three concepts alone is overwhelming. But if we understand fear, blame and disconnection as intricately woven together to create shame, it becomes very clear why shame is so powerful, complex and difficult to overcome.

The expectations that form the web are often based on characteristics like our race, class, sexual orientation, age or religious identity. They can be specific to the different roles we play like mother, employee, partner, sister or member of a certain group. But, at their core, the expectations that fuel shame are specifically about what is expected of us as **women**. Shame is organized by gender. The expectations that fuel shame for women are based on our culture's perception of what is acceptable for women. In my new research on men, I'm learning that the expectations that fuel shame for men are based on our culture's perception of masculinity—what should a man be, look like and act like.

Although these gender-based expectations are often born in our larger society, they can filter through our various communities in different ways. That is why I call them social-community expectations. For example, there are broad social expectations for women around the issue of appearance: We are expected to be young, beautiful, sexy, etc. However, in my community there are no expectations about hair texture or skin color, whereas in some communities, this can be an issue. I recently received a letter from one woman who wrote, "As a dark-skinned African-American woman raising multiracial children, I have experienced painful encounters

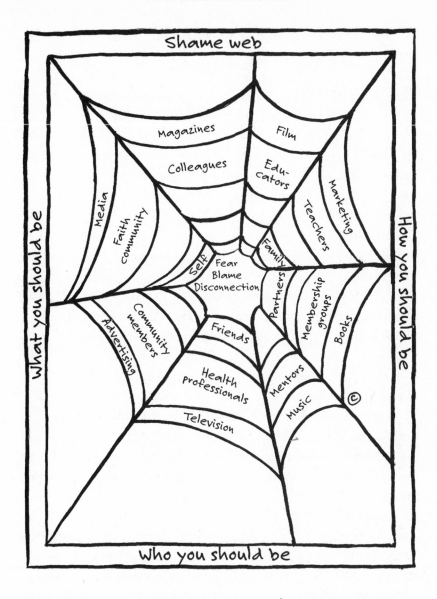

regarding race, skin color and beauty standards within the African-American community. Your work gives words and validation to the feelings that wash over me during those uncomfortable times when I am faced with explaining to my children that beauty is in everyone regardless of skin color, eye color or hair texture."

Another example might be mental health. There are general social expectations that only a certain level of "crazy" is tolerated or socially acceptable. However, in some communities, it can be shaming to take any mental health problems outside of the family, whereas in other communities, everyone has a therapist.

It is important to note that our communities are not just determined by geography; most of us belong to communities based on larger issues like race, ethnicity, social class, group membership, ideology, faith, politics, etc.

Shame and Fear

Shame is all about fear. As I wrote in the introduction, we are biologically, emotionally, socially and cognitively wired for connection. For many, there is also a deep need for spiritual connection. Shame is about the fear of disconnection. When we are experiencing shame, we are steeped in the fear of being ridiculed, diminished or seen as flawed. We are afraid that we've exposed or revealed a part of us that jeopardizes our connection and our worthiness of acceptance.

This fear is fueled by the sense that we are somehow trapped in our shame. This fear of being trapped relates to the way in which the shame web is baited with an impossible ratio of expectations and options. First, we have an unreasonable number of expectations put upon us, many of which are not even attainable or realistic. Second, we have a very limited number of options in terms of how we can meet those expectations. To bring the image of the shame web into focus, let's use an example that most of us find relevant—body image. Even with all our awareness about media manipulation and eating disorders, this issue just does not seem to be getting better. In fact, body image and weight emerged as a shame issue in approximately ninety percent of the women I interviewed.

As you can see on the web illustration, partners, family, friends and self are drawn closest to the center of the web. We most fear disconnection from the people closest to us. In other words, shame is the most powerful when we enforce the expectation ourselves, or when it's enforced by those closest to us (our partners, our family or friends). Radiating from the center, we have helping professionals (doctors, therapists, etc.), community members, membership groups, educators, colleagues and faith communities.

If we were raised in families in which unattainable body types were highly valued, we might continue to impose that unreasonable expectation on ourselves, even if we have found a partner who accepts us for who we are and who wants desperately for us to feel comfortable with our bodies. In other instances, our partners may enforce strict expectations, but our friends may either offer support or think less of us because we appear overly concerned about dieting. But even in the face of these opposing expectations, we all still want to be accepted and loved by these groups, so we struggle to find ways to please them all and then feel shame when we ultimately fail to meet the competing demands.

When it comes to the outer layers of the web, we may feel shamed by doctors, colleagues or fellow group members. And beyond these groups, there are even larger, more insidious systemic issues that we have to confront. For example, research shows that overweight and obese women have lower incomes ($6,700 a year less) and higher rates of poverty (ten percent higher) than their nonobese peers.

If you look at the perimeter of the shame web, you'll see the media. The culture of shame is reinforced by what we see on television, in advertising and marketing. It's what we see in movies, what we hear in music and what we read in newspapers and magazines. When it comes to body image, there's no question about the value of "thin." To make matters worse, as the "waif look" and "heroin chic" are recycled in yesterday's fashion magazines, the new ideal body is still tiny, except for a round, voluptuous bottom and huge breasts. This combination is not something that occurs very often in nature. The bone-thin, big-booty and boobs combo is more often a "carved to order" package.

Regardless of how hard we try to dodge the influence of the media, in our society we cannot escape it. Jean Kilbourne, one of my favorite researchers and writers, is an expert in helping us identify and deconstruct media messages—even the more subtle ones. According to her book *Can't Buy My Love: How Advertising Changes the Way We Think and Feel*, the average American is exposed to more than three thousand advertisements a day and watches three years' worth of television ads over the course of a lifetime. Trying to escape media influences in today's culture is as feasible as trying to protect ourselves from air pollution by not breathing.

Kilbourne also decodes the competing messages that grace the covers of women's magazines. She points out how the covers are usually plastered with catchy headlines like "Lose 15 Pounds in 10 Days" or "How to Get Healthy and Lighten Up by Summer." However, the pictures that go along with those tag lines never quite fit. The "lose weight now" slogan hangs over a double-chocolate mousse cake rather than a 175-pound woman sweating her butt off on a treadmill.

So, while we're lightening up for summer, we need to make time to whip up that "dessert of the month" and have a slice or two. And as Kilbourne points out, the back of that same magazine probably features a cigarette advertisement that associates smoking with being slim.

It is easy to see how quickly expectations become layered, competitive and conflicting. This is how the shame web works. We have very few realistic options that allow us to meet any of these expectations. Most of the options that we do have feel like a "double bind." Writer Marilyn Frye describes a double bind as "a situation in which options are very limited and all of them expose us to penalty, censure or deprivation."

When our options are limited, every choice violates another

expectation. Often we feel forced to choose between bad or worse:

- Be thin, but don't be weight-obsessed.
- Be perfect, but don't make a fuss about your looks and don't take time away from anything like your family or your partner or your work to achieve your perfection. Just quietly make it happen in the background so you look great and we don't have to hear about it.
- Just be yourself—there's nothing sexier than self-confidence (as long as you're young, thin, beautiful . . .).

If we can't pull it all off—lose the weight, bake and eat the cake, smoke the cigarettes and look cool, stay healthy and fit, buy all the products and, at the same time, love ourselves for who we are— GOTCHA! We get trapped in the shame web. That's when our fear starts to turn to blame and disconnection.

Shame, Blame and Power

When we are feeling shame and fear, blame is never far behind. Sometimes, we turn inward and blame ourselves and other times we strike out and blame others. When we blame ourselves, we often find ourselves in a cycle of self-loathing and shame. Quietly, we emotionally implode. When we try to get out from underneath the pain of shame and fear by blaming others, we often explode. We lash out at our child, our employee, our partner or maybe even the customer service person standing in front of us (we'll explore the relationship between blame and anger in Chapter 8). Either way, imploding or exploding, we are mostly unaware of what we are doing and why we are doing it. We use blame to deal with our feelings of powerlessness.

Power is a difficult topic for women. The majority of women I talk to are uncomfortable with the idea of a "powerful woman."

Many of them quickly associated the concept of a powerful woman with being unliked or being a "bitch." On the other hand, every woman I interviewed was quick to acknowledge how scary and desperate it feels to be powerless. This ambivalence about power poses a serious threat to our ability to be our best selves.

One of the issues that fuels our uncertainty about power is the fact that there are at least two forms of power—I call them "power-over" and "real power." Unfortunately, when most of us hear the word "*power*" we automatically jump to the concept of power-over—the idea that power is the ability to control people, take advantage of others or exert force over somebody or something. We think of power as finite—there's only so much, so if I'm going to get some, I'm forced to take it away from you.

Power-over is a dangerous form of power. Dr. Robin Smith, a psychologist and contributor to *The Oprah Winfrey Show*, described one of the most insidious forms of power-over as working like this: "I will define who you are and then I'll make you believe that's your own definition." This chilling explanation of power-over captures what shame does to us. It forces us into gender straitjackets, then convinces us that we put them on ourselves and that we enjoy wearing them. Over the past year, I've seen a potent example of "power-over" at work. I speak to many groups about shame and body image. When Dove's Campaign for Real Beauty was launched a couple of years ago, I asked women how they felt about seeing "real" women in their panties and bras (versus super-thin models). I was not surprised to hear half the women say they didn't like it. Many described their reaction this way: "I know it's probably a great thing, but I had a very negative emotional reaction when I saw it." Some women felt "embarrassed for the models" and others said, "It doesn't inspire me to look better or lose weight."

Basically, what I heard two years ago is what I still hear from women today: "I know it's empowering and wonderful, but my gut reaction is . . . *You're too fat and not perfect enough—put some clothes on.*" It's important to understand that most of the women who struggle with their emotional reaction to the Dove models look like the Dove models. This is "power-over" at work. Right in line with Dr. Smith's definition, beauty has been defined for us so often and in such insidious ways that we now support and buy into the definition, as if it were our own. The result is disastrous: We don't want to see ourselves reflected back to us in magazines because we're not perfect, thin or beautiful enough to be valued. Ironically, the only way to free ourselves from power-over is to reclaim our real power—the power to create and live by our own definitions.

The Merriam-Webster Dictionary defines *power* as "the ability to act or produce an effect." Real power is basically the ability to change something if you want to change it. It's the ability to make change happen. Real power is unlimited—we don't need to fight over it because there is plenty to go around. And the great thing about real power is our ability to create it. Real power doesn't force us to take it away from others—it's something we create and build with others.

When we talk about shame and powerlessness, we're really talking about three specific components of real power: consciousness, choice and change. In order to effectively make changes and address the problems in our lives, we need to first be conscious or aware of the problem. Second, we need to be able to problem-solve and identify the choices we can make to address the problem. Once we are aware of the problem and our options for dealing with it, we need to be able to facilitate change—we need to be able to act on those choices.

This is a great place to introduce Jillian. I interviewed Jillian in 2002 and then again in 2005. I'll tell you about our first meeting now. Later in the book, you'll learn how Jillian's life changed as she started building shame resilience. This story illustrates the way shame floods us with intense feelings of fear and blame. In our first interview, Jillian told me about a recent shame experience that had her believing she was "losing it."

Jillian had been enjoying an unusually relaxing Saturday with her two kids and her husband, Scott. Jillian and Scott were sitting on the patio while her kids played in the backyard. She was going through the week's mail when she came across a birthday invitation addressed to her five-year-old.

As she started reading it she was overcome with emotion—emotions that she described as a "terrible combination of fear, anger and anxiety." She described her reaction to the emotional flooding. "I swear. Out of nowhere I stood up and started yelling at my kids for being too loud and tearing into my husband for keeping the garage so messy. I ran into the house and slammed my bedroom door." Scott followed her into the house and stood outside the door jiggling the locked doorknob. She told me he just kept saying, "Jesus Christ, Jillian. What is wrong with you? Have you lost your frickin' mind?"

When I asked Jillian what had triggered the emotional flood, she said, "I really didn't know for days. I kept thinking I was going crazy, because it wasn't the first time. I finally figured out that the invitation was for a pool party and it said that parents have to swim with their kids." Jillian explained that she had terrible shame about being in a swimsuit in front of the "perfect, skinny moms." She said, "Sometimes, when I feel ashamed, I get fearful and I just go nuts. I feel so lost. I don't even know what's happening."

As Jillian and I continued to talk about her reaction to the birthday invitation and her fear of being in a swimsuit in front of the "perfect moms," she explained how she'd always been uncomfortable with her body, but since she had gained weight after her pregnancies, she had become very self-conscious. When I asked her to tell me more about motherhood and body image, she began to shake her head and said, "I can't believe it."

She explained that she had flipped through a fashion magazine while she was waiting to get her hair cut and there was a big spread featuring supermodels on the beach with their kids. She started reading it and one of the models was quoted as saying, "Just because

I'm a mom doesn't mean I can let myself go—kids don't want frumpy, fat mothers. My kids are proud of how I look." Jillian looked surprised as she told me about the magazine. "I didn't even realize how that has stuck with me."

Of course, a magazine alone might not trigger strong feelings of shame if we aren't already vulnerable. But, combine those pictures with that quote and the body image issues most of us struggle with, and you have a very powerful combination. It's clear in this example that Jillian felt fearful, trapped and powerless.

When we experience shame, it is very difficult to maintain our power. First, when we feel shame, most of us are not conscious of what we're feeling and why we're feeling it. Shame often produces overwhelming and painful feelings of confusion, fear, anger, judgment and/or the need to escape or hide from the situation. It's difficult to identify shame as the core issue when we're trying to manage all these very intense feelings. In their interviews, many women described the feelings of powerlessness that often overcome us in shaming moments:

- "Shame is that feeling that comes over you like a hot wave and the minute it comes over you think to yourself, 'Oh, my God, where can I hide? How can I disappear?'"
- "Shame is the feeling you get when you believe that you're not worthy of anyone caring about you or loving you. That you're such a bad person that you can't even blame other people for not caring about you. You just want the floor to swallow you up."
- "Shame freezes me. I totally lose my ability to respond."
- "All of a sudden everything goes dark and you're stuck. You don't know what's happening and you don't know what to do."
- "I just go away. I'm never ugly to people. I just disappear. If someone thinks I'm that bad, I'll just make myself invisible so no one has to deal with me."
- "One time I stopped to get gas and my credit card was declined. The guy gave me a really hard time. As I pulled out of the station,

my three-year-old son started crying. I just started screaming, 'Shut up . . . shut up . . . shut up!' I was so ashamed about my card. I went nuts. Then I was ashamed that I yelled at my son."

When we are experiencing shame we are often thrown into crisis mode. Most of the time we can barely handle all of the by-products of shame—the fear, blame and disconnection. In fact, there's new brain research that is helping us understand that shame can be so threatening that, rather than processing it in the neocortex—the advanced part of the brain that allows us to think, analyze and react—shame can signal our brains to go into our very primal "fight, flight or freeze" mode.

In this mode, the neocortex is bypassed and our access to advanced, rational, calm thinking and processing of emotion all but disappears. The primitive part of the brain springs into action and that's when we find ourselves becoming aggressive, wanting to run and hide or feeling paralyzed; sometimes, without any clue as to why. The good news is that by practicing shame resilience, we can actually change this response—we'll discuss this more in Chapter 3.

Shame and Disconnection

If feeling connected is feeling valued, accepted, worthy and affirmed, then feeling disconnected is feeling diminished, rejected, unworthy and reduced. When I asked Jillian why she didn't want to wear a swimsuit in front of her friends, the first thing she said was "I don't want to be put down or criticized. I cringe when I think of them talking about how I look behind my back. I just couldn't handle it." When I asked her if she thought they would care how she looked, she thought about it for a minute and said, "Probably not. I just can't risk being hurt like that. I'd feel totally alone."

While dealing with shame and feelings of disconnection can be a normal part of developing and growing relationships, disconnection can become more serious when it turns into feelings of isolation. When I talk about isolation I don't mean feeling lonely or alone. Jean Baker Miller and Irene Stiver, Relational-Cultural theorists from the Stone Center at Wellesley College, have beautifully captured the overwhelming nature of isolation. They write, "We believe that the most terrifying and destructive feeling that a person can experience is psychological isolation. This is not the same as being alone. It is a feeling that one is locked out of the possibility of human connection and of being powerless to change the situation. In the extreme, psychological isolation can lead to a sense of hopelessness and desperation. People will do almost anything to escape this combination of condemned isolation and powerlessness."

The part of this definition that really strikes me as critical to understanding shame is the sentence "People will do almost anything to escape this combination of condemned isolation and powerlessness." Shame can make us feel desperate. Reactions to this desperate need to escape from isolation and fear can run the gamut from behavioral issues and acting out to depression, self-injury, eating disorders, addiction, violence and suicide.

Personally, I've learned that when I'm experiencing shame, I often act out in ways that are inconsistent with who I want to be. Again, we see the fight, flight or freeze behaviors. Many of the participants expressed this same sentiment in their own language:

- "When I feel shame I'm like a crazy person. I do stuff and say stuff I would normally never do or say."
- "Sometimes I just wish I could make other people feel as bad as I do. I just want to lash out and scream at everyone."
- "I get desperate when I feel shame. Like I have nowhere to turn—no one to talk to."
- "When I feel ashamed I check out mentally and emotionally. Even with my family."
- "Shame makes you feel estranged from the world."

Using the web and the concepts of fear, blame and disconnection, I want to expand our earlier definition to address why and how women experience shame. Here is the full definition that we'll use throughout the remainder of the book:

> *Shame is the intensely painful feeling or experience of believing we are flawed and therefore unworthy of acceptance and belonging. Women often experience shame when they are entangled in a web of layered, conflicting and competing social-community expectations. Shame creates feelings of fear, blame and disconnection.*

TWO

Shame Resilience and the
Power of Empathy

How we do overcome shame? What can we do to avoid getting trapped in the shame web? The bad news is that there's no way to permanently rid ourselves of shame. As long as connection is critical, the threat of disconnection that leads to shame will also be a part of our lives.

The good news, however, is that we are all capable of developing shame resilience. Again, by *resilience*, I mean that ability to recognize shame when we experience it, and move through it in a constructive way that allows us to maintain our authenticity and grow from our experiences. And in this process of consciously moving through our shame, we can build stronger and more meaningful connections with the people in our lives.

In the same way we built an understanding of shame using definitions and descriptions, we have to build an understanding of resilience. First, shame resilience is not an all-or-nothing proposition. There are degrees of resilience. To illustrate this, I developed the Shame Resilience Continuum.

On the left-hand side of that continuum is shame. Under shame are the by-products of shame: fear, blame and disconnection. In

order to get to courage, compassion and connection, we have to discover what moves us away from shame toward resilience. To do that, we go back to the interviews with women about their experiences of shame.

Many of the women I interviewed shared their ideas and strategies for overcoming shame. I analyzed this information by asking:

- What is it that allows women to develop resilience to shame?
- How did they move away from feeling fearful, blaming and disconnected?
- What enabled women to work their way out of shame?

Over and over, the women I interviewed explained how *empathy* is the strongest antidote for shame. It's not just about having our needs for empathy met; shame resilience requires us to be able to respond empathically to others. **Women with high levels of shame resilience were both givers and receivers of empathy.**

Do you remember the petri dishes from high school science lab—those little round dishes? If you put shame in a petri dish and cover it with judgment, silence and secrecy, it grows out of control until it consumes everything in sight—you have basically provided shame with the environment it needs to thrive. On the other hand, if you put shame in a petri dish and douse it with empathy, shame loses power and starts to fade. Empathy creates a hostile environment for shame—it can't survive.

When I asked women to share examples of how they recovered from shame, they described situations in which they were able to talk about their shame with someone who expressed empathy. Women talked about the power of hearing someone say:

- "I understand—I've been there."
- "That's happened to me too."
- "It's OK, you're normal."
- "I understand what that's like."

Like shame itself, the stories of resilience shared a common core. When it comes to shame resilience, empathy is at the center.

Empathy—Easier Said than Done

Real empathy takes more than words—it takes work. Empathy is not simply knowing the right thing to say to someone who is experiencing shame. Our words are only as effective as our ability to be genuinely present and engaged with someone as she tells her story.

I define empathy as the skill or ability to tap into our own experiences in order to connect with an experience someone is relating to us. Another definition I like comes from a counseling textbook by writers Arn Ivey, Paul Pederson and Mary Ivey. They describe empathy as "the ability to perceive a situation from the other person's perspective. To see, hear and feel the unique world of the other." I believe that empathy is best understood as a skill because being empathic, or having the capacity to show empathy, is not a quality that is innate or intuitive. We might be naturally sensitive to others, but there is more to empathy than sensitivity. Here's an example of how my friend Dawn's empathic response helped me through a difficult, shaming moment.

Every now and then, maybe three times a year, my worlds collide. They aren't small schedule conflicts; they are major collisions involving almost every one of my roles. One weekend in May, a couple of years ago, I had one of those collisions. My daughter was having her first ballet recital on the same weekend as the university commencement ceremony. The graduation ceremony and ballet recital overlapped by two hours. This was a huge stressor because I had been elected by the students to play an important role in the graduation ceremony.

In addition to graduation and the ballet recital, that Sunday was Mother's Day and my entire family and my husband Steve's family were coming in from out of town for the festivities. The Friday leading into this monster weekend was my last day of teaching for the spring semester and Ellen's last day of school. For me, the last day means turning in the grades for my students. For Ellen, it means Teacher Appreciation Day.

Steve and I had signed up to bring cookies for the Teacher Appreciation party. In the midst of turning in grades, attending commencement practice, ballet dress rehearsal and getting the house ready for company, the cookies slipped my mind. Steve had dropped off Ellen on Friday morning and when I arrived to pick her up from school, the party sign-up sheet was still hanging on the front door. As I looked down and saw my name next to "dessert," I panicked. I really liked and respected Ellen's teachers. How could I have done this?

I quickly cased the joint and decided to slink in, grab Ellen and sneak out undetected. But as I was making my way down the hall, I came face to face with Ellen's teacher. I immediately went into my nervous, high-voice mode. "Hi, how are you? How was the party?" Ellen's teacher said, "Great, thanks—it was really fun. The food was great."

Oh, no, why did she say something about the food? She must know. I descended from high voice mode to liar mode. I said, "So did Steve bring the cookies this morning?" Ellen's teacher looked puzzled and said, "I'm not sure, I wasn't here when he dropped her off." So I stood on my tippy toes like I was looking over her shoulder, pointed my finger toward the back of the classroom, pretended like I was scanning the food table, and said, "Oh, there they are, right there—yum, they look good. Great, I'm so glad he brought them on time."

She looked at me kindly yet knowingly and said, "I'll see you in a couple of weeks when the summer session starts. Have a good break." I got Ellen, literally slithered back to the car, buckled Ellen in her car seat, sat in the front seat and tears just started pouring down my cheeks. As I sat there, clinging to the steering wheel, I didn't know which was worse: that I had forgotten the cookies, that I had lied about bringing cookies, or the shame of knowing Ellen's teacher must have been thinking, "Man, that was the worst working mom's shuffle I've ever seen."

Ellen looked a little worried so I kept telling her, "It's OK, Mommy has a little cry in her. It's no big deal." I cried all the way home. As soon as I got in the door I called my friend Dawn. She answered à la caller ID, "What's up?"

I confessed quietly and quickly, "I just stole cookies from some parent at Ellen's school. Then I lied to the teacher." Without skipping a beat she said, "What kind of cookies?" I replied, "No. Really. Listen to what I did." She stopped joking around and listened.

When I was done she said, "Look, you're doing the best you can; you have an impossible weekend in front of you. You're just trying to hold it together, and you don't want Ellen's teacher to think that you don't appreciate her. That's pretty understandable given the fact that you like her and she's great with Ellen. It's not a big deal."

I kept asking, "Are you sure? Are you sure?" She finally said, "Look, I know you don't think you're going hold it together for the next three days, but you will. You may not do it perfectly, but you're going to do it. I know that was probably really hard for you, but we've all been there and it's really OK."

In that split second, the shame turned into something else. Something I could handle. Something that moved me away from "I'm so stupid—I'm a terrible mother" to "That was pretty stupid—I'm an overwhelmed mother." She dropped just enough empathy in my petri dish to make it start fading away. She wasn't judgmental. She didn't make me feel I had to keep silent about my misstep. I really felt she had heard me and cared about me. She validated my fear of "barely hanging on" and she acknowledged how much I like Ellen's teachers. Most importantly, she saw my world as I was experiencing it and she was able to express that to me.

She didn't make it "OK" that I lied to Ellen's teacher, but she did make me feel accepted and connected. When I'm in shame, I can't be a good partner or a good teacher or a good mother or a good friend. If I had gone into that weekend feeling I was an unworthy mother and a liar who stole cookies from the mouths of babes, I wouldn't have made it.

She also held back her laughter. I can laugh about it now, but when it was happening, it wasn't the least bit funny to me. She could have laughed and said, "You're making a big deal out of nothing—it's fine. Don't worry." But that would not have been empathy. That might have reflected how she felt, but it certainly would not have expressed that she knew what I was experiencing. A joking response might have left me feeling unheard, diminished and even more ashamed because I was overreacting on top of stealing cookies.

I wasn't in a place where I could have said, "Look, Dawn, I did this really terrible thing. I was just trying to hold it together and I know I'm not perfect." I felt too fearful, trapped and powerless. If Dawn had not extended such great empathy, I probably would have gone into the weekend feeling very disconnected. I'm sure it would have been mere hours before I blamed Steve and blindsided him with a "You have no idea how stressful my life is!" fight. Not a good start to a big family weekend.

Empathy Education

When I was in graduate school, almost every one of my classes included a component on increasing empathy skills. This is true for most people pursuing graduate degrees in professions like psychology, social work, counseling and marriage and family therapy.

In the growing body of empathy research, we are finding that successful leaders often demonstrate high levels of empathy; that empathy is related to academic and professional success; that it can reduce aggression and prejudice and increase altruism. Studies also show that it's a vital component in successful marriages and effective organizations. The bottom line is that empathy is essential for building meaningful, trusting relationships, which is something we all want and need. Given its power to overcome shame and its key role in building many different types of connections, empathy is something we would all be wise to learn and to practice.

Fortunately, empathy is something that can be learned. Teresa Wiseman, a nursing scholar in England, identifies four defining attributes of empathy. They are: (1) to be able to see the world as others see it; (2) to be nonjudgmental; (3) to understand another person's feelings; and (4) to communicate your understanding of that person's feelings.

To understand the complexity of empathy, let's look at each attribute separately. By doing so, we can see how being authentically empathic is an incredible skill—one that takes commitment and practice.

To be able to see the world as others see it. Sometimes the skill of trying to see the world as others see it is called "perspective taking." I find the lens metaphor a very helpful way to understand perspective taking. We all see the world through multiple lenses. These lenses represent who we are and the perspectives from which we view the world. Some of the lenses are constantly changing and some have been with us from the day we were born. Conflict is easy to understand when we think about the lens metaphor. Twenty people can witness the same event, hear the same news story or analyze the same situation, but twenty different sets of lenses cause them all to see, hear and deduce very different things.

In order to be empathic, we must be willing to recognize and acknowledge our own lens and attempt to see the situation that someone is experiencing through her lens. For example, as a researcher, I need to understand how the world looks for the participants I interview. I must work very hard not to see their stories through my lenses, but to listen as they describe what they see, feel and experience. In the cookie example, Dawn was able to take my perspective on the situation and respond empathically from that perspective.

Children are very receptive to learning perspective-taking skills. They are naturally curious about the world and how others operate in it. They are also far less invested in their perspective being the "right one." Those of us who were taught perspective-taking skills as children owe our parents a huge debt of gratitude. Those of us who were not introduced to that skill set when we were younger will have to work harder to acquire it as adults.

Regardless of how hard we work, we are all human and there are times when we will push other people's lives and stories in front of our own lenses, rather than honoring what they see through theirs. Unfortunately, when it comes to responding empathically to someone who is experiencing shame, we're more likely to hold on to our own perspective if we have similar shame issues. If Dawn had recently had her own "mother-shame" experience, she might not have been able to put her lens down long enough to pick up mine. My cookie story might have hit too close to home. Over-identifying with someone's experience can be as much a barrier to perspective taking as not identifying at all.

While perspective taking is not easy, it can be accomplished. It takes commitment, effort, the courage to make a lot of mistakes and the willingness to be confronted about those mistakes. It also requires believing that what we see is *one* view of the world, not *the* view.

To be nonjudgmental. One of the greatest challenges we will face on this path to developing empathy will be to overcome the habit of judging others. We all do it and most of us do it all the time. Judging has become such a part of our thinking patterns that we are rarely even aware of why and how we do it. It takes a great deal of conscious thinking or mindfulness to even bring the habit of judging into our awareness.

Often, our need to judge others is deeply motivated by our need to evaluate our own abilities, beliefs and values. According to research conducted by Sidney Shrauger and Marion Patterson, judging others allows us to appraise and compare our abilities, beliefs and values against the abilities, beliefs and values of others. This explains why we most often judge others around the issues that are important in our lives.

For example, in my interviews with women, I heard over and over how women constantly feel judged by other women when it comes to appearance and motherhood. On the other hand, every man I interviewed talked about how other men are constantly sizing up each other's levels of financial success, intellect and physical strength as measures of power. Sometimes, when suffocating under our culture's rigid gender ideals, we mistakenly believe we can escape the pressure by judging others—"Look, compared to her, I'm great."

Shame, fear and anxiety are all major incubators of judgment. When we are in our own shame about an issue or when we are feeling anxious, threatened or fearful about an issue, refraining from judgment can seem impossible. In my interviews, there were three topics that consistently elicited painfully harsh judgments on the part of the participants. Surprisingly, they were not abortion, politics, religion or any of the big issues of the day. There were the issues that hit closest to home—addiction, parenting and affairs. In other areas, women felt remorse about being so judgmental toward others, but when it came to these issues, women felt absolutely justified in their angry judgments.

For example, I was talking to one woman who was telling me how shaming it is for her when her parents criticize the way she raises her kids. She told me, "When it comes to parenting, everyone is a critic. Very few people ever tell you what you do well; they just find fault in everything you do." She explained how she was working with a parenting coach and reading books and working really hard and that she'd just like someone to acknowledge how hard she's trying. Then, she went on to say, "Here's the thing. I work very hard to be a good parent. I try not to get angry and yell. I try not to lose my patience. When I do lose it and get angry, I feel really bad. I never hit or say hateful things, but sometimes I get angry. I work really hard to be a good mom. If you're that mother who hits, grabs, pushes or jerks your child around, I don't want to know you. If you spank your kids, we probably have nothing in common. If you say mean, hurtful things to your kids, I don't want to hear it and I don't want to be around it."

Given her own sensitivity to being judged, it would be easy to label her criticisms of others as "self-righteousness," but I'm not sure that's accurate, at least not in this example. I saw fear and shame more than anger.

This is the vicious cycle. The judgment of others leaves us feeling hurt and ashamed so we judge others as a way to make ourselves feel better. As I interviewed more and more women about this phenomenon, I realized that to move away from judging, we must be very mindful of what we are thinking, feeling and saying. You can't fake nonjudgment. It's in our eyes, our voices and our body language. Real empathy requires us to stay out of judgment and that's very difficult if we are not self-aware. We must know and understand ourselves before we can know and understand someone else.

To understand another person's feelings. In order to do this, we must be in touch with our own feelings and emotions, and we need to be comfortable in the larger world of emotion and feelings. For many, this world is completely foreign—it's a complex world of new language and thinking. For example, if we can't recognize the subtle, but important, differences between disappointment and anger in ourselves, it's virtually impossible to do with others. If we can't recognize and name fear when we are feeling it, how will we empathically connect to someone else who is in fear?

Emotions are often difficult to recognize and even harder to name. This is especially true if we weren't given the vocabulary and skills required to navigate this emotional world when we were growing up—which unfortunately is the case for most of us.

In the example with Dawn, she made it clear to me that she knew what I was feeling when she said, "You're just trying to hold it together," and "I know you don't think you're going to make it." She didn't have to say, "I hear that you're experiencing high levels of anxiety coupled with the fear of disappointing others." She could have said that—she's a social worker—but she didn't need to, and I'm not even sure that it would have felt as powerful to me. What she did need to do was convey to me that she understood my perspective and my feelings about the situation.

To communicate your understanding of that person's feelings. For me, this last step can sometimes feel risky. I know that when I teach empathy skills to graduate students, this is often where they stumble (where we all stumble). Let's imagine that Dawn misunderstood my feelings or didn't fully get my perspective, and her response was more along the lines of "I know, it's so frustrating. Steve could have remembered to bring those damn cookies to school. Why do we have to remember everything?" Would that have permanently damaged this opportunity for an empathic exchange? Absolutely not. Again, empathy isn't just about the words—it's about fully engaging with someone and wanting to understand. If I knew that Dawn was engaged, but missed my point, I probably would have said something like "No. I'm not pissed off at Steve. I'm freaking out because I screwed up and this weekend hasn't even started yet."

Now, if Dawn had not been engaged and had not really been listening, I might not have bothered to stay connected and to keep seeking what I needed from her. I might have just accepted her comment about Steve and said, "Yeah. The pressure is all on mothers," and moved on. But when I told her that it wasn't funny, she got very quiet and I knew she was listening and wanted to hear me.

Empathy, Courage and Compassion

Stories require voices to speak them and ears to hear them. Stories only foster connection when there is both someone to speak and someone to listen. In sharing my work on women and shame, I hope to accomplish two things: give voice to the voiceless and give ears to the earless. My first goal is to share the complex and important stories that women often keep to themselves because of shame. I want to share these voices because their stories are our stories. They deserve to be told. My second goal is to relay these stories in a way that allows us to hear them. Often, the problem isn't with the voices, but rather with our ears. The voices are frequently there—singing, screaming, yearning to be heard—but we don't hear them because fear and blame muffle the sounds.

Courage gives us a voice and compassion gives us an ear. Without both, there is no opportunity for empathy and connection. Again, I'm not talking about bravery or heroics, I'm talking about ordinary courage—the courage to tell our story from the heart. It took courage to call Dawn and tell her about the cookies. Dawn had to practice compassion. She had to be willing to make room in her world for my painful experience. In the next two sections, we'll explore these ideas of courage and compassion separately, but I first wanted to emphasize the importance of how they work together.

Empathy and Courage

In the Introduction, I talked about the important history of the word *courage*. While it's certainly not unusual for the meanings of words to change over time, many believe that the changing definitions of *courage* mirrors a cultural shift that has diminished the value of women's voices and stories. In the late 1990s, 150 therapists gathered in Vermont to talk about courage and the word's evolution. Elizabeth Bernstein, a therapist and one of the conference organizers, explained that courage is not just about slaying the dragon, but about being true to yourself and speaking your mind.

Reverend Jane Spahr, a Presbyterian minister and gay/lesbian rights activist, also attended the conference. Reverend Spahr told the stories of Saint George and Saint Martha to illustrate the different ways we think about courage. She explained that Saint George slew the dragon because the dragon was bad, but Saint Martha tamed and befriended the dragon. She went on to say, "This is one of our feminist myths that has been lost. Courage could mean to slay the dragon. But could it also mean to tame our fears?"

When I heard Susan, Kayla, Theresa, Sondra, Jillian and the rest of the women I interviewed tell their stories, I was struck by their openness. But as I listened, I realized it was more than openness. It was courage. Every woman who participated in this research willingly embraced her fears in order for us to learn. When we tell our stories, we change the world. I know that sounds dramatic, but I believe it. We'll never know how our stories might change someone's life—our children's, our friends', our parents', our partner's or maybe that of a stranger who hears the story down the line or reads it in a book.

But courage, especially the ordinary courage we need to speak out, is not simple or easily obtained. So often, we hear people say, "Just tell your story!" or "Speak your mind!" It's much more complicated than that. Sometimes we face real threats and consequences when we speak our minds or tell our stories. In fact, as you start to learn about the four elements of shame resilience, you'll see that most of us will have to do a lot of work before we can get to the element of reaching out and sharing our stories. Sometimes compassion is listening to someone's story and other times it's sitting with her in her fear about not being ready to share.

In her article on ordinary courage in girls' and women's lives, Annie Rogers writes, "One way to understand the etymology of courage is to consider its history as a series of losses. Over the course of five centuries, from 1051 to 1490, courage was cut off from its sources in time, in the heart, and in feelings. In other words, courage was slowly dissociated from what traditional Western culture considers feminine qualities, and came to mean 'that quality of mind that shows itself in facing danger without fear or shrinking,' a definition associated with the bravery and heroism of boys and men. The pattern of losses in the history of the word *courage* seems to reflect an increasing invisibility of girls' and women's courage in Western culture."

Without courage, we cannot tell our stories. When we don't tell our stories, we miss the opportunity to experience empathy and move toward shame resilience.

Empathy and Compassion

If empathy is the skill or ability to tap into our own experiences in order to connect with an experience someone is relating to us, compassion is the willingness to be open to this process. To prepare for writing this book, I read everything I could find on compassion. I ultimately found a powerful fit between the stories I heard in the interviews and the work of American Buddhist nun Pema Chödrön. In her book *The Places That Scare You*, Chödrön writes, "When we practice generating compassion, we can expect to experience the fear of our pain. Compassion practice is daring. It involves learning to relax and allow ourselves to move gently toward what scares us. The trick to doing this is to stay with emotional distress without tightening into aversion, to let fear soften us rather than harden into resistance."

When we hear and watch someone tell us the story behind her shame, can we lean into the discomfort of her pain? When Allison, the young woman whose mother committed suicide, tells us about her mother's death and what that's meant for her, can we sit with her in that pain? When the woman whose son is struggling in addiction tells us about her pain, can we be with her in her shame? Or do we feel the need to make it better or redirect the conversation? If we are willing to be open and present, we are willing to practice compassion.

I write "practice" because I believe compassion is a commitment and takes constant practice. Chödrön teaches that we must be honest and forgiving about when and how we shut down. "Without justifying or condemning ourselves, we do the courageous work of opening to suffering. This can be the pain that comes when we put up barriers or the pain of opening our heart to our own sorrow or that of another being. We learn as much about doing this from our failures as we do from our successes. In cultivating compassion we draw from the wholeness of our experience—our suffering, our empathy, as well as our cruelty and terror. It has to be this way. Compassion is not a relationship between the healer and the wounded. It's a relationship between equals. Only when we know our own darkness well can we be present with the darkness of others. Compassion becomes real when we recognize our shared humanity."

Better Late Than Never

I'm frequently asked if I think that it's ever too late to express empathy. Can we go back when we miss the opportunity to be empathic? Interestingly, many women spoke about this during the interviews and the resounding answer was "Better late than never." The impact of "late empathy" might be different from what we'd experience if someone responded empathically right away, but the potential for strengthening the relationship is still there. Let me give you a personal example.

Recently I was eating dinner with a friend. We both had newborns at the time. She stayed at home with her baby and her toddler, and I was getting ready to go back to work. She was telling me about the terrible sadness she felt about the fact that she and her husband were probably not going to have any more children. She explained that even though having two young children was overwhelming at times, she had always wanted three or four and that she was really having a difficult time letting go of that vision of a family.

As she was talking, I was listening; however, the voices in my head were drowning her out: "Oh, my God, what is she thinking? Two is awesome. I'm so happy. This is perfect for me."

My response to her was something like "Two is perfect. It gets a lot more demanding when they get in elementary school. Plus, you could go back to work or graduate school or something." She looked kind of shocked by my reply and stumbled to find the right words. "Well, I'm enjoying staying home with them right now. And if I had another child, it wouldn't stop me from going back to school or work—if I even want to do that. I'm not afraid of working or going back to school with three or four kids."

I scoffed, "Well, you should be afraid."

She very quickly changed the subject, and after doing the uncomfortable surface chat for the next ten minutes, we both got in our cars and headed home. I felt horrible. Two minutes after we drove out of the parking lot, I called her on her cell phone. "Where are you?"

She sounded surprised. "I'm at the corner. Why? Are you OK?"

I told her I needed to talk to her and asked her if she could pull into the gas station across the street.

I pulled in behind her and walked up to her car. She got out and asked, "What's wrong?" I explained, "I need to apologize for what I said . . . and . . . what I didn't say. When you told me that you were having a hard time about possibly not having more kids, I wasn't there for you. I'm really sorry. I want to understand and be here for you. I can tell you're really sad. Will you give me another chance?"

I'm lucky. She was courageous. She started crying and said, "Yeah, what you said felt bad. And, I am really sad. This is incredibly hard for me." I started crying. We talked about it for a while, then we hugged. She thanked me for pulling over and I thanked her for accepting my apology and, as important, giving me another chance.

It takes a lot of courage to share your hurt with someone. It takes even more courage to do it twice—especially after they shut you down the first time.

After reflecting on this situation, I finally figured out that when she started talking to me about not having more children, I instantly heard grief in her voice and that scared me. In fact, it shut down my compassion. I could have handled anger or fear, or maybe even shame. But not grief. I was experiencing high levels of stress and anxiety about my book deadline. I was also in my own grief about the time that I would be away from my new baby as I headed back to work. I filtered her story through my emotions. In other words, my own stuff just got in the way of my compassion.

There are times we will miss the opportunity to be empathic. Mental health professionals often call these "empathic failures." There are also times when the people around us will not be able to give us what we need. When this happens on occasion, most of our relationships can survive (and even thrive) if we work to repair the empathic failures. However, most relationships can't withstand repeated failed attempts at empathy. This is especially true if we find ourselves constantly rationalizing and justifying why we can't be empathic with someone or why someone is not offering us the empathy we need.

I could have easily told myself, "You know what—she needed to hear that. She's crazy for thinking about another baby so soon. I'm sorry if it hurt her feelings, but someone has to tell it like it is." And my friend could have responded to my request for her to let me in again by saying, "No. It's not a big deal. I'm fine."

Developing our empathy skills is not easy. Shame is a complex problem that requires a complex solution. Each of the four attributes of empathy requires us to know ourselves, act authentically and engage with others using our minds and our hearts. This act of empathy produces resilience to shame by countering fear and disconnection.

Empathy and Connection

For women, connection is about mutual support, shared experiences, acceptance and belonging. As you can see in the illustration on page 48, individuals and groups that may enforce the expectations that create shame in one area can turn out to be a valued source of connection building in another area.

In relationships, we are given threads. We can use these threads to weave webs that trap others or to weave blankets of support. It's our choice. For example, a colleague might be a tremendous source of connection around shame experiences that develop from professional situations, yet he or she might make comments or re-inforce stereotypes that trigger shame in other areas, like mother-hood or sexual orientation.

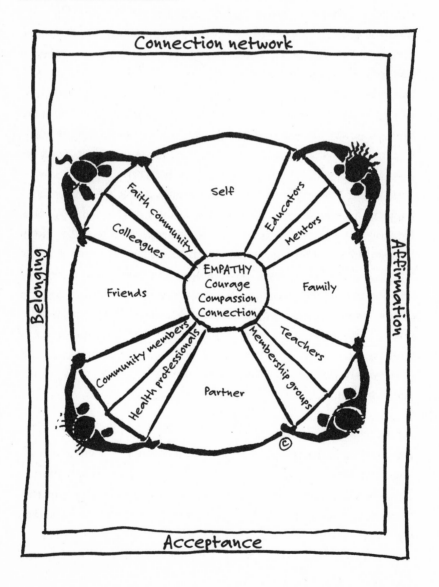

Researchers and activists Lorraine Gutiérrez and Edith Anne Lewis's concept of connection captures its ability to counter the messages, expectations and stereotypes that form the shame web. They write, "Connection serves two purposes: the development of social support networks and the creation of power through interaction. Involvement with others in similar situations provides individuals with a means for acquiring and providing mutual aid, with the opportunity to learn new skills through role modeling, with strategies for dealing with likely institutional reprisals, and with a potential power base for future action."

When we develop and practice empathy, courage and compassion, we move from disconnection to connection. This creates the liberation we need to enjoy the things we value rather than be imprisoned by what others expect. When we are ready to start practicing empathy, we should start with our most important relationship—the one we have with our "self." I write about self-empathy in Chapter 9, but I want to address it here as well. It is important to understand that we cannot practice empathy with others unless we can be empathic with ourselves.

If, for example, we judge ourselves harshly and are incapable or unwilling to acknowledge our own emotions, we will struggle in our relationships with others. If we make a mistake and our self-talk is, "I'm so stupid. I can't do anything right," then we are more likely to turn to our child or partner who has made a mistake and convey the same feelings (even if we don't say them out loud). Empathy and connection require us to know and accept ourselves before we can know and accept others.

Barriers to Empathy
Sympathy Versus Empathy

When we talk about empathy, we often confuse it with sympathy. Yet, during the interviews, women were very clear about the differences between sympathy and empathy. When they talked about their ability to overcome shame, they clearly pointed to empathy:

sharing their feelings with someone who would understand and relate to what they were saying. Conversely, women used words like *hate, despise* and *can't stand* to describe their feelings about sympathy seeking—looking for sympathy or being asked for sympathy.

Empathy seeking is driven by the need to know that we are not alone. We need to know that other people have experienced similar feelings and that our experiences don't keep us from being accepted and affirmed. Empathy helps us move away from shame toward resilience. Sympathy, on the other hand, can actually exacerbate shame.

To illustrate the difference between sympathy and empathy, let's go back to the cookie story. About a week after my conversation with Dawn, Steve and I were eating dinner with some friends who really appear to be the super working parents. During dinner, they told a story about parents who had had the gall to bring sugary "store-bought" treats in plastic bags to their seven-year-old son's homeroom party.

Of course, I'm one notch below store-bought treats; I'm the treat thief. I reacted to their story by saying, "Well, when I remember to bring treats they're normally store-bought—it's a rare occasion that I have the time to make something homemade." They gave me the quasi-friendly upside-down smile like they were thinking, "Hmm—let's make a note of this."

So, for some reason, this response compelled me to tell the cookie appropriation story. Maybe I was trying to test the waters—given their comments about store-bought snacks, could we possibly belong to their club? Dawn had shown empathy, but she wasn't a mother at the time. Maybe I was seeking redemption from these Super Parents. If they could understand, I must be OK.

It was one of those stories you begin telling with enthusiasm and a strong commitment to be genuine, but in the middle, when you sense it's not going over very well, you skip the worst details and try to wrap it up as quickly as possible. I don't know what I was expecting, but I certainly didn't expect them to literally gasp and put their hands over their eyes (like looking at me might blind them). When I was done, they shook their heads in unison and looked at me with pity. She leaned toward me and said, "Oh, my God, that's so horrible. I can't imagine doing that. I'm so sorry."

Their sympathy slapped me across the face. Like all sympathy, it said, "I'm over here and you're over there. I'm sorry for you and I'm sad for you. AND, while I'm sorry that happened to you, let's be clear: I'm over here." This is not compassion.

In most cases, when we give sympathy we do not reach across to understand the world as others see it. We look at others from our world and feel sorry or sad for them. Inherent in sympathy is "I don't understand your world, but from this view things look pretty bad." Looking back, I think the worst thing that she said to me was probably "I can't imagine doing that."

When she said that, it was very clear that she didn't see the world as I saw it. She saw my experience from her world, and again, that's not empathy. Secondly, I certainly felt judged. I heard nothing that told me she understood my feelings, and in no way did she communicate her understanding of my experience. When our need for empathy is met with sympathy, it can often send us deeper into shame—we feel even more alone and separated. Empathy is about connection; sympathy is about separation.

Sympathy Seeking
On the flipside of responding to empathy seeking with sympathy is the complex issue of trying to express empathy when someone is seeking sympathy. One sentiment underlying sympathy seeking is often "Feel sorry for me because I'm the only one this is happening to" or "my situation is worse than everyone else's." This naturally creates disconnection and separation. People seeking sympathy are not looking for empathy or evidence of shared experiences—they are searching for confirmation of their uniqueness.

When I talk about sympathy seeking in workshops, the audience members usually start to look agitated and crusty. I learned early on how to diffuse the situation—I just have to ask, "How many of you know someone who sympathy-seeks and are thinking of that person as I describe this concept?" Without fail, hands shoot up across the room—the participants are anxious to talk about the person they're envisioning and how irritating he or she is.

I've had many people tell me that they feel manipulated and controlled by the people in their lives who are sympathy seeking. I even hear these descriptors from therapists who often feel stuck when they're working with someone who is in sympathy-seeking mode.

It's not unusual to feel resentful or dismissive when someone requests our sympathy. When people look for sympathy, it feels like a no-win situation. On the one hand they are telling us that they have it worse than anyone and no one can understand, but on the other hand they are looking for our validation.

I interviewed one woman who said, "In my family, my husband is the only one who is entitled to have it hard. Even if I'm going through something just like him or something worse, the attention needs to be on him. He's not asking for help. He just wants me to tell him that his life is hard and unfair and worse than mine. He thinks he works harder, sleeps less and does more. Trust me, he doesn't."

Sometimes the best we can do with someone who is sympathy seeking is to fake a "Yeah, that's really hard" or "Wow, sounds rough." But on the inside we're probably thinking, "Please . . . get over it," or "Hey, that's nothing," or "Enough of the pity party." Sometimes these requests for sympathy make us so angry and resentful that we can't even muster a benign response. However they play out, it's easy to see why these exchanges rarely produce real connection and understanding.

While sympathy seeking is often about casting ourselves in a unique light, we can certainly communicate "feeling alone" and "feeling like the only one" without sympathy seeking. What separates sympathy and empathy is our motivation for sharing struggles. And, ironically, our motivation for sympathy seeking is often shame.

My first year as a doctoral student, I did a lot of sympathy seeking. Unsurprisingly, the more I sought sympathy, the more alone I felt. I was so overwhelmed by my classes that the shame and fear of potential failure was too real and immanent for me to say, "I'm drowning. I feel like I'm in over my head and if I quit or fail, my life is going to be over." While that sentiment is relatable for almost everyone I know, I just wasn't in a place where I could clearly understand, much less articulate, my true feelings.

I would say, "You have no idea what the pressure is like—it's not like getting an undergraduate degree or the office." For the people around me, this translated to "This is more important than anything you've ever done, so feel really sorry for me." When friends and family responded to my plea with halfhearted sympathy, I would dig myself in even more by thinking, "I knew it! It's not like any of them is in a doctoral program."

When we find ourselves seeking sympathy, it is helpful to step back and think about what we are really feeling, what it is we're seeking and what we really need. On the other hand, when we are asked to give sympathy, we have to decide if we want to simply give it and move on or really try to connect and develop empathy.

If we want to develop connection and understanding, sometimes the best way to practice compassion is to say, "It sounds like you are in a hard place, tell me more about it," or "You're right, I don't know what that's like. What is it like? Help me understand."

Sometimes, when I facilitate groups, I'll even say to someone, "You are telling us that no one can understand, yet you're asking us to understand. What should we do? We want to connect, but you're telling us it's impossible." Often, a dialogue grounded in these questions can lead to genuine empathy and connection.

Stacking the Deck

Another barrier to developing empathy is a phenomenon I call "Stacking the Deck." In many ways this is related to sympathy-seeking behavior. Over and over, women described how devastated they were after they finally mustered up the courage to reach out to someone, then had their story trumped by the "you think you've got it bad" card:

- I'll see your "drunk mother" and raise you a "drug-addict sister."
- I'll see your "unmarried and thirty" and raise you a "single mom."

When we compete to see whose situation is worse, whose oppression is the most real or whose "-ism" is the most serious, we lose sight of the fact that most of our struggles stem from the same place—powerlessness and disconnection.

If we spend our resources attempting to outdo one another, competing for "last place," or stepping on each other to climb out of shame, shame will always prevail. It will prevail because being told "That's nothing" can make us feel like nothing. Most of us will feed shame with our silence before we risk sharing something that we fear might not be as bad as someone else's situation, or bad enough to warrant empathy.

Lorraine, a woman in her early twenties, talked about the shame she felt when she finally opened up with her college roommate about the fact that her teenaged brother was schizophrenic and had a history of violence before he was stabilized on his medications. "She had asked me about him several times. I finally told her about him and I started crying. I explained that I'm not ashamed of him, but I'm ashamed that my parents have him living in a treatment center. She didn't say anything back to me."

When I asked her what happened next in the conversation Lorraine said, "My roommate just stood up and said, 'That's no big deal. Kendall's [their suitemate] little sister was killed in a car wreck. That's got to be way worse.' Then she walked into the bathroom. I felt so small. I wish I hadn't said anything at all."

We don't know why Lorraine's roommate was unable or unwilling to respond empathically. Perhaps she was fearful about the level of emotion she saw in Lorraine or maybe she just didn't want to know. There are many reasons. Let's look at a couple of other common responses as examples of how easy it is to skip right over empathy.

"I feel like my marriage is falling apart right before my very eyes."

Response A: "Oh, no, you and Tim are a great couple—I'm sure everything will be fine."
This is the "you have NOT been heard" and "they're not going there" response.
Response B: "At least you have a marriage. John and I haven't had a real marriage for years."
I call this the "I'm bringing it back to me" response. It lacks concern and empathy completely. There aren't many hard and fast rules about empathy, but this might be one: *At least* is not a good lead-in for an empathic response:

"I had a miscarriage." "At least you know you can get pregnant."
"I've been diagnosed with cancer." "At least you caught it early."
"My sister is really struggling with her alcoholism." "At least it's not drugs."

This "at least" response is primarily about our own discomfort. "At leasting" someone is equivalent to shutting her down.
Response C: "I'm really sorry—that can be a very lonely place. Is there anything I can do?" This response demonstrates empathy. It is not judgmental. It's an attempt to reflect back how someone might be feeling. Even if she's not feeling lonely, she has a chance to respond and she knows you are trying to understand her world.

The pressure "to get it right" or to "say the perfect thing" can be the biggest barrier to empathy and compassion. We start to experience anxiety about saying the right thing and before we know it, we've missed the opportunity to be empathic and compassionate. We diminish, change the subject or walk away. Lorraine's roommate didn't have to say anything magical. She could have just said, "Gosh, that must be so hard for everyone in your family," or "That would be hard for me too—how is your brother doing in the center?"

Often, just hearing about someone's shaming experience can cause us to want to shield ourselves. We don't want to hear it. It's too painful just to listen. One reason empathy and compassion are so powerful is the fact that they say to someone, "I can hear this. This is hard, but I can be in this space with you."

Digging Deep

Another way we avoid empathic connection is by convincing ourselves that we can't really understand experiences that we haven't actually had. Lorraine's roommate might have thought, "I have no idea what it's like to have a brother with a mental illness—how am I supposed to know what to say?" The bottom line is this: If we want to build connection networks—networks that really help us move from shame to empathy—we cannot reserve empathy for the select few who have had experiences that mirror our own. We must learn how to move past the situations and events that people are describing in order to move toward the feelings and the emotions they're experiencing.

For example, one of the participants spoke about the difficulty of being an African-American medical student. Here's how she described her experience:

- For me shame is about being too black at school and too white for my family and friends at home. In medical school everyone looks at me like I don't belong. I feel like they wonder if I'm the "affirmative action" case. It's not just about race either. I'm also from a pretty poor family. I went to college on scholarships. Most of my friends didn't even finish high school. When I'm at school, it's clear that I'm different. When I go home they give me a hard time. One time my grandmother said, "Leave that white coat and that white attitude at the door. Don't be thinking you're Marcus Welby around here." Even though I act the same, they assume I think I'm better than they are. I don't. I just want to feel like I fit someplace.

Now, I would venture to say the majority of us are not black medical students. Most of us have not had the experience of straddling the very white, male world of medicine and black family life. If we read her quote and we walk away thinking, "Wow, that sounds pretty tough, but I can't really relate to that," then we've missed an opportunity for empathy. This is critical because our level of shame resilience depends equally on both our ability to receive empathy and our ability to extend empathy.

On missing the opportunity to be empathic, Jean Baker Miller and Irene Stiver (researchers and therapists from the Stone Center) write, "The phenomenon of empathy is basic to all our relationships. Either we deal with the feelings that are inevitably present in our interactions by turning to each other, or we turn away. If we turn away from others without conveying recognition of the existence of their feelings, we inevitably leave the other person diminished in some degree. We also are inevitably turning away from engaging fully with our own experience, dealing with it in a less than optimal way—that is, in isolation."

If we reach far enough into our own experiences, most of us can relate to trying to keep one foot in one world and the other foot in another world. Most of us know what that feels like. When I open myself up to hearing beyond the struggles of balancing medical school and family life, I immediately think about trying to keep one foot in motherhood and one foot in a very male-defined academic world.

When I'm in one world the message is "It's great that you're a mother, but we don't really want to see any evidence of that around here. If your children are sick, you'll still need to be here; if their day care closes, we would prefer you not bring them here." So I have one foot in this world where I'm allowed to be a mother, but only if it doesn't detract from my focus as an academic. And my other foot is in motherhood, where it's OK that I work at pursuing something I think is important, but not if it disrupts anything that goes on at home.

On some days I can stay balanced. On other days, I feel fearful that the worlds will drift so far apart that I'll end up losing my footing in both. The worst feeling for me is that sense that I am the only person about to be split in half.

I'm not an African-American medical school student, but I've had similar experiences in terms of trying to balance two worlds that often seem mutually exclusive. For me, this experience makes me feel lonely, unworthy and like something is wrong with me. So when I read her statement about shame, while I certainly do not want to project my experiences onto her, I do want to be able to touch, in myself, some of the emotions that she might be feeling so that I can try to connect with what she's saying.

I don't have to tell her my story. I certainly wouldn't say, "I know exactly what you mean," because I don't. I may know what it feels like to try to balance different roles, but I don't know what racism feels like. I don't know how exhausting it is to have to constantly shift from one culture to another in order to "fit in." I don't believe we can fully understand racism, sexism, homophobia, ageism or any other form of oppression, unless we've experienced it. However, I do believe that we are all responsible for constantly developing our understanding of oppression and recognizing our part in perpetuating it. Empathy is a powerful place to start.

So often I find that our feelings of unearned privilege kill empathy. By unearned privilege I mean the privileges afforded us simply because we are white or straight or members of certain groups. We get stuck in what I call privilege shame. This is very different from privilege guilt (or white guilt). It's appropriate to feel guilt over forwarding a racist e-mail or telling a hurtful joke. Guilt can motivate change. Guilt helps us reconcile our choices with our values.

Shame doesn't help. If we feel ashamed because we don't know how to relate to someone who is different or connect with someone who faces unfair discrimination, we get stuck. If we think, "I'm a bad person because I can't relate to her" or "I'm a bad person because I have this and they don't"—we get paralyzed. For me, I've come to a place in my life where unlearning prejudice is more important than avoiding situations where I might be accused of saying or doing the wrong thing. I've learned that it is better for me to accept the fact that I struggle with many of the same learned biases that other people do. This had allowed me to spend my energy unlearning and changing my prejudices rather than proving that I don't have any.

When we are honest about our struggles, we are much less likely to get stuck in shame. **This is critical because shame diminishes our capacity to practice empathy.** Ultimately, feeling shame about privilege actually perpetuates racism, sexism, heterosexism, classism, ageism, etc. I don't have to know "exactly how you feel"—I just have to touch a part of my life that opens me up to hearing your experience. If I can touch that place, I stay out of judgment and I can reach out with empathy. This is where both personal and social healing can begin.

Imagine what it would be like if we could only reach out to folks who have had our exact experiences. We would all be very much alone. Life experiences are like fingerprints; no two are exactly alike. Furthermore, even if we've had what we believe is the exact same experience as someone else, we can never know exactly how they feel. Going back to the lens metaphor, there are just too many variables for any of us to experience anything the exact same way.

Below are five more shame experiences from my research. Under each, I've labeled some of the emotions that I heard in the interviews, and I've posed empathy questions that might help us connect with that experience.

Experience: When I think of shame I think of being sexually abused when I was growing up. I think about what that's done to my life and how it's changed everything. It's not just the abuse itself. It's everything you have to deal with the rest of your life. It's like you feel different from anyone else; nothing is ever normal for you. Everything is about that. I'm not allowed just to have a regular life. That is the thing that made me who I am and so everything is stained by that. That's what shame is for me.

Emotions: Feeling labeled, dismissed, misunderstood and reduced. Emotions might include grief, loss, frustration and anger.

Dig Deep: Have you ever been defined by an experience? Found yourself unable to get out from under a reputation or "an incident"? Have you ever been unfairly labeled? Have you ever had people attribute your behaviors to an identity you don't deserve? Have you ever fought to overcome something, only to find others less than willing to move past it?

Experience: I'm ashamed because I always hate my life. No matter what I have and no matter how much I have, I'm always disappointed with my life. I always think to myself, "If I only had this or that I'd be happy." I get this or that and I'm still not happy. It's a horrible part of me and I don't know how to make it go away. I can't talk about it with anyone because everyone is sick of hearing how disappointed I am about everything all the time. That's what's shameful to me. I just can never seem to pull it all together and find happiness.

Emotions: Stuck, angry, overwhelmed, disappointed, confused, lost, alone.

Dig Deep: Do you ever feel like happiness is always in front of you? Do you ever set yourself up to be happy when you lose twenty pounds or get a new house or have another baby or get promoted? Do you define success by what you don't have? Do you ever dismiss what you do have because it must not be that great if you have it? Do you ever feel like people are sick of hearing you complain or vent?

Experience: Shame is when my husband left me for another woman and my son told me it was because I was a "fat-ass." He's only fourteen and I don't think he meant it, or at least I hope not. He's just used to hearing it from his father. Plus he's angry and maybe he does think it's my fault. Maybe I think it's my fault.
Emotions: Hurt, loss, anger, fear, grief, self-blame, confused, isolated, trapped.
Dig Deep: Have you ever struggled not to blame yourself? Have you ever been the target of someone's anger and grief? Have you ever had to take care of someone when you could barely take care of yourself? Have you ever had a child parrot a partner's insults?

Experience: When I made partner at the law firm I went into a terrible depression. Everything I had worked for seemed like nothing. Every day I went to work thinking, "Oh, my God, when are they going to catch on to the fact that I really don't know what I'm doing? I didn't deserve this promotion; I don't deserve partnership. They're going to find out that I'm really not good." The pressure was so much that I finally had to step down. I don't think people respect me anymore. I just couldn't do it. I don't know if I was really that good and I deserved it or that I really was never that good and I was faking it. It just got too confusing.
Emotions: Fear, self-blame, confusion, overwhelmed, isolation, insecure, loss, disappointment.
Dig Deep: Have you ever felt like an imposter—like people think you are more capable than you really are? Have you ever feared "getting caught" when you didn't do anything wrong? Have you ever felt the pressure of disappointing others? Yourself?

It is easy to think that it is safer to distance ourselves rather than dig for empathy, but as social worker Marki McMillan writes, "Empathy is a gift of validation that, no matter how many times it is given, always returns us to our own truth. Empathy heals another at exactly the same time it is healing me."

Don't We Need a Little Shame to Keep Us in Line?
Another barrier to being empathic centers around our beliefs about shame. If we believe that shame is a constructive emotion, we might not be interested in being empathic. We might listen to someone's experience and think, "You should feel ashamed!"

When I started this research I wasn't sure about the distinction I had seen drawn between good shame and bad shame. There is a small group of researchers, especially those working from an evolutionary or biological perspective, who believe that shame has both negative and positive consequences. The positive consequence of shame, they contend, is its ability to serve as a compass for moral behavior. They believe that shame keeps us in line. Seven years of testing the proposition that shame can't be used to change people, combined with a lack of actual data supporting this claim, made me a little suspicious, but I was willing to let the research speak for itself.

It didn't take very long for me to reach the conclusion that there is nothing positive about shame. In any form, in any context and through any delivery system, shame is destructive. The idea that there are two types, healthy shame and toxic shame, did not bear out in any of my research.

When I talked to women about the possibility of shame having positive outcomes or serving as a guidepost for good behavior, they made it clear that shame is so overbearing and painful that, regardless of the intent, it moved them away from being able to grow, change and respond in any kind of genuine or authentic way. Guilt, on the other hand, was often a strong motivator for change.

Again, there are researchers who disagree with this proposition and continue to believe in a concept of healthy shame, but there is now a growing body of evidence against that idea. One of the most comprehensive books on shame research is *Shame and Guilt* by June Price Tangney and Ronda L. Dearing. In it, Tangney and Dearing offer an excellent overview of the shame and guilt literature, and they present some of their original research on these emotions.

In a section of their book entitled "Does Shame Serve Any Adaptive Function?" Tangney and Dearing explain how earlier conceptualizations of shame may not take into consideration the current way people self-evaluate and relate to one another. They write, "With increasingly complex perspective-taking and attributional abilities, modern humans have the capacity to distinguish between self and behavior, to take another person's perspective, and to empathize with others' distress. Whereas early moral goals centered on reducing potentially lethal aggression, clarifying social rank, and enhancing conformity to social norms, modern morality centers on the ability to acknowledge one's wrongdoing, accept responsibility, and take reparative action. In this sense, guilt may be the moral emotion of the new millennium."

If you're interested in additional reading about shame—the distinctions between shame and guilt and how shame is measured in research—this is an excellent book, though it may feel a little research-heavy for some. To help clarify the difference between shame and guilt when it comes to positive behavioral outcomes, I'd like to tell you about two important studies described in their book.

The first is Tangney and Dearing's eight-year study of moral emotions in which they followed a group of almost four hundred children. Using a measurement instrument that presented potentially shaming or guilt-eliciting situations, they found that shame proneness in fifth-graders (that is, a susceptibility to shame) was a strong predictor of later school suspension, drug use (including amphetamines, depressants, hallucinogens and heroin) and suicide attempts. On the other hand, when they compared children who were guilt-prone, the guilt-prone fifth graders were more likely to later apply to college and to be involved in community service. They were less likely to make suicide attempts, use heroin or drive under the influence of alcohol or drugs, and they began having sex at a later age.

The second is a substance abuse study conducted by Dearing, Stuewig and Tangney. The researchers found that when shame proneness increases, substance abuse problems increase. In the same study they found that guilt proneness may have a protective effect against the development of problematic alcohol- and drug-use patterns. I've written more about this study in Chapter 9.

As we learn more about the positive aspects of guilt, I believe it's important to remember that feeling guilty is only adaptive if we are the ones who are actually responsible for a specific outcome, event or behavior. Too often, in our society, women are blamed when they bear no responsibility, and socialized to take responsibility for things they shouldn't. In her book *Changing Course: Healing from Loss, Abandonment and Fear*, Dr. Claudia Black refers to this type of guilt as "false guilt." She writes, "Feeling guilty for other people's behaviors and actions is a 'false' guilt. Taking on guilt for things over which we had no control is false guilt. There are enough things in life for which we are responsible and therefore can experience 'true' guilt."

This is also not a call to raise guilt-prone kids; more than anything, these findings are additional evidence that seriously call into question shame's ability to produce good behavior. I think all of us are capable of remembering a time when we were experiencing profound shame. I can honestly say that in those moments of shame when I felt rejected, worthless and degraded, I was far more likely to engage in inappropriate behaviors than I was to choose the healthier behaviors that seem so natural when I am feeling accepted and good about who I am.

When we start to explore the concept that all shame is bad

and destructive, it really forces us to reevaluate how we use shame to parent, how we use shame to fight with partners and, on a community and societal level, how we use shame to punish. In a world that still falls back on "You should be ashamed of yourself," "Shame on you" and "Have you no shame?" the time has come to explore the possibility that we are safer in a world where people aren't mired in shame.

To help you think about these concepts I invite you to compare the following two approaches to working with men who batter their partners. As a social worker, domestic violence is a very important subject to me, and one that I spend a lot of my time and energy trying to understand. In Harriet Lerner's book *The Dance of Connection*, she tells a story about Ron, a man who punches his wife, Sharon, in the face and stomach and is forced to attend court-ordered therapy sessions. Dr. Lerner explains that Ron resists being in a group of batterers but is willing and even interested in joining a group of men who have trouble controlling their anger.

Dr. Lerner writes, "Ron was resisting the notion that his crime defined him. You might argue that Ron is a batterer and that any language that softens or obscures this fact leaves him less accountable for his actions, but Ron will be more likely to accept responsibility and feel remorse if he can view himself as more than a batterer. For people to look squarely at their harmful actions and to become genuinely accountable they must have a platform of self-worth to stand on. Only from the vantage point of higher ground can people who commit harm gain perspective. Only from there can they apologize."

Dr. Lerner goes on to explain that refusing to take on an identity defined by one's worst deeds is a healthy act of resistance. If Ron's identity as a person is equated with his violent acts, he won't accept responsibility or access genuine feelings of sorrow and remorse, because to do so would threaten him with feelings of worthlessness. Dr. Lerner concludes the section in her book by writing, "We cannot survive when our identity is defined by or limited to our worst behavior. Every human must be able to view the self as complex and multidimensional. When this fact is obscured, people will wrap themselves in layers of denial in order to survive. How can we apologize for something we are, rather than something we did?"

Now, let's contrast Harriet Lerner's thoughts on battering and the need for self-worth to the views of Judge Ted Poe. Judge Poe, who is now a member of the U.S. House of Representatives, has received local and national attention for his "shame and humiliation punishment" of criminals. In two separate cases, Judge Poe ordered men who assaulted their wives to make public apologies in front of the Family Law Courthouse in downtown Houston.

The apologies were delivered in front of hundreds of downtown employees during the lunch hour. In an editorial piece written by Poe and published in the *Houston Chronicle*, Poe defends his actions by writing, "Let those who would beat their wives, steal their neighbor's property and abuse children feel the sting of the community's intolerance, hear their names on our lips and pay the price in full view of the public. Shame on them or shame on us."

I leave you with these questions. If your husband was battering you and he was forced to apologize on the steps of City Hall in front of hundreds of people, would you like to be the woman he comes home to after his day of public shaming? Given what we know about shame and how it affects us, are we safer with him when he's in shame or when he is repairing shame? Are we using shame as a punishment because we think it will foster real change in people? Or are we shaming others because it feels good to make people suffer when we are in fear, anger or judgment?

Developing Shame Resilience

Developing shame resilience, this ability to move toward empathy in the face of shame, is not an easy process. If it were, shame would not be such a prevalent and destructive force in our lives.

One of the greatest challenges to developing shame resilience is the way shame actually makes us less open to giving or receiving empathy. Shame protects itself by making it very difficult for us to access its antidote. When we are in shame, reaching out for empathy feels very dangerous and risky. And when we are in shame and someone reaches out to us, it is very difficult to dig deep and find anything beyond fear, anger and blame.

As I read through the interviews I conducted with these courageous women, I tried to identify the qualities that helped women develop shame resilience. Did the women who were successful in overcoming shaming experiences have anything in common? Did the women who were able to give and receive empathy have different information or skills from the women who struggled more with their shame?

The answer to both questions is yes. I found four elements that were shared by all the women who demonstrated high levels of shame resilience. They are:

1. The ability to recognize and understand their shame triggers
2. High levels of critical awareness about their shame web
3. The willingness to reach out to others
4. The ability to speak shame

For the sake of an organized presentation on paper, the four elements are forced into linear order (1–4). I'm presenting them in the order that reflects what I heard most often in the interviews. It's important to understand, however, that this is different for everyone. Some women start with the fourth element of speaking out. Others start with the second or third element. You know yourself best. Please think about the information in this book in the context of your own life and experiences, and begin developing resilience or practicing empathy in the areas where you are most comfortable. Success there will likely give you confidence to being working in the areas you consider more difficult.

Additionally, in the chapters describing the four elements of shame resilience, I've included some written exercises. I've used these exercises with thousands of women. Most find them to be an extremely helpful start to the process. You are welcome to follow along and keep your own journal with the exercises or you can just read them and think about them. If you go to my Web site (www.brenebrown.com), you can download the preformatted exercises.

I've had many people tell me that they worked through the exercises with a friend, siblings or with a group of friends. I've talked to many women who read them as part of their group therapy. I actually think working through the process with other people is one of the most effective ways to develop shame resilience. Shame happens between people and it heals between people. It's just important that you have some level of trust and confidence in your relationship so you feel safe exploring these ideas.

I also think there is power in writing down our thoughts, reading them and reflecting on them. All of the exercises were developed with writing in mind. Again, you are welcome to read them and think about them or write them all down—find a way that is meaningful for you.

THREE

The First Element: Recognizing Shame and Understanding Our Triggers

If we're going to build shame resilience, we have to start by recognizing and identifying shame. Because shame floods us with strong emotions like fear and blame, we often can't recognize what's happening until after we've already reacted in a way that moves us away from our authenticity and, in some cases, exacerbates our shame.

For example, the mother whose credit card was declined—she was overwhelmed with feelings of shame and took it out on her crying child. Most of us with children are not strangers to that phenomenon. It happens in a split second. The goal is to learn to recognize when we are experiencing shame quickly enough to prevent ourselves from lashing out at those around us. Or if, as in this example, we have already yelled at our child, we want to learn to immediately stop, calm down, take a breath and make amends.

Somewhat paradoxically, our bodies often to react to shame even before our conscious minds do. People always think it's strange when I ask them where and how they physically feel shame. But for most of us, shame has a feeling—it's physical as well as emotional. This is why I often refer to shame as a full-contact emotion. Women have described various physical reactions to shame, including stomach tightening, nausea, shaking, waves of heat in their faces and chests, wincing and twinges of smallness. If we can recognize our physical responses, sometimes we can limit the powerlessness that we feel when we are in shame.

When I started this research project, I was unaware of my own physical responses to shame. I only started investigating them after interviewing the first fifty women. At that point in the research, it became clear to me that women with high levels of shame resilience recognized and could describe their physical reactions to shame. One woman told me, "My mouth gets really dry and I feel like I can't swallow. I try to recognize it and name it right away." When I asked her how, she said she starts whispering, "Pain, pain, pain, pain, pain, pain." She explained, once she can acknowledge what's happening, she can make better choices about how to deal with it.

I thought it was a little strange until I tried it. I doubt it will work for everyone, but I think it's a great example of how recognizing a physical indication of shame increases our opportunity to be mindful and to react consciously.

The questions below are designed to help us focus on recognizing our physical reaction to shame. Spend some time thinking about these or answering them on paper. Some may fit for you and others might not.

I physically feel shame in/on my _____
It feels like _____
I know I'm in shame when I feel _____
If I could taste shame, it would taste like _____
If I could smell shame, it would smell like _____
If I could touch shame, it would feel like _____

Recognizing shame is an important tool for regaining our power. For example, I know that I need to be alone for at least fifteen or twenty minutes when I'm experiencing shame. Now that I recognize the physical symptoms, I often use those as a cue to make a quick exit. Once I'm alone, I can feel my feelings in private. I can cry or take deep breaths. Most of the women I interviewed talked about the importance of being alone for a few minutes, so they could "pull themselves together" or "sort through their feelings." I also had women tell me they liked to jog, go for walks or be outside.

When we know how shame feels, we have an important resilience tool. Often, we feel shame before we think it. Recognizing our shame allows us to find the space we need to process the experience and gain some clarity before we act out or shut down. The next step in examining our experiences is to better understand our shame triggers.

Shame Triggers

When I first began my research, one of my goals was to develop a list of shame triggers. My thinking was pretty simple—if we knew what issues triggered shame, we could stay alert and, if not avoid them, at least increase our awareness about the potential of experiencing shame. Of course, it didn't take long to learn that shame is a highly individualized experience and there are no universal shame triggers. Along with other researchers, I found that the issues and experiences that trigger shame appear to be as individual and different as women, their relationships and their cultures. I also learned that we face shame every day—no matter how well we can recognize our triggers, avoiding shame is not possible.

However, as I spoke to women, I saw a very strong pattern emerge in the interviews: *Women with high levels of shame resilience recognize shame and understand their shame triggers.* When women with high shame resilience talked about their shame, they clearly knew what triggered it and why some issues were greater triggers than others.

Recognizing and understanding our triggers is not something that we instinctively know how to do. It's a process. Sylvia's story is a great example of this first element of resilience in action.

Sylvia, an event planner in her thirties, jumped right into our interview by saying, "I wish you could have interviewed me six months ago. I was a different person. I was so stuck in shame." When I asked her what she meant, she explained that she had heard about my research from a friend and volunteered to be interviewed because she felt her life had been changed by shame. She had recently had an important breakthrough. Sylvia said her breakthrough happened when she found herself on the "losers' list" at work.

Apparently, after two years of what her employer called "outstanding, winner's" work, she had made her first big mistake. The mistake cost her agency a major client. Her boss's response was to put her on the "losers' list." She said, "In one minute I went from being on the winner's board to being on top of the losers' list." I guess I must have winced when Sylvia referred to the "losers' list" because, without my remarking at all, she said, "I know, it's terrible. My boss has big dry-erase boards outside of his office. One's the winners' list and one board is for the losers." She said for weeks she could barely function. She lost her confidence and started missing work. Shame, anxiety and fear took over.

Then one evening, Sylvia was talking to her sister about the "loser" board and it all started to make sense. Sylvia and her sister had been very competitive athletes in high school. Sylvia had even been offered a scholarship but turned it down. As Sylvia and her sister talked, her sister reminded Sylvia about their father's constant use of the word *loser*. "No one likes a loser." "Losers never change." He would post their track times on the refrigerator door along with sticky notes that said things like *Be a winner!*

Sylvia said, "I got off the phone with my sister, cried and started working on my résumé. I realized that I couldn't work there anymore. It's not just the word *loser* that throws me into shame. It's the whole idea of believing that you're either good or bad. You can't be good and have a bad day or make a bad decision. You can't be a good runner and run a bad race. I'm embarrassed, or I guess it's really ashamed, that I used to be like that. I laughed at the people on the losers' list. Until I was on it. I made fun of the losers just like my dad and my boss. I regret not competing in college. I could have gone to a better school with the scholarship. Now I know I didn't go because I wouldn't have always been a winner with that level of competition. Now I'm afraid of being less than perfect, and my sister is still struggling with an eating disorder. That's how bad it was to be a loser in my family." Sylvia later told me that she and her sister made a pact to call each other whenever they felt what they called "loser shame."

Does this mean that Sylvia is no longer vulnerable to feeling shame around failing or being cast as a loser? Absolutely not. No level of shame resilience provides us with immunity. What it means is that Sylvia will have much more awareness about what she's feeling when it happens again. This process gives her better tools to step back and think about what happened and why it happened. Then she can start to work her way out of it—constructively.

Unwanted Identities

To start the process of recognizing our shame triggers, we need to look at the concept of *unwanted identities*. Over the course of the interviews, twelve categories emerged as areas in which women struggle the most with feelings of shame. These categories are appearance and body image, motherhood, family, parenting, money and work, mental and physical health, sex, aging, religion, being stereotyped and labeled, speaking out and surviving trauma.

What makes us vulnerable to shame in these areas are the "unwanted identities" associated with each of these topics. For example, many women used adjectives like *loudmouth* and *pushy* to describe unwanted identities associated with speaking out. These specific unwanted identities surfaced in the interviews as women described the difficulty of navigating all of the messages and stereotypes that discourage them from taking an unpopular stand on an issue or sharing opinions that might make others feel uncomfortable.

Researchers Tamara Ferguson, Heidi Eyre and Michael Ashbaker argue that "unwanted identity" is the quintessential elicitor of shame. They explain that unwanted identities are characteristics that undermine our vision of our "ideal" selves. Sometimes we perceive others as assigning these unwanted identities to us, and other times, we pin them on ourselves. For example, I don't think any of us would ideally describe ourselves as pushy loudmouths, nor would we want others to describe us this way. These hurtful stereotypes are often used (successfully, I might add) to keep women quiet. We don't even have to be pushy or boisterous to fear these labels—it's been socialized in us.

So where do unwanted identities come from? The messages and stereotypes that are the most powerful are those that we learned from our families of origin. The term family of origin refers to the family in which we were reared. In my interviews with both men and women, it was obvious that many of the "unwanted identities" that cause us to feel shame stem from messages we heard growing up and the stereotypes we were taught by our parents or immediate caregivers. Sometimes, teachers, clergy and other important adults in our lives may have helped shape our thinking; however, parents and caregivers are by far the most influential. I would venture to say that, when it comes to the twelve shame categories, every family has identities they value and, likewise, unwanted identities that are seen as shameful, unacceptable or unworthy.

For example, in my family, being "sick" was an unwanted identity. We never really talked about illness. I never heard my parents say anything negative about sickness or health issues; however, I grew up believing that illness was weakness. Interestingly, my parents didn't shame us for "being sick" and they were empathic and helpful with neighbors or family members who were sick. However, they were both hard on themselves when they got sick—

which was rare. When they were sick, they toughed it out. They didn't slow down. If they had surgery, they were back on carpool duty or back at work right away.

So, if you combine this upbringing with a culture that despises the sick, you can see how being sick became a powerful unwanted identity for me. This was never a problem, until I became very ill when I was pregnant. Not only did I get sick, I was diagnosed with hyperemesis gravidarum—a pregnancy-related condition characterized by extreme nausea, vomiting and dehydration. So there I was, throwing up twenty-five times a day, unable to keep down ice chips, hospitalized for severe dehydration and spending what little energy I had trying to figure out if any of the hospital rooms had Internet access or if maybe Steve could videotape me teaching from my bed. That way the dean wouldn't need to bring in another instructor to take over my class.

I kept telling Steve, "This can't be happening. I'm tough. I don't get sick." Finally, out of frustration he lovingly held my face in his hands and said, "Well, apparently you do get sick. And right now, you're not so tough. You're human like the rest of us. You really need to work through this—you're not going back to work for a couple of months. This is serious. You need to apply some of your own shame medicine right now."

Family messages die hard. And many times, they're very insidious. The messages become part of the fabric of our families. Until we can recognize and understand why and how they influence our lives, we just keep living by them and passing them down to the next generation. I don't believe my parents consciously introduced the messages about illness and weakness to our family. In fact, as I get older I'm able to look back with more clarity and perspective. I'm sure they were also prisoners of this message. Both my parents were raised in families where these beliefs about toughness and weakness seemed to be encoded in the genes. I think, if anything, they just unknowingly passed them along.

I've had to work very hard to break the cycle with my children.

And as my experiences demonstrate, it doesn't have anything to do with what I say or how I treat others. I have to watch what I do and how I treat myself when I'm feeling sick. Being married to a very compassionate physician helps. He often reminds me that "being tough" is more about being lucky—that when illness strikes, toughness has nothing to do with it. We're all vulnerable.

Of course, families don't operate in a vacuum. Like individuals, they are influenced by the culture and history. I interviewed Deidre, a woman in her sixties, who told me that she had spent years being shamed by her mother about money and "indulgent behavior." Deidre described her house as nice, but "not over the top." Yet, when her mother would come visit she would walk through the house picking up things and saying, "Look at this place! Who do you think you are? The Queen of Sheba? All you do is spend, spend, spend. You've spoiled your kids rotten and you live like there's no tomorrow. I can't believe you're my child." Deidre's mother was a child of the Depression. For her, any material possession that wasn't a necessity was extravagant and wasteful. And both extravagance and wastefulness were major unwanted identities that she used to shame her daughter.

In addition to the messages and stereotypes passed down through our families of origin, we also live in a world with partners, colleagues, friends and community members, where TV and magazines do nothing but set expectations and define what is and what is not acceptable. I don't want to dismiss the important role that all of these factors play in our lives; however, in my research it was painfully clear that the shaming wounds inflicted in our first families often set the stage for many of our greatest shame struggles.

I've been asked many times if I think that shame can only be experienced in areas where we have been shamed by our parents or caregivers, but I don't think this is the case. I do believe we are more vulnerable to shame triggers that developed from our families of origin; however, I interviewed many people who struggle with shame around issues that stem from other places—namely cultural messages and stereotypes. This is especially true of women and men who are under forty. For many people in this age group, the media has become the primary storyteller in their lives. Along with their families, TV is now setting the expectations and defining the unwanted identities.

The Strength of Vulnerability

When I first started writing on shame, I actually referred to this element of shame resilience as "Acknowledging Our Vulnerabilities" rather than "Understanding Our Shame Triggers." I changed it for a couple of reasons. First, over the past two years, I've received hundreds of letters and e-mails from people who are applying the strategies that are outlined in this book to build shame resilience. In the vast majority of these letters, people write about the power of "discovering their shame triggers." In many ways I think the term *shame triggers* just rings truer for people than the term *acknowledging vulnerability*. Second, I think people still struggle with the term *vulnerability*. We equate vulnerability with weakness, and, in our culture, there are very few things we abhor more than weakness.

Regardless of the words we choose, recognizing and understanding our triggers is essentially the same as recognizing and understanding our vulnerabilities, and this is a source of strength. Vulnerability is not weakness. Sometimes we are afraid that acknowledging that something exists is going to make it worse. For example, if I acknowledge that being perceived as a good mother is really important and if I accept the fact that motherhood is a vulnerable issue for me, is the shame around this issue going to grow? No. This is simply not true. When we feel shame about an experience, we often feel some overwhelming combination of confusion, fear and judgment. If it happens in an area where we know we're vulnerable, we're much more likely to come out of that confusion, fear and judgment with an instinct about what we're feeling and what we need to do to find support.

Again, my cookie appropriation story provides a good example. I want to be a good mother and I want to be perceived as a good mother. So, when someone says something to me, or when I do or feel something that threatens my "good mom" status, my shame is triggered. I'm not surprised when I'm overcome by feelings of shame around this issue. I may still feel pain, confusion, fear and judgment, but I have just enough information to react a little more quickly than I would if it were an area of unacknowledged vulnerability—like if I didn't know that motherhood was a shame trigger for me.

When we experience shame we often feel confused, fearful and judged. This makes it very difficult to access the awareness we need to evaluate our choices. We're in a fog. That's how shame makes us powerless. After my exchange with Ellen's teacher, I knew I needed to talk to someone in my connection network, but it was still a difficult call to make. Here's how four other women described the importance of recognizing their triggers or acknowledging their vulnerabilities:

- I only see my therapist three or four times a year—one time after each trip to visit my parents. I know they love me, but I also know they use shame and judge me about being fat and unmarried. I make the trips for all of us, but I see my therapist afterward for myself.

- If there's one thing I've learned, it's to never bring up money around my mother-in-law. If she starts worrying about me and my husband, she starts shaming us about buying too much. It took me several years to learn that, but it makes a big difference; we don't fight and I don't avoid her like the plague.

- In my second year of fertility problems, I finally accepted the fact that I couldn't go to baby showers. When you're in your early thirties, it seems like there's a baby shower every weekend.

I found myself going and making an ass out of myself. I would talk about how great it was to have the freedom and flexibility of not having kids; I'd ask stupid questions about the horrors of labor. The only person who knew we were trying to get pregnant was my best friend. After one particularly bad shower, she confronted me. She said I was being "mean and not like myself." She asked me if it was about the fertility problems. When I realized it was, I had a total breakdown. She helped me through it. She also helped me understand that it was OK to not go to all the showers.

- A few years after my husband died, I started going out with a gentleman from our dominos club. About six months after we started spending time together I asked my daughter if I could talk to her about sex. I wasn't looking for the "birds and bees" conversation; certainly her existence would prove that I knew how things worked. She's a health teacher at a junior high school and I had heard her talking about AIDS. Well, my friend had had a blood transfusion some years back and I wanted to know about the risks. When I sat down with her and started explaining my questions, she said, "You've got to be kidding me, Mother! That's disgusting! I don't ever want to talk about that again." I was completely mortified. I said, "What do you mean, disgusting?" She told me that I was disgusting for even thinking about having sex with someone at my age. Up until that minute I didn't think much about it. I thought it was natural. I thought it was good that I was asking the right questions. When she said that to me, when she called me disgusting, it was so belittling. I completely lost my confidence. I regressed, you could say. I thought to myself, "What am I thinking? What am I doing?" But I know my daughter can really get me stirred up. She can act very "holier than thou"—like her father. Luckily I have some very dear friends. I talked to them and they helped me make sense of it. I went right along with my plans, but I keep her out of it. I guess you could say we have a "don't ask, don't tell" policy.

It's not just shame resilience that is increased when we acknowledge our vulnerabilities. Several other fields of study, including health psychology and social psychology, have produced very persuasive evidence on the importance of acknowledging vulnerabilities. From the field of health psychology, studies show that perceived vulnerability, meaning the ability to acknowledge that we're at risk, greatly increases our chances of adhering to some kind of positive health regime. For example, we can know everything about an illness. We can score perfectly on a hundred-question test, we can know people who have that illness; however, if we don't think we're vulnerable to that illness, we won't do anything to prevent it from happening. Health psychology researchers have determined that in order to get patients to comply with prevention routines, they must work on perceived vulnerability. And just like building resilience to shame, the critical issue is not about our level of vulnerability, but the level at which we acknowledge our vulnerabilities.

From the field of social psychology, influence and persuasion researchers have studied personal vulnerability. These are researchers who examine how people are influenced and persuaded by advertising and marketing. In a very interesting series of studies, researchers found that the participants who thought they were not susceptible or vulnerable to deceptive advertising were, in fact, the most vulnerable. The researchers explained, "Far from being an effective shield, the illusion of invulnerability undermines the very response that would have supplied genuine protection."

Again, this is a very counterintuitive concept because it challenges everything we think about vulnerability. Judith Jordan, a Relational-Cultural theorist from the Stone Center at Wellesley College, points out another difficulty in acknowledging personal vulnerability. Jordan writes, "Acknowledging vulnerability is possible only if we feel we can reach out for support. To do so, we must feel some competence in our relationships." The likelihood of our finding the insight and courage to acknowledge our personal vulnerabilities is dependent on our ability to share and talk about those vulnerabilities with someone we trust and with whom we feel safe.

If we don't have people we can trust in our lives or we have yet to build those kinds of relationships, we must reach outside of our existing connection-network of friends and family for professional help. Therapists and counselors spend a large part of their practice helping people identify and understand their vulnerabilities, and as a result they are frequently able to help clients build or identify relationships that can serve as connection networks.

For most of us to successfully begin to recognize and understand our shame triggers, we first need to accept that acknowledging our vulnerabilities is an act of courage. We must be mindful in our attempts not to see vulnerability as weakness. I'm very lucky when it comes to this difficult endeavor. My mother taught me a tremendous lesson about vulnerability and courage. In the late 1980s, my mom's only sibling, my uncle Ronnie, was killed in a violent shooting. Just months after his death, my grandmother basically checked out mentally and emotionally. Having been an alcoholic most of her life, my grandmother didn't have the emotional resources she needed to survive a traumatic loss like this. For weeks she roamed her neighborhood, randomly asking the same people over and over if they had heard about his death.

One day, right after my uncle's memorial service, my mom totally broke down. I had seen her cry once or twice, but I certainly had never seen her cry uncontrollably. My sisters and I were afraid and crying mostly because we were so scared to see her like that. I finally told her that we didn't know what to do because we had never seen her "so weak." She looked at us and said, in a loving yet forceful voice, "I'm not weak. I'm stronger than you can imagine. I'm just very vulnerable right now. If I were weak, I'd be dead." In that split second, I knew my mom was probably the strongest, most courageous woman I would ever know. She did more than give us permission to use the word *vulnerable*—she taught us that acknowledging our vulnerability is a true act of ordinary courage.

The Shame Trigger Questions

How do we start to recognize our shame triggers? What do we need to do to start acknowledging our vulnerabilities? I think we begin by examining each of the shame categories and trying to unearth the unwanted identities that cause us shame. As I was interviewing both men and women, many of the same phrases kept coming up in the interviews—the ones that I heard over and over were "I don't want to be seen as . . ." and "I don't want people to think I'm . . ." There were many variations on this including, "I would die if people thought I was . . ." or "I couldn't stand people thinking I'm . . ."

As these phrases indicate, shame is about perception. Shame is how we see ourselves through other people's eyes. When I interviewed women about shame experiences, it was always about "how others see me" or "what others think." And often, there is even a disconnect between who we want to be and how we want to be perceived. For example, one woman in her seventies told me, "I'm OK when I'm alone. I know I'm changing. I know things are slowing down and everything is not what it used to be. I just can't stand the thought of others seeing it and dismissing me as a person. Being dismissed is shameful."

Another good example is body image. We might stand in front of the mirror, naked, thinking, "Hmmm, not perfect, but OK." But the moment we think of someone else seeing us—especially someone who is critical—we can just feel the warm wave of shame wash over us. Even if we are totally alone, we rush to cover up. Once we are covered, we fight to push the thought of "being exposed" out of our mind. That's shame.

To help us begin to recognize some of our shame triggers, let's look at the questions I use in my workshop sessions. We start with these fill-in-the-blank statements, which should be answered separately for each of the shame categories:

I want to be perceived as _____, _____, _____, _____ and _____.

I do NOT want to be perceived as _____, _____, _____, _____ or _____.

These are fairly simple statements; however, when you start to think about these questions in relation to the twelve shame categories, this can be a probing and powerful start to the process. But it's important to remember that it is only a start. As I've said throughout the book, there are no easy answers or quick fixes.

The next step is to try to uncover the source of these triggers. When the research participants spoke about their shame triggers, they were able to express an understanding of how and why these triggers developed in their lives. Sylvia's story is a good example of this. The winner/loser dynamic is a shame trigger for Sylvia. The source of this trigger goes back to the enormous pressure she was under from her father when she was a competitive athlete.

If we look at our unwanted identities, three questions that can help us start to uncover the sources are:

1. What do these perceptions mean to us?
2. Why are they so unwanted?
3. Where did the messages that fuel these identities come from?

When it comes to shame, understanding is a prerequisite for change. We can't consciously make the decision to change our behavior until we are aware of what we are thinking and why we are thinking it. Before she understood the source of her shame, Sylvia actually used the winner/loser framework to shame others.

Changing that behavior required her to recognize the power it had in her own life and to understand the source of that power.

In the Introduction we met Susan, Kayla, Theresa and Sondra. Let's take a look at the shame triggers they describe and how these unwanted identities played out in their experiences.

- Susan was contemplating returning to work until a shaming conversation with her sister. In this exercise, Susan focused on perceptions around motherhood. She wrote, "I want to be perceived as dedicated to my child, putting motherhood before everything else, confident and easygoing. I do not want to be perceived as selfish, too ambitious, uncaring or uptight." Susan told me that, after spending some time looking at these, she wasn't the least bit surprised that her sister's comment threw her into shame: "She painted a picture of me that struck at my biggest fears. My parents don't believe mothers should work. They attribute the world's problems to the breakdown of the traditional family. I guess now my sister has adopted that belief. If you combine my family's beliefs with the whole 'working mothers versus stay-at-home mothers' mentality—there you have it."

- After confiding in her boss about becoming a caregiver for her father, Kayla was criticized at work for always being caught in "family drama." She wrote about how she wants to be perceived at work: "I want to be perceived as competent, strong, dependable, focused and committed. I don't want to be perceived as scattered, untrustworthy, too emotional, hysterical or flaky." As Kayla studied what she wrote, she came to an important realization. She said, "When I think about the people I've worked with who are normally very professional, but sometimes act scattered and emotional at work, I'm hard on them. I've never bothered to find out what's going on or why they're having a hard time. My attitude has always been, 'Hey. Check your personal crap at the door—we have work to do here.' I'm not sure where those messages come from. I guess everywhere. No one likes a slacker and no one likes the kind of people who bring their personal stuff to work. Both of my parents were in the newspaper business, so they were all business. They also didn't like overly emotional people. I also think it's the very competitive work environment. Women have to work twice as hard. All of these unwanted characteristics get slapped on women all the time. Nancy, my boss, is the worst. She survives in our agency by attacking other women who bring any family stuff to work. Her favorite put-downs are to call someone a drama queen or say, 'Don't get so hysterical.'"

• Theresa's quest for the perfect body, house and family resulted in a breakdown, witnessed by her child. She examined her identities as they relate to her family. "I want my family to be perceived as fun-loving, laid-back, organized, happy and good-looking. I don't want people to think that we are always stressed, falling apart, chaotic or unhappy." Theresa found it very difficult to talk about her "ideal" perceptions. She told me, "I can't believe I care about my family being good-looking. That's a horrible thing to care about. It's just you see these families where everyone is dressed nicely, no one is wrinkled or messy. The moms are pretty, the dads are good-looking and the kids are super cute. Their houses look like something out of a Pottery Barn catalog. Then you look at yourself and your kids. You wonder how they do it. What are they doing that you don't know about? We're late everywhere we go. By the time I get the last kid dressed, the first one has stuff all over them." I asked her if she knew any family that met her "ideals," and after thinking about it, she said, "Yes. My family growing up." She told me that her family was perfect-looking on the outside and that everyone always complimented her mother on how well-dressed and well-behaved her children were. She told me her mother was very appearance-conscious and was always watching her weight and dressing to the nines. Theresa started crying as she told me, "There was a price, though. After my mom tucked us in every night, she started drinking. My parents have always had a cold, quiet marriage. She stopped drinking a few years ago, but we don't talk much. We've certainly never talked about this issue."

- Sondra was able to quickly identify her triggers. She had a notepad in front of her and she wrote down: "I don't want people to see someone who is stupid, always saying the wrong thing, uninformed or uneducated. I want people to see a strong woman who is smart, well-read, knowledgeable, intelligent, well-spoken and can balance her passion and her knowledge." Sondra explained, "The minute my husband told me that I embarrassed him when I talked politics and religion with Don, I knew I'd never say another word. He knew how much that would hurt. He went in for the kill." She thought for a minute and said, "Maybe I'm just hurting myself by trying to show him, but that's where I am right now." Sondra explained that her parents had raised her to "live proud and out loud," but they did not prepare her for the consequences of doing that. She said growing up, her teachers shamed her, her minister told her she talked too much and never made sense, her husband was always trying to get her to "tone it down" and even her in-laws gave her a hard time for being too excitable and opinionated.

As you look at these assessments of their shame triggers (and maybe your own), I want to talk about the issues that always surface when I do this exercise at the workshops. First, we are very hard on ourselves. When we identify these desired and unwanted identities, we give ourselves very little room to be human. Second, we cannot deny the power of the messages we heard growing up. Last, most of us judge others whom we perceive as having the traits we dislike in ourselves.

When participants do these exercises in large groups, I often ask how many people found the "I want to be perceived" questions more difficult to answer and how many found the "I do *not* want to be perceived" questions more difficult. It is always about fifty-fifty. Those who find the "ideal perceptions" more difficult to acknowledge often talk about feeling bad for placing so much value on these identities and sometimes feeling ashamed for even thinking anyone would ever see them this way. For those who find the unwanted identities more difficult to talk about, I often hear that it is "painful" and "scary" to look at this list.

There's a third set of questions that is very important to this exercise. Examine your list of unwanted identities and ask yourself, "If people reduce me to this list, what important and wonderful things will they miss about me?" For example, if all Kayla's colleagues see is a co-worker who is "scattered, untrustworthy, too emotional and flaky," they'll miss the fact that Kayla is very dedicated to her work, talented, and a committed, loving daughter who is doing the best she can to manage a stressful, painful experience. It's very important that we acknowledge that we are complex, vulnerable people with both strengths and challenges—this is what makes us human and real.

Most everyone agrees upon the importance of actually writing down these exercises. I know, for me, it is more difficult to write these words out and stare at them on a piece of paper. I also know that it is more meaningful. I can get my head around them. I can be still and reflect. Sometimes we believe that acknowledging our

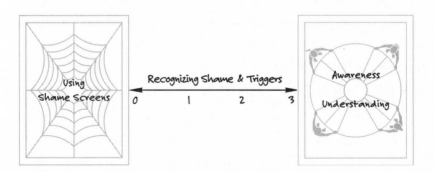

triggers will make them worse. We convince ourselves that if we pretend they don't exist, it's somehow easier. It's not. Our feelings, beliefs and actions are motivated by these triggers regardless of whether we write them down and acknowledge them or we pretend they don't exist. Recognizing and understanding them is the only path to change.

In the next section, I'm going to introduce the concept of shame screens. As you can see in the illustration on the previous page, when we don't recognize shame and understand the messages and expectations that trigger our shame, we often rely on our shame screens to protect us. As you'll learn, not only is relying on shame screens ineffective, it can often be shame-inducing in itself.

Shame screens

I came up with the term *shame screen* after analyzing data from the first hundred interviews. As women explained the unpredictable and sometimes unconscious ways they reacted in response to shame, I realized the experiences shared something in common—when we are in shame we are often overcome with the need to hide or protect ourselves by any means possible. As I thought about our protective reactions to shame, I kept envisioning smokescreens— the canisters of dense smoke used by the military to hide their activities from the enemy.

Unfortunately, shame screens don't work. We're not dealing with tanks and infantry behind enemy lines; we're dealing with people and relationships. Wouldn't it be great if we could just carry those canisters on our belts and when someone hurt our feelings, shamed us or made us angry, we could just whip out our canister of thick smoke, launch it and run? Or we could even just stand there, behind the wall of smoke, and make rude gestures. Please. I'd order them by the case if I thought they'd work. Unfortunately, we can't do that. The reality is that when we throw up the shame screen, we're usually the ones who end up choking on the smoke.

When we experience shame, our first layer of defense often

occurs involuntarily. It goes back to our primal flight, fight and freeze responses. Dr. Shelley Uram, a Harvard-trained psychiatrist, is currently the consulting psychiatrist at The Meadows, a trauma and addiction treatment facility. In her work, Dr. Uram explains that most of us think of traumatic events as *big* events (like car wrecks and disasters). But Dr. Uram points out that we tend not to recognize the small, quiet traumas that often trigger the same brain-survival reaction. After studying Dr. Uram's work, I believe it's possible that many of our early shame experiences, especially with parents and caregivers, were stored in our brains as traumas. This is why we often have such painful bodily reactions when we feel criticized, ridiculed, rejected and shamed. Dr. Uram explains that the brain does not differentiate between overt or big trauma and covert or small, quiet trauma—it just registers the event as "a threat that we can't control."

In her work on "remembering the wound" versus "becoming the wound," Dr. Uram explains that most of the time when we recall a memory, we are conscious that we are in the present, recalling something from the past. However, when we experience something in the present that triggers an old trauma memory, we reexperience the *sense* of the original trauma. So, rather than remembering the wound, we become the wound. This makes sense when we think of how we are often returned to a place of smallness and helplessness when we feel shame.

After our physical fight, flight or freeze response, "strategies of disconnection" provide us with a more complex layer of shame screens. Dr. Linda Hartling, a Relational-Cultural theorist, uses Karen Horney's work on moving toward, moving against and moving away to outline the strategies of disconnection we use to deal with shame. According to Dr. Hartling, in order to deal with shame, some of us **move away** by withdrawing, hiding, silencing ourselves and keeping secrets. Some of us **move toward** by seeking to appease and please. And, some of us **move against** by trying to gain power over others, being aggressive and using shame to fight shame.

During a recent workshop, I was presenting these strategies of disconnection and they were lettered on my slide *(a, b, c.)*. A woman raised her hand and asked, "Is there a *d* for all of the above?" We all laughed.

I think most of us are *d*'s—most of us can relate to all three strategies of disconnection. I know I've used all of them, depending on why and how I feel ashamed and who I'm with. I'm less likely to move against when there is a power differential (bosses, doctors) or someone I'm trying to impress (new friends, colleagues). In those situations I'm more likely to move toward or move away.

Unfortunately, I think I reserve moving against for the people with whom I feel the deepest connection—my family members and close friends. This is often where it feels safest to dump our anger and fear.

We develop our shame screens over years. Sometimes, the way we handle shame has become so deeply ingrained in us that we can't even see it. Other times, we'll read books or listen to other people's stories and recognize our own patterns. Either way, it takes much more than reading a book to change how we feel, act and believe.

We can learn and become wiser about who we are and how we behave from reading a book, but we need to put these ideas into practice. We change in and through our relationships with others. Sometimes we can do that with friends and families, other times we need the support of a therapist or counselor who can walk us through the process. It's a unique and individual journey; how we get there depends on who we are.

Another thing to keep in mind is that resilience is not a one-time cure. Don't think that I've spent all this time and energy dissecting my experiences and the payoff is "No more shame screens for me." I still use ineffective shame screens. It happens all the time. I'm just much more likely to move through it quicker and with fewer casualties.

The next exercise is identifying our shame screens. As you think about each of the shame categories and the triggers associ-

ated with each category, try to think of a specific shame experience. How did you respond? Is that a pattern? How do you protect
yourself in those situations?

Let's take a look at Susan, Kayla, Theresa, Sondra and Jillian.

Susan: I'm definitely someone who moves away or moves toward.
I don't like conflict. I don't get aggressive or mean; I just try to
make everyone happy. Of course, it never works and I can get resentful. It will be very difficult to tell my mom and sister that their
comments are shaming to me. I'm not quite ready but I think I'll
eventually do it.

Kayla: There should be one called "copycatting"—I think I just
turn into Nancy and mimic everything she says. It's how I deal
with her—if you can't beat them, join them. I just never realized
how much it hurts to be on the receiving end. I guess a combination of moving toward and moving against. I suck up when I'm
with her—I confide in her when I shouldn't. Then, I shame other
co-workers for the things she shames me for. That's my shame
screen.

Theresa: I definitely move toward. I want to please and live up to
the expectations.

Sondra: I do it all. I shut down, act up, act out—you name it. In
this case, I shut down until I started figuring out what was going
on. I couldn't set that kind of example for my girls. It's too dangerous. My tendency is to move away—especially with my husband.
It's like a form of punishment because I know he'll miss my normal
rowdy self.

In the next chapter, I'll discuss the importance of "reality-checking"
our shame triggers. This helps us build resilience by connecting our
own unwanted identities with the larger societal expectations that
drive shame. This is essential to developing shame resilience, because, no matter how alone shame can make us feel, we are all in this
together.

FOUR

The Second Element: Practicing Critical Awareness

A couple of years ago, I was giving a noontime lecture to a large group of medical students, residents and medical faculty. During these daily lectures, pharmaceutical companies or other sponsors often provide lunch to the attendees. About twenty minutes into my talk on shame and health, I started explaining the concept of critical awareness. Very quickly I noticed a swelling wave of lost faces. I looked out on the audience, almost all of whom were busy eating, and abruptly asked, "How's the pizza?" Everyone stopped chewing, leaned forward in their chairs and stared back at me with blank expressions on their faces.

I pointed to a long table of empty pizza boxes and said, "I'm aware that there were pizzas on that table and that most of you took a couple of slices on your way to your seat. That's awareness." They looked very unimpressed. Then I said, "I'm also aware that you have very little time for lunch and the drug company sales rep is offering lunch as an incentive to get you to attend this presentation. If there were no pizza, you probably wouldn't be here. If you weren't here you wouldn't get to hear me talk, but more importantly, you wouldn't get the pen and the pad that has the drug company's newest logo on it and patients wouldn't see you carrying that pen and so on. . . . That's critical awareness."

They turned and looked at one another then looked back at me and, in unison, looked down at their plates. I smiled. "Awareness is knowing something exists, critical awareness is knowing why it exists, how it works, how our society is impacted by it and who benefits from it." I think they started to get it.

The concept of critical awareness is sometimes called critical consciousness or critical perspective. It's the belief that we can increase personal power by understanding the link between our personal experiences and larger social systems. When we look at the shame categories—appearance and body image, motherhood, family, parenting, money and work, mental and physical health, sex, aging, religion, being stereotyped and labeled, speaking out and surviving trauma—most of us have not been taught how to see the connection between our private lives and social, political and economic influences.

Shame works like the zoom lens on a camera. When we are feeling shame, the camera is zoomed in tight and all we see is our flawed selves, alone and struggling. We think to ourselves, "I'm the only one. Something is wrong with me. I am alone."

When we zoom out, we start to see a completely different picture. We see many people in the same struggle. Rather than thinking, "I'm the only one," we start thinking, "I can't believe it! You too? I'm normal? I thought it was just me!" Once we start to see the big picture, we are better able to reality-check our shame triggers and the social-community expectations that fuel shame.

I think the best way to learn critical awareness is to apply the concepts to a real issue. Let's start by looking at the issue of appearance and body image. I like to use this issue as an example because it is an almost universal shame trigger. To begin to understand the big picture we need to ask the following big-picture questions about appearance:

- What are the social-community expectations around appearance?
- Why do these expectations exist?
- How do these expectations work?
- How is our society influenced by these expectations?
- Who benefits from these expectations?

While each of us would probably have specific answers to these questions based on our age, race, ethnicity, etc., for the purpose of the example I'm going to respond with broad, general answers.

First, what are the social-community expectations of appearance? From a societal level, appearance includes everything from hair, skin, makeup, weight, clothing, shoes and nails to attitude, confidence, age and wealth. If you pile on community-specific expectations, you might have to add things like hair texture, hair length, skin color, face and body hair, teeth, looking "done-up," not looking "done-up," clothing and jewelry.

Why do appearance expectations exist? I would say they exist to keep us spending our valuable resources—money, time and energy—on trying to meet some ideal that is not achievable. Think about this: Americans spend more each year on beauty than we do on education.

How does it work? I think the expectations are both obvious and subtle—they are everything we see and everything we don't see. If you read fashion magazines or watch TV, you know what you are "supposed to" look like and how you are "supposed to" dress and act. If you look hard enough, you also see everything that's missing—the images of real people. If you combine what's there and what's missing, you quickly come to believe that if you don't look a certain way, you become invisible; you don't matter. What is the impact of these expectations? Well, let's see. . . .

- About eighty million Americans are obese.
- Approximately seven million girls and women suffer from an eating disorder.
- Up to nineteen percent of college-aged women are bulimic.
- Eating disorders are the third most common chronic illness among females.
- The latest surveys show very young girls are going on diets because they think they are fat and unattractive. In one American survey, eighty-one percent of ten-year-old girls had already dieted at least once.
- A research survey found that the single largest group of high-school students considering or attempting suicide are girls who feel they are overweight.
- Twenty-five years ago, top models and beauty queens weighed only eight percent less than the average woman; now they weigh twenty-three percent less. The current media ideal for women is achievable by less than five percent of the female population—and that's just in terms of weight and size.
- Among women over eighteen looking at themselves in the mirror, research indicates that at least eighty percent are unhappy with what they see. Many will not even be seeing an accurate reflection. Most of us have heard that people with anorexia see themselves as larger than they really are, but some recent research indicates that this kind of distorted body image is by no means confined to those suffering from eating disorders—in some studies up to eighty percent of women overestimated their size. Increasing numbers of women with no weight problems or clinical psychological disorders look at themselves in the mirror and see ugliness and fat.
- According to the American Society for Aesthetic Plastic Surgery,

since 1997, there has been a 465 percent increase in the total number of cosmetic procedures.

- Women had nearly 10.7 million cosmetic procedures, ninety percent of the total. The number of cosmetic procedures for women has increased forty-nine percent since 2003.
- The top five surgical procedures for women were: liposuction, breast augmentation, eyelid surgery, tummy tuck and facelift.
- Americans spent just under $12.5 billion on cosmetic procedures in 2004.

Who benefits from the appearance expectations?
- The $38 billion hair industry.
- The $33 billion diet industry.
- The $24 billion skincare industry.
- The $18 billion makeup industry.
- The $15 billion perfume industry.
- The $13 billion cosmetic surgery industry.

That's a whole bunch of folks depending on us to see and believe messages that sell the social-community expectations of appearance. If we don't believe we're too fat, ugly and old, then they don't sell their products. If they don't sell their products, they don't make their house payments. The pressure is on!

When we ask and answer these big-picture questions, we begin to develop critical awareness. The next step is learning how to use this information to reality-check our shame triggers. We do that by looking at our shame triggers and asking these six reality-check questions:

- How realistic are my expectations?
- Can I be all these things all of the time?
- Do the expectations conflict with each other?
- Am I describing who I want to be or who others want me to be?

- If someone perceives me as having these unwanted identities, what will happen?
- Can I control how others perceive me? How do I try?

During our second interview, Jillian shared her answers to these reality check questions with me. (Jillian's ideal identities are thin, sexy, confident, natural and young. Her unwanted identities are middle-aged, tired, fat and frumpy.) Here's how she answered these questions:

How realistic are my expectations? Not realistic at all. I am middle-aged and I'm tired a lot. I don't always look tired, but you can't change my age. The truth is that I'm not going to look thin and sexy all the time. When I first started this process, I thought it was realistic. But the more I learn about the expectations I put on myself and the images I measure myself against, the more I realize that I literally can't have that. The girls in these magazines are sixteen or maybe twenty at the oldest. I might be able to feel sexy and fit, but I won't look it by the movie standards. The truth is that it's not OK to look forty. It's OK to be forty, as long as you look like you're twenty-five or thirty. I saw a commercial the other day where the model said, "I don't mind being my age. I just don't want to look it." Why not? If she said, "Hey, America! This is what forty looks like!" then we'd all want to look our age.

Can I be all these things all of the time? No. I can't. I do look good sometimes. I'm proud of how I look every now and then. But, I'm still hard on myself because I don't look great all the time. I'll be at home with my gown and slippers on and my hair pulled back, and think, "What a slob." Even then, I think I should have on Victoria's Secret lingerie. I'm starting to hate the television.

Do the expectations conflict with each other? Yes! This was the most eye-opening question for me. I can't look confident when I am afraid that people will think I'm fat and frumpy. And I don't look so natural when my girdle is squeezing the life out of me.

I also think about fake tanning. It's so cold here six months out of the year. When spring comes, everyone wants to look tan. By summer everyone is bright orange from the tanning beds. That's not very natural. You can't pretend to be natural and confident. I admire the women who say, "I'm fifty and this is what I look like. Take it or leave it."

Am I describing who I want to be or who others want me to be? Some of both. I want to be confident and natural and want people to describe me that way. I don't care as much about sexy and thin. I want to be healthy, but I think I want to look young and sexy because you are supposed to be those things. I've talked a lot about this with my husband. He doesn't make comments very much anymore. When I talked to him about it, he was shocked about how much it hurt me. My mother-in-law is still pretty judgmental.

If someone perceives me as having these unwanted identities, what will happen? At one time I would have said that I'd be embarrassed if I thought people saw me as fat, frumpy and old. Now I know that it's shame. I guess nothing would happen. I'd just feel made fun of or ridiculed. But truthfully, I don't think anyone would say that about me, except for me.

Can I control how others perceive me? How do I try? Before I learned about shame I thought I could control how others perceive me. Now I know that no one can, so my answer is cheating a little. I really did believe that you could control perception if you stayed on top of it. Now I know that it's a no-win situation. I don't try as much as I used to, but I still fall back into that thinking. I used to try to control it by not getting myself in situations where I'd be judged. I wouldn't swim at the party so I could stay in my shorts. But then, they're judging you for that. No matter what you do, you can't control how other people see you.

As you read Jillian's answers, you can see that reality-checking our shame triggers is not easy. And, it's almost impossible if we don't have some sense of the big picture. Jillian has certainly "zoomed out" around her appearance issues and the media. She doesn't just see herself as flawed and incapable of meeting reasonable expectations. She knows what she's up against—it's all women versus a huge beauty industry that's very effective at making us feel bad about ourselves. She seems to have a good sense about how her triggers work and how they affect her.

During our second interview, Jillian said, "It's tiring. You can't just know this stuff and think about it once or twice. You have to constantly remind yourself or you get sucked back in. It's hard. Especially when the people around you don't get it."

Jillian is right. This element is called **practicing** critical awareness. If we only ask and answer the questions, we are likely to feel stuck, angry and overwhelmed. It's bad enough that we are under immense pressure to be unattainably beautiful, but when we learn that this pressure is supported by the weight of multibillion-dollar industries, we can feel defeated and resigned.

Practicing critical awareness means linking our personal experiences to what we learn from the questions and answers. When we do this, we move toward resilience by learning how to:

- Contextualize (I see the big picture);
- Normalize (I'm not the only one); and
- Demystify (I'll share what I know with others).

When we fail to make the connections, we increase our shame by:

- Individualizing (I am the only one);
- Pathologizing (something is wrong with me); and
- Reinforcing (I should be ashamed).

I always find examples helpful, especially when I'm trying to get my head around new concepts, so in this chapter I've also included how Susan, Kayla, Teresa and Sondra answered their big-picture and reality-check questions.

Understanding the big picture often requires us to investigate issues. For example, the list of beauty facts and statistics earlier in this chapter all came from books or the Internet. I really encourage you to do your own detective work—it can be very empowering. Of course, you'll want to make sure that you are pulling information from reputable sources—especially on the Internet—but there are many individuals and organizations doing wonderful work on exposing how social-community expectations impact the way we think, feel and act.

On my own Web site (www.brenebrown.com), I have critical-awareness resources for all of the shame categories, including exercises, links and lists of recommended books. During a recent workshop, one woman told the larger group that she struggled with serious shame issues over money. After the workshop she came up to me and said, "Rather than shopping, I'm going to spend my time investigating how credit card debt hurts women." Right on!

Let's look at how Susan, Kayla, Theresa and Sondra applied the principles of critical awareness to their situations:

After Susan answered the big-picture and reality-check questions, she wrote, "I'm surprised to find myself in this big 'motherhood' war. I didn't think that would happen to me. I'm not a very political person and I don't really have strong opinions one way or the other when it comes to working or staying at home. I had no idea my decision, which is very personal, to go back to work part-time would spark such emotion in my sister." She went on to say,

"I'm not sure who benefits from all of this pressure—it certainly is not mothers." Susan said, "I had no idea, until I wrote it down, how much I worry about what other people think. I know I'm a good, committed mom. Why do I care if people see it or not?" In her final thoughts, Susan told me that the most difficult thing for her was letting go of the idea that she could control how people see her, especially her mother and sister. "I just keep working to convince them that this is a good decision for me and our family. I want them to change how they see it. Maybe they will. Maybe they won't. I have no control over it and that's hard."

Kayla read over both sets of critical awareness questions and wrote down one simple but powerful sentence: "I have bought into the messages that are being used to shame me." She explained that she cared what Nancy, her boss, thought and said because she looked up to her and her tough approach about mixing business and family. Kayla said, "No one benefits from this. No one. Everyone has a life outside of work and that life can be hard. It's not just hard on the women either. There was a guy whose child was sick, and it got so stressful for him that he had to quit. I felt bad for him when it happened, but not enough to say anything." I asked her if the company benefits by this informal policy, and after thinking for a minute she said, "No. Not really. Everyone is too stressed. That guy who quit to take care of his son was awesome. We needed him and now he's gone. Maybe people think it's good for the bottom line, but it's not." Kayla told me her next step was to actually consider leaving for another agency. She said, "It might be the same competitive culture everywhere I go, but I could start over with new boundaries and new expectations."

Theresa had a difficult time with these questions. She explained, "I just don't know if I'm making excuses for how I feel or doing something that's going to make me feel better. I can't stop thinking that some better, more put-together version of what I have is possible." She said, "One thing is clear—I definitely can't be as stressed and overwhelmed as I am now and have a family that's fun-loving, laid-back and happy." Even though Theresa and her mother had a distant relationship, she told me that she thinks she sometimes judges her family through her mother's eyes. "My constant disappointment in my life wears on my husband and our marriage. It's hard on my kids. They certainly don't care about it being more perfect. They just want me to be happy. I'm pushing these expectations. My mom is in my head."

When Sondra examined how her experience of speaking out fit in the big picture in her community, she came across a complicated intersection of race and gender. She said, "On the one hand, black women are respected for being strong and assertive. This is especially true when we're dealing with white folks. But when it comes to black men, we are supposed to back down. I don't think that Don believes that, but certainly my husband and in-laws don't think I'm showing him enough respect when I challenge his opinions." Sondra went on to say that she believes this takes a toll on black women and girls. She said, "I can't be superhuman sometimes and then back down others. I'm really somewhere in the middle." As she used these ideas to reality-check her ideal perceptions, she wrote, "All of these expectations keep me quiet. If I'm not perfect, I can't speak. I need to be OK with being wrong. I need to be allowed to say, 'I don't know.' I also need to be OK with asserting myself. Sometimes it's as hard to be right as it is to be wrong."

In the next sections, we will explore the strategies that move us toward resilience and the common barriers that stand in our way.

Contextualizing Versus Individualizing
The word *context* is derived from the Latin word *contexere*, meaning "to weave or twine together." When we understand the context of an experience, we see the big picture. It goes back to the zoom lens. When we are in shame, we just see our own struggle. As we zoom out, we start to see others engaged in similar struggles. When we pull completely back, we start to see an even bigger

picture—how political, economic and social forces shape our personal experiences. Contextualizing is the key to making the shame connection.

If I understand how industries and individuals benefit from my appearance shame, does that mean the shame goes away? No, unfortunately not. But identifying the contexts in which we feel shame helps us build resilience. If we feel shame because, despite our best efforts, we can't look like the model on the cover of a magazine, it helps to know that the model probably doesn't look like that either. Her blemishes are airbrushed, her legs are stretched using a computer, her smile is whitened and her clothes are borrowed.

Magazines make money by selling advertising space, not subscriptions. The goal is to have us look at the woman on the cover, feel bad and then buy all the lotions and potions advertised in the magazine. If we buy a lot of products, the cosmetic companies buy more advertising space in the magazine and so on. . . .

If we buy into the whole package of what we are supposed to look like, and think we can't achieve that look only because we don't have enough willpower or genetic advantage, we sink in shame. Context helps us understand how social-community expectations, economics and politics are all woven together to produce one cohesive image. We can't unravel the truth without recognizing the threads.

As the categories indicate, many of us actually fall prey to the same sources of shame, and we experience very similar reactions. However, due to the isolating and secretive nature of shame, we feel like it is only happening to us and that we must hide it at all costs. This, in turn, has led to our false belief that shame is a personal problem—even a psychological defect of some kind. It's not.

Yes, shame can lead to personal problems and even play a role in mental illness, but shame is also a social construct—it happens between people. Shame is how I feel when I see myself through someone else's eyes. I have labeled shame a psychosocial-cultural construct.

I like to explain it this way: If you stick shame under a psychological microscope, you'll only see part of the picture. If you do the same thing with a social lens or cultural lens—same outcome—you'll only see pieces of the problem. If, however, you combine all three of these lenses—the psychological, social and cultural—you get the full picture of shame. I think the most dangerous view is looking at shame strictly as a personal problem. When we do that, we seek only personal and highly individualized solutions, which leave the layers of competing and conflicting expectations that drive shame intact and unchanged.

If one or two or even a hundred women said they were ashamed of their bodies, that probably wouldn't point to a larger social connection. But it wasn't just a few women—it was more than ninety percent of the women I interviewed. If it was just Sondra who talked about the fear of experiencing shame when she voiced her opinion or spoke out on public or private issues, then "speaking out" wouldn't be a shame category. It's a category because a strong pattern emerged across the interviews, indicating that a significant number of women remain quiet rather than deal with their fear of being put down and ridiculed or appearing stupid.

The Myth of Shirking and Blaming

Many people mistake contextualizing for a means to shirk our personal responsibilities and "blame the system." For example,

- It's not my fault I can't find a job—it's because I'm a woman.
- It's not my fault that I can't lose weight—it's the diet industry.
- It's not my fault that I'm in debt—it's those evil credit card companies.

I think contextualizing is the opposite of blaming and shirking. When the women I interviewed talked about the importance of getting the big picture, they didn't talk about making excuses.

They talked about finding the power to make changes by understanding the big picture and knowing they weren't the only ones struggling:

- During my senior year, my mom made me join a group with other girls with "trich." At first I was really pissed. I didn't even believe that other girls had it. In this group I found out that several million people have it. It didn't make it go away, but at least I know other people; I'm not a total freak. There was even a girl three years younger than me and I was able to help her by telling her how I explained it to my friends.

  Note: TRICH is short for trichotillomania—an impulse control disorder that causes people to pull out body hair (skin, head, eyebrows, eyelashes, etc.). It seems to occur most frequently in pre- or early adolescent years.

- I'm one of those people who have a lot of fear about rape. I'm very aware of things like sexual assault and "no means no." I support that and I believe in it. But I feel a lot of shame because when I think about "hot sex" or when I imagine something to make me more excited or more into sex, those are the kind of fantasies and scenarios I think about in my head. I think about those scenes in the movies when the girl says, "No, no, no," and then it turns into great, hot sex. What is that about? How can that be our biggest fear in real life but also be a big fantasy? I asked my older sister about it and she said it's because you never see gentle, loving, vulnerable sex in the movies. She said no one would buy tickets. She said people want to see forbidden or fearful sex, and after a while, you start believing that's what it takes to have good sex. I asked her if I was normal and she said a lot of people buy into that but no one talks about it because it's shameful. She said the dangerous part is men also believe that women like to be forced.

- I think you grow up feeling shame about the stuff your parents didn't allow you to talk about when you were little. So anything that a parent makes "off-limits"—that's the shit that's going to make you crazy when you get older. If you want your kids to be normal, let them talk about everything, then they won't have any shame around it; then it's just not a big deal anymore. If you grew up with a lot of "off-limit" things, you have to ask people and figure it all out. The more you know, the more you realize you're not the only one.

When we strive to understand the context or the big picture, we don't give up responsibility. We increase it. When we identify a personal struggle that is rooted in larger issues, we should take responsibility for both. Maybe it's not just our job to make things better for ourselves; maybe we have a responsibility to make things better for our children, our friends or our community.

If we understand how larger systems are contributing to our shame and we choose only to change ourselves, we become as negligent as the person who says, "I'm not changing myself, because the system is bad." Context is not the enemy of personal responsibility. Individualism is the enemy of personal responsibility.

A good example of the importance of context and collective action is breast cancer. For many of us, there couldn't be a more personal issue. But, however personal it is, we still need the big picture. There have been very important advances in breast cancer research over the past ten years. These advances could not have happened without advocates who recognized the political, social and economic contexts of health research.

These advocates have pushed breast cancer to the top of the national health agenda, raised millions of dollars and drastically increased federal funding of breast cancer research. We might be able to make individual choices that lower our risks for breast cancer, but without collective action, we wouldn't know how to manage those risks, and we certainly would not get the level of treatment available today.

When we talk about putting issues into context in order to increase our critical awareness and increase our shame resilience, we need to realize that getting mired in blaming systems is as destructive as being mired in self-blame. When the most effective way to change a situation is to look at the big picture and we individualize the problem, there is little chance that we're going to change it.

Normalizing Versus Pathologizing

When it comes to raising critical awareness and increasing our resilience to shame, the most powerful words we can hear are "You are not alone." When the research participants talked about critical awareness, the actual words "You have to find out you're not alone" or "You need to know you're not alone" or "You need to find out you're not the only one" came up, verbatim, in at least eighty percent of the interviews. Shame works only if we think we're alone in it. If we think there's someone else, a group of women, a city full of women, a country full of women, a world full of women, struggling with the same issue, the concept of shame becomes bankrupt.

However, unless we understand our shame triggers and practice critical awareness, chances are we're not ever going to reach out far enough or often enough for someone to have the opportunity to say, "Hey, you're not alone."

On the opposite side of the continuum from normalizing is pathologizing. Pathologizing is classifying something as abnormal or deviant. Without critical awareness, we might believe that the social-community expectations are attainable. Individually, it is easy for us to believe that we are the only person who doesn't meet the expectations; therefore, there is something abnormal or deviant about us. If we're going to develop and practice critical awareness, we have to be able to normalize experiences to the point of knowing we're not alone.

Driving It Home with Divorce

I talked to many women who spoke about the shame of divorce. Some women spoke about their own divorces and other women spoke about their parents' divorces. One thread running through many of the experiences was the economic consequence of divorce. For many women, divorce takes a serious financial toll in addition to the emotional toll. Here are four examples:

- I went from being the perfect mom and the perfect wife to broke, unemployed and alone. No one calls you poor when you're married and staying at home with your kids—not even when all the money really belongs to your husband. You think, "His money is our money," and so on. Then one day, he leaves and takes everything with him—except the kids, thank God. I didn't even know where to mail the mortgage. Now my kids and I live at home with my parents. When you're in your twenties and you move back in with your parents, people think you're lost and trying to find your way. When you're forty and move back in, everyone thinks you're pathetic. The truth is we're just lost and trying to find our way.

- People tell you not to feel shame for your parents' divorce. That's easier said than done. Try telling your son that his grandparents aren't coming to his Bar Mitzvah because they can't stand to be in the same place. Who feels that shame? What about begging your father for money so you can fill your mother's prescriptions? My father always tells me, "You're on her side." He just won't understand—he left her with nothing. I'm not on anyone's side, but of course I'm going to care for my mother.

- My parents divorced when I was ten. I've spent the last eight years listening to my mom tell me horrible stories about my father. She's constantly saying, "If he loved you, he'd do more for you." He left her in pretty bad shape, but he was also broke. If she had more money, she'd probably get off his back. I love my father. He's a good, decent person and a good dad. She makes me feel ashamed to love him. Ironically, he's the one that makes me feel better about my mom. He never says anything bad about her—he actually defends her sometimes. It's so confusing.

- I knew we needed to get divorced. He had several affairs and our fights were starting to affect our children. I had this idea in my head that I could start over—make a new life. I thought I could get a small, cute house, a part-time job and we'd be OK. Six months after we sold our house, I was fourteen thousand dollars in debt, I had a job that paid six dollars per hour and I could barely make rent. Rather than helping, my ex-husband suggested he take the kids until I got back on my feet. I was so ashamed that I couldn't take care of my own children. I should have known better than to ever let that happen. I got a second job, but that leaves me no time to be at home with the boys. They still live with him.

Like most women, when I read these stories I feel some combination of sadness, fear and a need to protect myself from acknowledging that this could ever happen to me. When we do that, however, we reinforce the stereotypes of women who struggle financially after divorce by individualizing their situations:

- "She brought that on herself."
- "That's a personal problem, not a community problem."

And, in many ways, we make women out to be flawed, damaged or somehow abnormal:

- "It's stupid not to know about the family finances."
- "She'd look harder if she really wanted a good job."

If we want to develop critical awareness, we start by acknowledging the importance of context. Once we have a better understanding of the big picture, we can start linking. What political, social, and economic realities do divorced women face? Here's what we know:

- Researchers consistently find that women suffer significant economic losses after divorce, much more than their male ex-partners.
- Researchers agree that a woman's postdivorce income is driven by labor force participation. Women who work, especially those who have an education and can secure high-income jobs, do better after a divorce. Women who have not worked during their marriage face larger economic obstacles.
- Ninety percent of children stay with their mothers.
- Only one in four divorced mothers does not have a court-ordered child support award.
- Among divorced mothers who have a support award, fifty percent receive the full amount, twenty-five percent receive only a part and twenty-five percent receive nothing.
- Divorced parents (both men and women) are more likely to pay child support if they have an ongoing relationship with their children.

Research also shows that the ability for women to financially recover after divorce has increased over the past few years. When we talk to women in my mother's generation, it is easy to understand why many of them suffered great personal and financial losses when they divorced. They didn't participate in the workforce as much as women do today. When they did work, it was often in traditional support or service jobs. If they had high-status jobs they were paid much less than men, and there were no child support laws.

As we strive to understand issues in their social, political and economic contexts, we are better able to move away from individualizing problems and making them about someone's character flaw. We also become less likely to pathologize women and more likely to understand how and why things work.

When we tear down the myths of divorce and really examine the realities and contexts, we build a new understanding that makes us far more critically aware and far less likely to blame women—including ourselves.

Critical awareness also requires us to question this notion of blaming the victim. In particular, some pop psychologists preach that "There is no such thing as reality, just perception." Not only is this inaccurate, it's dangerous. Racism is real, domestic violence is real, homophobia is real. The economics of divorce are real.

When you tell people their situation is only "perception" and they can change it, you shame them, belittle them and, in the case of domestic violence, you put them in extreme physical danger. Rather than dismissing someone's experience as perception, we might want to ask, "How can I help?" or "Is there some way I can support you?"

It might be accurate to say that we all see things differently, but the world trades in both reality and perception. Try paying your mortgage with paper you perceive as money, or try walking out of the store with that Kate Spade bag and telling the police, "It matches my shoes so I perceive it's mine."

Demystifying Versus Reinforcing

The last benefit of practicing critical awareness is demystifying. If we want to demystify something, we simply break it down and take the "mystery" out of it. How many times do we see something unusual or interesting and, even if we are dying to know about it, feel too unworthy to ask what it is, how much it costs or how it works? If we start demystifying by asking the critical awareness questions, we often find that the answers are kept secret for a reason.

When individuals, groups or institutions want to exclude people or raise their status, they have a tendency to shroud themselves, their products or their ideas in mystery. One example from my life is the mysterious power of getting a Ph.D. Every semester, without fail, I have female students come to my door and, with their heads hung low, say, "I think I might be interested in getting my doctorate and I don't know that I can really do it, but I'm wondering, if you're not too busy, if you could tell me about your experiences or how it works?"

Well, I love getting that question because for me, part of building critical awareness is not only seeking to demystify issues for myself, but helping other people do it too. I firmly believe that if we have "mysterious powers"—if we know how something sacred works—we are obligated to share what we know. Knowledge is power and power is never diminished by sharing it—it is only increased. My degree doesn't lose value if I help other women figure out how to get into graduate school. I love peeling the layers of mystery off that process.

The opposite of demystifying is reinforcing. Reinforcing is protecting the mystery of something so we can feel more important and secure. I think we're most susceptible to reinforcing when we feel shame around an issue. But when we reinforce, we weave webs that not only entangle other women but eventually trap us.

Here are two sample responses to the questions women ask me about applying to graduate school:

- "That's exciting—I'm glad you asked. I was really nervous about applying, but a couple of people gave me some good pointers. I'm happy to share what I know."
- "Well, we can talk about the fit between this program and your epistemological interests because it's very important to develop

a strong program of inquiry before you start applying. You want to make sure, methodologically, that your research agenda is compatible with the research agenda of the college and the scholars with whom you will do your training."

These are actual responses that I received when I asked for help with my graduate application. After that second response, what saved me from shame and yielding to intimidation was my level of acknowledged vulnerability. When I reached out, I knew I was vulnerable. I knew being perceived as "not smart enough" was a major trigger for me.

The research participants frequently discussed the important relationship between understanding their shame triggers, demystifying and reinforcing. When we don't understand something and "not understanding" is a shame trigger, we are often too fearful to even ask for an explanation. I've named this "The Edamame Threat."

The Edamame Threat: It's More Than a Soybean

The word edamame *means "beans on branches." Edamame is a green vegetable soybean that is incorporated into many types of dishes and often eaten as a snack. It is pronounced "ed-a-mommy."*

A couple of years ago, Steve and I went to a dinner party at an acquaintance's house. These were new, "fancy friends" and I was anxious to make a good impression. When we got there, they offered us an appetizer—a big silver bowl of beans. When I first saw them I thought they were beans that needed to be shucked for dinner, so when they offered them to us as an appetizer, I'm sure I looked shocked.

I said, "Really, what is it?" I'll never forget the look on their faces. They were absolutely floored.

"What do you mean 'what is it?'"

I immediately felt the warm wave of shame. I apologetically asked, "Are they beans?"

The host replied, "Of course. It's edamame. Don't tell me you've never had edamame. Don't you eat sushi?"

Then, as if it were both unbelievable and fascinating, she started turning to other dinner guests and announcing, "They've never had edamame—can you believe it?" I desperately wanted to turn right around and go home. I was filled with shame.

A couple of weeks later, I was in my office working and eating some beans (I ended up really loving edamame). A student knocked on the door and asked if she could come in to talk to me about a paper. I'm not sure why this student pushed my buttons, but she did. It was probably because she reminded me of myself when I was in my late twenties—smart, but at times painfully insecure and trying harder than necessary.

She looked at my bag of beans and said, "What are those?" In that split second, I felt the dinner party shame all over again. In what must have been an attempt to "shift shame" by putting some of my shame onto her, I said, "Edamame, of course. Haven't you had them?" She looked embarrassed. "No, I don't think so. Are they good?"

And then, in a very Joan Crawford way, I said, "I can't believe you haven't tried them. They're the super food. They are fab-u-lous."

By the time she left my office I was numb. I couldn't believe it. Why had I done that? Why did I care so much? I'm not a food snob. I have no stake in soybeans. I thought about it for several days before it hit me.

I didn't feel shame because I had never tried edamame. I didn't "reinforce" because it was important for me to feel smarter than the student. I felt shame because, for me, not knowing about Japanese food was a class and culture issue. The people at the dinner party were real food elitists. They were the kind of people who travel the world and know all about art and wine. Their toddlers eat food I can't even pronounce.

The more I thought about it, the more I realized that class was a major shame trigger for me. That's hard for people to understand at times because I'm a college professor and my husband is a pediatrician. Our professional peers frequently assume that we share their background, but often we don't.

When I was in my twenties I was not eating sushi and studying at Harvard to fulfill my legacy to become an academic. I worked for the phone company and I was a member of the same local union hall that my parents belonged to when they were in their twenties. My parents worked hard to expose us to different cultures, music, books and food, but we were certainly not exposed at the same level as the "fancy friends."

A few months after the reinforcing incident, Dawn came to Houston for a visit. When it comes to demystifying class issues, she is my go-to girl. When I'm with her I can ask anything, or safely share anything; we came from the same place and we have ended up in the same place. As I started fixing our lunch I said, "Hey, I'm going to make some edamame. Have you tried it before?" She looked at me and said, "No, but I've heard of it. What is it?" I smiled. "I think it's the Japanese word for soybeans. You boil them, sprinkle them with salt, pop the seeds out and eat them. They're really good—I just had them for the first time a few months ago."

Demystifying is a choice. If you know something and you have the opportunity to demystify it or reinforce it, you have the opportunity to move along on the shame resilience continuum. When we choose to reinforce, we should ask ourselves why we feel better keeping what we know a mystery.

I've told this story in my talks and seminars many times and I can't tell you how many e-mails and letters I've received about it. Some of them are just about the general concept of demystifying, but strangely enough, many of the letters are specifically about edamame. One young woman wrote in an e-mail, "I had never had edamame before, and though I'd seen it on menus I never wanted to order it because I didn't know how to pronounce it. After reading your story, I laughed, asked a good friend who wouldn't judge me to order some when we were eating sushi and asked her to show me how to eat them. I love the dish now and I think of you every time I have it. Having come from a very poor Mexican immigrant background, I really related to your story."

Demystifying Credentials

During the interviews, many women associated shame with educators and helping professionals. As an educator, I was not at all surprised to hear shame identified as an issue in the classroom. In fact I believe that shame is one of the greatest barriers to learning. I'm afraid the social-community pressure to appear *learned* has become more important than actually *learning*. When we spend our time and energy building and protecting our image of "knowing," it is highly unlikely that we will risk admitting we don't understand or asking questions—both of which are essential to real knowledge building.

I was, however, shocked to learn that the mere concept of credentials evoked shame in women. Women talked about shame preventing them from returning to school, going to psychotherapy, going to the doctor, visiting the dentist and even talking to members of the clergy. In this section, I want to share my observations on credentials and how we often turn our power over at the first glance of initials strung behind someone's name.

Folks with credentials have three distinct advantages over the folks they are working with: (1) they have permission to "not know," (2) they have permission to "not tell," and (3) their objectivity is not questioned. When most people are asked a question or put on the spot for information, they feel tremendous pressure to come up with an answer—preferably the right one. If we can't produce an answer or we supply the wrong information, we often feel judged. If we are credentialed, however, we automatically have the right not to know or the right not to answer.

Credentials can be excellent "get out of jail free" cards. For example, in my bachelor's program, an incorrect answer or no answer reflected my lack of preparation or my lack of knowledge. Most of the time I felt embarrassed, but occasionally I felt shame. But in my master's program, I could reply to questions with a simple "I really don't know." It wasn't the best answer, but more times than not, I was validated for answering honestly.

At the doctoral level, if someone asked me a question that I couldn't answer, they'd either assume they had asked a bad question or that I was too smart or busy to concern myself with such foolish matters. One of the perks of earning credentials is gaining permission to know nothing. This privilege is rarely afforded to those who aren't protected by plaques, titles, certificates or initials strung behind their names.

The second advantage is what I call the "Do Ask—Don't Tell" policy. In all fields where credentials are issued, elusiveness is either formally taught or, at the very least, informally modeled. Most educators and helping professionals—therapists, physicians, social workers, clergy, etc.—have been trained to extract information from reluctant consumers while sharing as little as possible about their lives. The unspoken rule states the greater the credentials and status, the more you're allowed to know about others and the less you have to reveal about yourself.

Think about it. Your doctor may know your sexual history, your weight and how many bowel movements you have per week. Yet it's questionable for you to ask if she's married or has children. Many professionals will quip back, "We aren't talking about me" or "That's not relevant."

Here are four examples:

• When I got pregnant, rather than going to the doctor and getting prenatal care, I waited until I was six months pregnant.

I waited until it was too late for me not to be pregnant anymore. I was so afraid the doctor was going to say, "You're too fat to have a baby. You shouldn't be pregnant." It scared me and I was so ashamed that I just waited and waited. I can't believe I put myself or my baby at risk because I was so humiliated about my weight. I just hate doctors.

- My daughter died of cancer when she was six. My preacher said that I was being selfish by grieving her death because she was in a better place—she was with God. He is a very smart and educated man, but I think what he said was cruel. It made me hate him, it made me hate my church and it made me hate God. I still hate the preacher. I still don't go to church and I'm working on things with God. But how dare someone shame you about grieving the death of your own child. No collar, no degree, should allow you to do that. Do you have any idea how many years it took me to get over the shame of being sad? I'm allowed to grieve. A part of me will always grieve. What he said was a terrible, terrible injustice—he took advantage of his position.

- The very first time my son got an ear infection, my pediatrician said, "Well, what's it going to be? Your career or your son's hearing?" Only a doctor would feel entitled to say something like that. I asked him if his kids went to day care and he said, "My kids aren't in the doctor's office with an ear infection." You resent them for acting so much better than everyone else, yet you totally depend on them.

- I was fifty-eight when I went back to graduate school. I didn't even know how to e-mail or use the computer. The last time I was in school we thought erasable bond was revolutionary. I knew it would be intimidating, but when I'm in class I turn into a bumbling idiot. If I want to ask a question or make a point, I trip all over myself. Not because of the other students but because of these young professors—they make me so nervous. A few of them are younger than my kids. I hate feeling foolish in front of them.

The third advantage of the credentialed is the assumption of objectivity. Most credentialed professionals do indeed receive some type of training regarding objectivity, but there is ongoing debate about what is truly achievable. Some are taught that objectivity is possible, and they are trained to try to replace their personal lenses with professional lenses when they are with clients or patients.

Others, including me, are taught that pure objectivity does not exist and that people can't ever completely put away their personal lenses. We are trained, instead, to understand the biases and power of our experiences so we understand how they might affect our interactions with clients. We believe this is the most ethical way to work with clients.

In my experience, the most serious threat to objectivity is the very belief that "pure objectivity" and "value neutrality" exist. I have greater trust in those who question objectivity and who believe that people, values and experiences influence our research and practice—they are the ones who make the greatest effort to present their opinions in the appropriate context.

When we interview doctors, therapists and other credentialed professionals, we can't assume objectivity. We don't have the right to infringe on their private lives, but we do have the right to understand their professional values, ethics and their motivation for working with us. This is especially true for professionals who offer advice or guidance.

I want a pediatrician who supports mothers in the workforce. I want an ob-gyn who shares some of my basic beliefs about pregnancy and childbirth. I want a CPA who understands my values and ethics. And I certainly want a therapist who shares my basic values about how people change.

Given the power of credentials, it is easy to understand why shame often results from interactions with the credentialed. To build connection and power in these situations, we need to practice our critical awareness skills. We need to determine who benefits from our fear and shame and decide how we can find support. Toward that end, we should not hesitate to get referrals from friends, and we must also accept that we have an absolute right to interview credentialed professionals about how they practice, before we expose our most personal information or vulnerabilities.

In the next chapter we will learn about the power of reaching out. While the four shame resilience elements don't always happen in a particular order, I have found that understanding our triggers and having some level of critical awareness about our issues make reaching out to others less scary. This is important because, as the next chapter will demonstrate, reaching out is the single most powerful act of resilience.

FIVE

The Third Element: Reaching Out

I'd like to start this chapter by sharing three letters I received from women who have been applying the concepts in this book to their own lives. The first woman, Leticia, e-mailed this experience to me:

> One afternoon I was on the phone with my mother telling her about a guy who wanted a relationship with me, but in whom I was not really interested. My mother was still in favor of him and in explaining why, she said, "He likes you even though you aren't skinny. It doesn't matter to him that you are heavy—he still thinks you are pretty." On the other end of the line my jaw dropped. A few years ago I'd undergone treatment for an eating disorder—I was seeing up to four doctors at a time for it. My mom is well aware of my medical history.
>
> The first thing that came through my mind was "Wow, a few years ago that would totally have thrown me into despair." I would have hung up with her and then cried with shame over my size and felt that no one could ever really love

me with this body and that I had to be grateful for anyone who did.

Having read about shame, though, I realized that both my mother and my weight were triggers for me and I was able to step back from the situation and see my mother's comment as her (poorly executed) attempt at support rather than react in anger as I would have in the past. It still shook me a little and bothered me that her attitude was so negative, but I had aware-ness of the situation and was able to call a good friend to dis-cuss the situation and diffuse the emotional buildup. It also gave me better insight to where so many of my body issues came from.

This second piece is a longer letter about putting the elements of shame resilience to work:

Dr. Brown,

I have been affected by your work in two areas. One, I learned to identify what I was feeling as shame and second, I learned how to act on it by "speaking shame." I learned that I am very shame-based, that I had all of the "symptoms" of shame that you speak of, but never really related them to the concept of shame. It's kind of like having a lot of strange and disparate symptoms but not knowing what to attribute them to. If you don't know what the disease is, you can't treat it. When painful things happened, my face would flush, my stomach would tighten, and I would want to hide. But since the situations were all different, even though my reaction might be the same, I never could specifically identify the emo-tion I was feeling. So I never really could deal with it. Plus, I was so busy trying my old methods of coping, that is, trying to develop amnesia about the events, that I didn't spend much time trying to figure out what was going on and how to deal with it more effectively.

In fact, I was so disassociated from the concept of shame that I wasn't sure that it even applied to me. Somehow "shame" was for other people. Only through reading your work was I able to see how pervasive shame was in my life and how ineffective I had been at both identifying it and dealing with it.

My favorite part of Shame Resilience Theory is "speaking shame." For me that means identifying shame and then dealing with it in more appropriate ways. I now can more effectively identify those situations in which I feel shame. It is usually prompted by a strong physiological reaction, such as face flushes, stomach tightens, and I replay the incident over and over in my head while actively trying to forget it ever happened. This strategy doesn't work well, and years later the recall of a shameful incident will cause me to wince and flush. But now I am able to catch myself and label this reaction "shame."

So now I have a name for it and some effective action that I can take. My most effective action now is finding someone supportive to tell my shame story to instead of holding it in. I love the metaphor of the petri dish, for when I kept my shame silent and in the dark, it grew exponentially. However, exposing it to the light of day causes it to lose its power and even shrink. Now instead of cringing, I can almost laugh at some of my experiences. Sometimes I am even eager to tell my shame story to others; other times I more reluctantly share my stories.

For example, one day I had a group of old neighbors over to my new home. I had always felt insecure around these old neighborhood friends, as they were the type of women that dressed really lovely and decorated their homes to perfection. I was friendly with this group, but always felt a little on the outside, as I cared less about clothes and home décor. In turn, they seemed to view me with paternalistic bemusement, "poor bumbling Barbara." I always felt "less than" in their presence.

Well, I had moved to a new home and had spent a lot of time decorating it and was very proud of my more sophisticated taste. So I invited them over, along with other old friends from the neighborhood. I was so eager to please and impress that I went really overboard on the food and my large dining table nearly groaned with platter after platter piled high with wonderful cheeses, chips and dips, and desserts. However, the party was not well attended, except for this one group of women that I was so desperate to impress. So they came, and loved the house and we caught up on our lives, and then there was this table covered with food and they ate only a few bites (did I mention they were all thin too?!).

After they left I was mortified. Up into that point I had not realized how hard I was trying to impress them and make up for my perceived past poor showing by inviting them to my new place. And now instead of rectifying the past shame, I created more shame by having this table full of food that was untouched. The heaping trays of food represented my shame to me. And it was piled high and deep!

I saw myself as looking foolish, and trying so hard to impress this group of women and I had failed, yet again. In the past I would have tried to hide the shame and maybe thrown out the food as a way to hide my shame. However, with my new skills, I reached out to a friend who I could trust to understand and share my pain. I called her and told her the story and cried. And she came over the next day and we ate the leftovers for lunch.

After talking seriously about the issues, I was even able to laugh about my attempts to garner approval and joked about the food, and I felt better. Having it all out in the open I could more clearly see that I was looking for approval in the wrong places, from the wrong people. I could let go of the shame.

Today when I think of the experience I generally smile rather than wince. I think of my friend and I sitting at the table and laughing and eating the food rather than the botched party. This was a real change for me, for in the past I would stuffed down the shame instead of the food.

My husband had an opportunity to hear an abbreviated version of your shame presentation and that has been helpful as well. We "talk shame" together and use it to better our communication as a couple.

I also think learning about shame has made me a more empathetic person. I have always prided myself on listening to and not judging others. However, knowing about shame has taken that to new levels. I realize what is at stake when someone chooses to share their shameful stories with me and I know the damage that can be done by greeting such a story with judgment instead of empathy.

So I am more aware of trying to comfort that person and let them know that all of us end up in the shame soup at times, that I might be the person on shore throwing the life vest this time, but next time I will be in the shame soup and need some help myself. I am so much more aware that that distancing from others and using "us" and "them" strategies separates people and instills a false sense of superiority. So I am much more aware of my shame and the shame of others and really work to develop compassion for us all.

This is an e-mail from a therapist who uses the work with her clients and in her personal life:

Dear Brené,

As a counselor for survivors of domestic and sexual violence, dealing with shame has always been a difficult part of my work. Your work has been a great tool for working with my clients. I use the activities in my groups and with my individual clients. I think the most helpful part of this book for me has been that I'm now able to identify shame and how it is

affecting my clients more frequently. I have the tools of help-
ing them acknowledge personal vulnerability, using critical
awareness and facilitating their ability to speak shame. It's al-
most like magic. Being able to dissolve shame and move for-
ward is a powerful part of healing.

In my personal life, I have used your work as well. I talk
about shame with my friends. Many of them have read your
work. Just being able to talk about shame helps so much.
Dealing with my own issues of shame has helped me in areas
of my life where I felt stuck. As a survivor myself, I've talked
to my friends about shame relating to violence against
women. But this book helped me identify other areas of shame
in my life. The more common, everyday areas that it was easy
for me to ignore. Being able to talk about my shame, whether
it is about my body (feeling too fat) or about my work (not be-
ing good enough) is so powerful. It took a lot of courage in the
beginning to even bring up feelings of shame. I never want to
talk about shame but every time I do, I feel so relieved. The
more I do it, the easier it gets. And usually I no longer feel
ashamed. Without your work I might not have been brave
enough to speak.

When I read these letters, the first thing that comes to mind is this: I didn't invent the strategies in this book. It's deeply meaning-ful to know that the ideas presented in this book are helping women, but these ideas belong to others besides just me. I listened to hundreds of women tell their stories and explain their strategies for dealing with shame. I studied their experiences, organized them and put words to them. To better understand what I was hearing, I studied the work of many different clinicians and re-searchers. Their work, which is quoted throughout the book and referenced in the Notes at the end, makes my work possible.

Reading these letters only confirms what I've learned from

studying Relational-Cultural Theory: We heal through our connections with others. Relational-Cultural Theory grew out of a collaborative process of theory building initiated by the scholars at the Stone Center at Wellesley College. In their book, *The Healing Connection*, Jean Baker Miller and Irene Stiver write, "If we observe women's lives carefully, without attempting to force our observations into preexisting patterns, we discover that an inner sense of connection to others is the central organizing feature of women's development. By listening to the stories women tell about their lives and examining these stories seriously, we have found that, quite contrary to what one would expect based on the governing models of development emphasizing separation, women's sense of self and of worth is most often grounded in the ability to make and maintain relationships."

The need for connection and the capacity to use these shame resilience strategies is within all of us. And as Barbara points out in her letter, sometimes we're in the shame soup and need help and other times we are the ones who can throw the life preserver to the person who is drowning.

There are certainly real differences that separate us all in many ways, but in the end, we are more alike than we are different. We all need to feel valued, accepted and affirmed. When we feel worthless, rejected and unworthy of belonging, we feel shame. Long letters or short e-mails, letters from young women or experienced professionals, it doesn't matter. The message is the same: One of the most important benefits of reaching out to others is learning that the experiences that make us feel the most alone are actually universal experiences.

Regardless of who we are, how we were raised or what we believe, all of us fight hidden, silent battles against not being good enough, not having enough and not belonging enough. When we find the courage to share our experiences and the compassion to hear others tell their stories, we force shame out of hiding and end the silence. Here's how three women turned their shame experiences into connection:

- I got pregnant when I was sixteen. I always had weird periods, so I didn't even know until I was about three months along. The only person who knew was my sister. I didn't even tell my boyfriend. About a week after I found out, I had a miscarriage. It was really scary—my sister took me back to the doctor. On the way home from the doctor's office, my sister said losing the baby was the best thing that could have ever happened. That was twenty-five years ago and every year I still remember the day that would have been my baby's birthday. I knew that I was not allowed to be sad about it because I wasn't supposed to be pregnant. I'm ashamed that I got pregnant, but I'm also ashamed that I wasn't allowed to be sad. Now, when I see someone who is ashamed to be sad, I tell them how important it is to tell someone and let it out. I tell my daughters, my friends, my nieces—anyone who seems to be scared to grieve. Everyone has the right to grieve and be sad.

- My dad's wife is younger than I am and my mom's new boyfriend has been married six times. My family is ridiculous. We're supposed to be comfortable with that and that's "supposed to be OK" because all families are crazy. Well, that only works when you're around other people who also talk openly about their families being crazy. When you're around people who pretend their families are perfect, it's not OK. In fact, it's very shameful because they judge you based on your crazy family members. You try to avoid the discussion and start talking about something else. When I see people admit something about their weird family and someone starts judging them and saying shitty things, I jump right in. I start talking about my family. If we all told the truth, no one would feel like they were the only one with a screwed-up family. I try to help people in that situation because I've been there—it's really lonely.

- I think not knowing the truth about something is really shameful. Especially when you're growing up and you hear things or get bad information. When I was growing up I thought a tampon could make you pregnant and if you masturbated you would become a porn star. I don't even know how I learned these things but for one year I wouldn't use a tampon. When my friends asked me why I wore gross pads, I couldn't tell them, because I wasn't sure if the "pregnancy thing" was true. It's not like I could ask my parents. Finally I saw a tampon in one of my baby-sitter's purses and I asked her about it. She just laughed and told me everything about periods, sex and guys. Parents have no idea what bad information does to kids. When young kids ask me questions or even make references to bad information, I tell them everything they want to know. I try to save them the misery I experienced.

When we don't reach out to others, we allow them to sit alone in their shame, feeding shame the secrecy and silence it craves. Just like we can't use shame to change people, we can't benefit from other people's shame. We can, however, benefit from shared empathy.

We don't reach out to "fix" or "save" others. We reach out to help others by reinforcing their connection network and our own. This increases our resilience by:

- Sharing our story
- Creating change

When we don't reach out, we fuel our shame and create isolation by:

- Separating
- Insulating

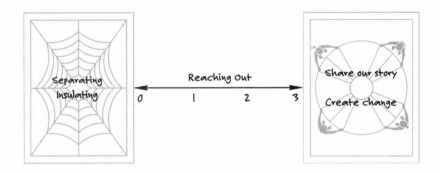

One of the benefits of sharing our story is experiencing "knowing laughter." I define knowing laughter as laughter that results from recognizing the universality of our shared experiences, both positive and negative. It embodies the relief and connection we experience when we realize the power of sharing our shame. Hopefully, if you laughed when you read the cookie story, you were laughing with me, not at me. That's "knowing laughter."

Knowing laughter is not the use of humor as self-deprecation or deflection; it's not the kind of painful laughter we sometimes hide behind. Knowing laughter is acknowledging the absurdity of the expectations that form the shame web and recognizing the irony of believing that we, alone, are trapped and entangled in that web. When I think of knowing laughter I think of the incredible volume of work written by Erma Bombeck and the poignant humor of *Cathy*, the comic strip written by Cathy Guisewite. Their creative work targeting motherhood and single life captures our vulnerabilities in a way that makes us laugh and feel normal.

There is something moving, spiritual and essential about sharing knowing laughter with people who understand our struggles. My favorite definition of laughter comes from the wonderful writer Anne Lamott. I once heard her describe laughter as a "bubbly, effervescent form of holiness."

Over the past several years, I've had the opportunity to work with some wonderful graduate students on this project. We spent many hours reading and analyzing interviews and discussing shame. I remember when the research team first started exploring the concept of knowing laughter. Intuitively, we knew laughing about shared shame experiences played a significant role in our meetings, but as we heard an increasing number of research participants talk about it, we were a little surprised. Finally we realized that the universal language of laughter gave all of us a way to talk about shame; a concept that otherwise resists words and descriptions.

Here's what Marki McMillan, one of the researchers, writes: "Laughter is the evidence that the chokehold of shame has been loosened. Knowing laughter is the moment we feel proof that our shame has been transformed. Like empathy, it strips shame to the bone, robs it of its power and forces it from the closet."

When we reach out to others and share our stories, we increase our power and potential to create change. For most of us, reaching out to others results in tremendous individual change, and inspires some still further to engage in collective change.

Creating Change

Believing that we truly do have the ability to create change in our lives may seem difficult, or even impossible, at first, but it is one of the most empowering steps along the path to developing resilience. When we talk about individual and collective change, it's important to realize that not all of us are going to engage in political action, advocacy or even small group efforts. Some of us may create change by changing the way we interact with people or changing our relationships. Others may raise critical awareness with friends and family members.

We need to find a method of change that moves and inspires us. Sometimes, as individuals, our efforts vary depending upon the issue. There are some issues that motivate me to fully engage in collective action. There are other issues where I feel my strongest contribution is making personal changes. When we talk about ways to create change, I like to think of the six *P*s—personal, pens, polls, participation, purchases and protests. Whether we are trying to change something at our child's school, fighting to have offensive magazines removed from our local convenience store, trying to get better maternity leave at work or struggling to change national policy, the six *P*s work.

Personal: Even the most personal changes often have a powerful ripple effect through the lives of our families, friends and colleagues. Jillian, for example, started monitoring the shows her children watch and now limits her fashion magazine subscriptions. Sondra, the woman silenced by her husband's remarks, has returned to debating politics and religion with her brother-in-law. She's also passing down her parents' wonderful legacy of "living out loud and proud" along with tools her daughters can use to effectively deal with the shaming that some people use to keep us quiet. Change can take many forms—there is nothing more inherently political than breaking through social-community expectations so we can live our lives at our full potential and help others do the same. Practicing courage, compassion and connection in the face of shame is a political act.

Pens: Write a letter. Most organizational leaders and legislators will respond to letters, e-mails or faxes. My friend and colleague Ann Hilbig lobbies for children's issues. She told me that U.S. Congress members need only twelve letters before they ask someone in their office to research the issue. I send e-mails all the time. If you see an advertisement that's incredibly offensive, e-mail the company. The National Organization for Women sponsors Love Your Body Day. On their Web site, they collect offensive advertisements that promote appearance shame, teen smoking and alcohol consumption. They have a ready-made petition form that you can pass around to your friends and send to companies. The petition reads:

Dear Marketing Director:

We refuse to starve our bodies to fit into this year's fashions. We reject your idea of tobacco as a diet aid and we denounce the diet industry for making us doubt our dignity. We won't be pushed up, squeezed into, reduced, flattened, straightened, or touched-up. You will not map my face or my body for the perfect eyes, nose, neck, breast, tummy, hip, thigh or butt . . . we will not be cut up like meat for your profit. We're beautiful just like we are!

We KNOW that cigarettes addict and kill. We KNOW that starvation diets rob us of muscle tissue and brainpower. We KNOW that the images of women you place in magazines and on TV are offensive, harmful, dangerous and disrespectful. These ads are an attack on women and girls. These ads are an affront to my intelligence. These ads are an assault on women's equality.

Polls: Vote. Find out how candidates feel about the issues that affect your life and vote.

Participation: Learn about the organizations that support your issues. Join them in the fight. Most organizations make it very easy to stay up to date on issues by e-mailing or faxing updates. They'll also help you speak out by offering preformatted e-mails and faxes; you just enter your zip code, and send them right from the computer. It takes two minutes and they make sure it gets to the right person.

Purchases: The dollar is mightier than the sword; stop buying from people who don't share your values. Marketing research shows that women are the decision makers in an estimated eighty-five percent of household buying decisions. Here's an example. About two years ago, Ellen and I went to our local video rental store to rent a couple of DVDs. I was reading the back of movie cases when Ellen tugged on my shirt and asked, "Are they princesses?" I looked down and rather than seeing one of her regular picks, I saw three young women in string bikinis. The title of the movie was something like *Want Ads: Trouble in the Suburbs*. I grabbed it out of her hand and examined it cover to cover. It was an "adult" movie.

I immediately picked up Ellen, power-walked to the register and asked to speak to a manager. After a couple minutes' wait, a young woman walked up to me and introduced herself. "When did you start carrying these?" I asked. She looked down at the box and sighed, "We got the porn about the same time they cut our benefits and extended our hours." She went on to explain that a huge telecommunications company had bought this national chain of video rental stores. After the buyout, they started renting adult movies. She explained that her store received only fifty adult movies, but the stores in "poor neighborhoods" stock hundreds of them.

On the drive home I explained to Ellen why I was angry and why I think some movies hurt girls and women. She helped me cut up my membership card. We mailed the shredded card and a letter to the company's district manager. I found a great online service that delivers DVDs straight to my door—no late charges and no adult movies. Our old store may never stop renting pornography, but Ellen and I are not participating.

Protests: A protest is not always a million people marching on the capital. Sometimes a protest is four or five people showing up at a school board meeting or in someone's office. Regardless of size and scope, when we come together to ask for what we need, some people will label our actions as "protest." If that stops us, we have to ask, "Who benefits by that?"

In *The Dance of Intimacy*, Harriet Lerner writes, "Although the connections are not always obvious, personal change is inseparable from social and political change." I believe this is true. Reaching out to others allows us to identify and name what we share in common and creates the opportunity for both personal and social change.

Barriers to Reaching Out

As we practice reaching out, we need to be very aware of the barriers that might get in the way. In the remainder of this chapter, we're going to examine the two main issues that often prevent us from practicing courage and compassion. The best way to introduce these concepts is by telling the story of Jennifer and Tiffany. Their story beautifully illustrates these barriers to reaching out and why it's worth the fight to overcome them.

When I first interviewed Jennifer over the phone, she and her husband, Drew, were both finishing their MBAs and they had a three-year-old son, Toby. Our interview mostly focused on her struggle with speaking out in her predominantly male classes and the shame of sending her toddler to day care while she worked and went to school every other weekend. I got to meet Jennifer in person several years later at a shame resilience workshop I was conducting. She approached me at break and asked if she could share an important reaching-out story with the group. This is her story.

After finishing their degrees and getting jobs, Jennifer and Drew moved into their first house in their dream neighborhood. They moved in across the street from Tiffany and her husband, Andy. Jennifer and Tiffany both had sons the same age and Tiffany had a baby daughter. Jennifer was pregnant at the time of our second interview.

While their sons grew to be best friends, Jennifer and Tiffany's friendship moved a little slower. Jennifer told me, "Things never got very deep between us. It was mostly talk about kids. I tried a couple of times, but she just didn't seem to want to go there. After one year, I didn't know much about her and she really didn't know much about me . . . well . . . until this whole thing started."

Jennifer explained that her younger sister, Carly, had struggled with alcoholism since her teens. Their mom, who was a recovering alcoholic, had called Jennifer to tell her that Carly had been admitted into a rehab hospital and that her mom would be caring for Carly's daughter, Emma, until Carly got out. Jennifer's mom asked her if she and Drew could attend family weekend at the rehab center, and Jennifer assured her that they would be there. Jennifer had never left her son with a sitter overnight, so she decided to ask Tiffany if her son could spend the night.

Here's how Jennifer recalled the scene: "I walked across the street, knocked on the door and took a deep breath. Tiffany answered the door and I said, 'My sister, Carly, just went into rehab and Drew and I need to go and see her in a couple of weeks. Could Toby spend one night with you? I'd ask my mom to drive down, but she'll be with my sister too.' " Jennifer said that Tiffany looked shocked.

Tiffany quickly answered, "Of course he can spend the night. No problem." Jennifer was relieved. Then Tiffany's questions started. "Which sister—I thought you only had one sister?"

"Yeah, Carly, you met her a couple of months ago when she was here with her daughter. She lives upstate, close to my mom," answered Jennifer.

Tiffany looked confused, "Carly! You're kidding? She's so cute, right? She was the one with the little girl? The two of them were wearing matching Lilly Pulitzer dresses?"

"Yes, that's her," replied Jennifer, who was starting to get increasingly uncomfortable while Tiffany seemed to be trying to put it all together in her head. Here's how the rest of the conversation went:

Tiffany: "She doesn't look like a person who goes to rehab. What's the problem?"
Jennifer: "She's an alcoholic."
Tiffany: "You're kidding. She doesn't look like an alcoholic. What does her husband think?"
Jennifer: "She's not married."
Tiffany: "You're kidding. What does your mother think?"
Jennifer: "About her being an alcoholic or being a single mother?"
Tiffany: "Gosh, I don't know."

Jennifer: "She thinks Carly and Emma are great and she's also a recovering alcoholic."
Tiffany: "Wow. That's some family. Very complicated."
Jennifer: "Yes, I guess so. So, Toby can stay with you that night?"

As you can imagine, this conversation didn't do much to deepen the connection between Jennifer and Tiffany. And things would get worse before they got better.

A couple of months later, Jennifer and Tiffany's boys started kindergarten. Two weeks into school, there was a horrible incident in the carpool line. Jennifer had already picked her son up and was in the kitchen when Tiffany pounded on the door. Jennifer answered the door and Tiffany excitedly reported every detail of the incident. "You are not going to believe this. Did you see the police cars? Did you see the ambulance?" Jennifer got scared. "No! What happened?"

"One of the cars didn't pull forward in the carpool line and people started honking. A mom got out of her car and walked up to the car that wasn't moving. A woman was slumped over the steering wheel. The mom started screaming and a bunch of teachers ran up. They thought she was dead. Someone called 911 and by the time the ambulance got there they realized that she wasn't dead. She was passed-out drunk! Can you believe it?"

Jennifer could barely respond. Her eyes welled up with tears. "Oh, my God. That's horrible . . ." she replied.

Tiffany interrupted her. "I know! Can you believe—at our school? In our neighborhood? I mean this woman could have killed someone. She could have run over our kids. I know I almost started crying too. Just thinking about that crazy woman driving up to our school like that."

Jennifer was speechless.

Tiffany responded to her silence by saying, "I know, I know. It's horrible. I'm devastated too. It happened right here—down the street. In our neighborhood."

Jennifer shook her head and said, "I'm devastated for that mom. And her kids. And her family. But I don't think we're devastated for the same reasons, Tiffany."

Tiffany, who was looking out the door, didn't respond to Jennifer's comment. She was distracted as she saw another neighbor pull up in their driveway and said, "Oooh, I'm going to talk to Leena about it—I'll see you later."

Jennifer was angry and hurt. As she recounted the story, she kept telling me that she couldn't believe she could be friends with someone so superficial—so clueless. Tiffany knew that Jennifer's mother and sister were alcoholics; yet, she failed to make the connection. Jennifer said, "I'll never forget her saying that she couldn't believe that this could happen in our neighborhood, at our school, in front of our kids." Jennifer explained, "I wanted to ask her, 'Where do you think this should happen? Whose kids should see this?'"

Their friendship became a little more distant, but this didn't stop Tiffany from asking Jennifer if she wanted to work together on the school's winter carnival. Tiffany pitched the idea by saying that it would be a great opportunity to get to know some of the PTA moms—especially Amber Daniels. Jennifer reluctantly agreed. She figured it would be a good way to ease some of her working-mom guilt.

Amber Daniels had three kids in the school—a fifth-grader, a third-grader and a second-grader. She was the president of the PTA and, according to Jennifer, "about the most perfect person you'll ever meet." Jennifer described her as smart, beautiful, nice and, by all accounts, a perfect mom. Tiffany idolized her to the point that she couldn't even talk to her. Amber had a following of friends—mostly the mothers of older kids. If Amber or any of her friends said hello to Tiffany, she stammered. Jennifer wasn't quite as starstruck but did find this "PTA in-crowd" a little intimidating.

Jennifer and Tiffany were put in charge of the silent auction.

One evening, after a carnival-planning meeting, Jennifer and Tiffany were walking out of the cafeteria when Amber, who was sitting with two of her friends, shouted, "Hey, come join us for some coffee." Jennifer and Tiffany looked at each other and slowly started walking toward the table.

Jennifer laughed and used her Valley Girl voice when she told me about the moment. She said, "I kept thinking—Oh! My! God! Like, we've been invited to sit at the cheerleaders' table."

They sat down and Amber introduced herself and her friends. Then Amber asked, "So do either of you have exciting holiday plans?"

At this point in her story, Jennifer looked at me and said, "Brené, honestly, I don't know what came over me." She went on to say, "I looked right at Amber and said, 'Yeah. I'm going upstate to see my family. My sister just got out of rehab, so we're going to spend some time with her and her daughter. She's a single mom and it's been hard.'"

Apparently, Tiffany was so taken aback by Jennifer's candid answer that she slumped forward in her chair at the miniature cafeteria table, knocking her forehead against the table.

Jennifer told us, "If she was trying to divert attention from the conversation, she did a good job. Amber even asked her if she was OK."

Tiffany pulled herself together, looked right at Jennifer and said, "C'mon, Jennifer! I doubt Amber wants the details of your complicated family."

Amber responded by laughing and saying, "Hey. Aren't all families complicated?"

Jennifer started to reply, but Tiffany interrupted and quickly said, "Not like hers." At this point, Jennifer said she was starting to feel ashamed. She was staring down at her coffee cup and was somewhat startled when Amber broke the awkward silence by asking, "So, how's your sister doing?"

Jennifer described the moment like this: "Amber was directing the question to me, but she was staring right at Tiffany with a look that said, 'You better not say a word.'"

Jennifer quickly answered, "Better. Thanks."

"Where was she in treatment?" Amber asked.

"Moorewood," Jennifer replied.

Amber nodded and said, "Yeah—my husband sponsors a guy who went through their program. It's supposed to be pretty good."

Tiffany was speechless.

One of Amber's friends started laughing and asked, "What about you, Amber? Going to any holiday parties this year?"

Amber and her friends started laughing and Jennifer told me that she could sense that there was some kind of inside joke at work. Amber shook her head and said, "Talk about complicated."

Amber went on to explain that, the previous year, they had taken their kids to her mom's house for the holidays. Amber's mother begged them to attend a holiday party hosted by one of her closest friends, who just happened to be the mother of Amber's first husband—her ex-mother-in-law.

Jennifer told us that right in the middle of her story, Tiffany blurted out, "You've been married before?" Amber apparently nodded and just kept telling the story.

Amber explained that all of her kids knew she had been married before, but she and her husband were shocked when her ex-husband showed up with his new boyfriend. Jennifer said, "By this point in the story we were all laughing and getting on great. All of us except for Tiffany. She didn't even crack a smile. I almost felt bad for her until she asked Amber if it was hard to expose her kids to the 'gay thing' at such a young age."

Jennifer said Amber handled it really well. She explained that she wasn't sure what Tiffany meant by the "gay thing" but that her husband's youngest brother and his partner also lived in town and baby-sat the kids all the time, so the "gay thing" was a "normal thing" to their kids.

Jennifer described the ride home from the carnival meeting as incredibly uncomfortable. Tiffany didn't say a word. About a week later, Jennifer asked Tiffany if they could talk. Tiffany agreed and they talked about Carly, the carpool incident and Amber.

As hard as Jennifer tried to explain how she felt, Tiffany just kept saying, "I don't know why you talk about these things like you're proud of them."

Jennifer said, "I tried to explain that I'm not proud of them, but I'm just not going to be ashamed of them. I tried to explain to her that I'm working on my shame issues, but she just didn't get it."

Tiffany responded by saying, "Am I supposed to think more of Amber because her husband's an alcoholic with a gay brother and she's been married before? Well, I don't think more of her. I like honest people. When you see Amber, what you see is not what you get!"

Jennifer said, "I got so pissed, I gave up. I knew if it kept going we'd end up not speaking."

From that point, their relationship solely focused on the kids and school. Jennifer did become good friends with Amber. Tiffany remained convinced that Amber was overrated and turned down all of Jennifer's invitations to hang out with them.

One morning, almost six months later, Tiffany called Jennifer. She was crying so hard that her voice was barely audible. Jennifer ran to Tiffany's house. The front door was open and Jennifer walked in. Tiffany was sitting on the kitchen floor, sobbing.

"I was sure someone had died. I sat down next to her and asked her what had happened," Jennifer explained.

Tiffany looked at Jennifer and said, "I'm not perfect. I'm really not. My life is as fucked up as everyone else's. I swear."

Jennifer said, "I must have looked shocked, because Tiffany angrily said, 'Yes, I said the *f*-word. That's right. I'll say it again too.' Then she just started sobbing even harder."

Jennifer held Tiffany and said, "I know you're not perfect. Trust me I know. It's fine. It's better than fine. It's great."

They both laughed a little, but then Jennifer said that Tiffany turned toward her, held both of her hands and reached out in the most powerful way. Tiffany explained to Jennifer that she really didn't understand.

Tiffany explained that she didn't even know her father—she had never seen or met him. She told Jennifer that her mother didn't visit because Tiffany was too ashamed of her so she didn't invite her.

Tiffany said, "She doesn't have normal problems—like the kind you and Amber laugh about. She's poor. She's missing teeth. She doesn't speak like us. I didn't grow up in a neighborhood like this. No matter what I did growing up—no matter how good my grades were or how hard I worked to dress nice—I was still shit."

When Tiffany met Andy at college, he was everything she wanted. He had the seemingly perfect family and he taught her how to look good. Tiffany went on to tell Jennifer, "I didn't even invite my mom to my wedding. Andy met my mom after we were married. He didn't like her either. He hates where I'm from. It's not like I told him that I wasn't sure what to do about inviting my mom to the wedding and he tried to talk me into inviting her. He said it would be easier on everyone if she didn't come."

At this point Jennifer and Tiffany were both crying. Tiffany told Jennifer, "I want to be normal. But I'm exhausted. I keep it all in because Andy would freak out if anyone knew our problems. I miss my mom. I don't know what to do. I want to be able to talk to you."

Jennifer told me, "I didn't know what to say or do. I just sat and listened and cried."

Jennifer said the hardest thing was when Tiffany stood up and walked over to a drawer in the kitchen and pulled out a folded piece of paper. She looked at Jennifer and said, "When you told me you were working on your shame, I Googled the word *shame*. I found this poem. If you read it, you'll understand me better. Do you want to read it?"

Jennifer said she could barely force herself to look at the paper, but she read it. It was Vern Rutsala's poem, *Shame*. I had never heard of it until Jennifer gave me a copy. I've since shared it with several people and I do believe it's one of the most courageous acts of truth telling that I've come across. This is it:

*This is the shame of the woman whose hand hides
her smile because her teeth are so bad, not the grand
self-hate that leads some to razors or pills
or swan dives off beautiful bridges however
tragic that is. This is the shame of seeing yourself,
of being ashamed of where you live and what
your father's paycheck lets you eat and wear.
This is the shame of the fat and the bald,
the unbearable blush of acne, the shame of having
no lunch money and pretending you're not hungry.
This is the shame of concealed sickness—diseases
too expensive to afford that offer only their cold
one-way ticket out. This is the shame of being ashamed,
the self-disgust of the cheap wine drunk, the lassitude
that makes junk accumulate, the shame that tells
you there is another way to live but you are
too dumb to find it. This is the real shame, the damned
shame, the crying shame, the shame that's criminal,
the shame of knowing words like* glory *are not
in your vocabulary though they litter the Bibles
you're still paying for. This is the shame of not
knowing how to read and pretending you do.
This is the shame that makes you afraid to leave your house,
the shame of food stamps at the supermarket when
the clerk shows impatience as you fumble with the change.
This is the shame of dirty underwear, the shame
of pretending your father works in an office
as God intended all men to do. This is the shame
of asking friends to let you off in front of the one*

nice house in the neighborhood and waiting
in the shadows until they drive away before walking
to the gloom of your house. This is the shame
at the end of the mania for owning things, the shame
of no heat in winter, the shame of eating cat food,
the unholy shame of dreaming of a new house and car
and the shame of knowing how cheap such dreams are.

© Vern Rutsala

As you can imagine, this marked a huge turning point in Jennifer and Tiffany's friendship. The first few times they were together after this sharing, they both felt a little awkward, which was to be expected.

Jennifer said, "At one point I knew that it would be easier for us to pretend that afternoon didn't happen. But we didn't. It was too big."

According to Jennifer, she and Tiffany are best friends today. Jennifer's family is still complicated, but aren't they all? Tiffany and Andy are in couples counseling. Jennifer said that Tiffany threatened to leave if he didn't go and that would be worse for his image than going to counseling. Tiffany and her mom are working on mending their relationship, and that's been very tough on both of them.

Amber didn't run for PTA president again because she decided to become a yoga instructor. Jennifer laughed. "She has a huge following. Tiffany and I take her class together."

In this next section, we'll look more closely at the concepts of insulating and otherness—two of the barriers that we face when we try to reach out. These are two of the barriers that almost prevented Jennifer and Tiffany from building the connection they now seem to value so deeply. These barriers affect all of the shame resilience elements. If we don't understand how these barriers work in our lives, shame resilience is almost impossible. Let's start by exploring the concept of "insulating."

Insulating

In a culture of shame, we are constantly overwhelmed with feelings of fear, blame and disconnection. This creates an "us and them" world. There are people like us, and then there are "those other people." And, we normally work very hard to insulate ourselves from "those people." As children, there were the people that we were allowed to hang out with and then there were the other kids. There were the people we were allowed to date and then there were the other kids. There were the schools we went to and there were schools for the other kids. As adults, we live in the neighborhood where our kind live—the other neighborhoods are for the other folks. We emotionally and physically insulate ourselves from "the other." It never seems to end. We've developed language to describe the others—sometimes we refer to them as "those people" or the even more mysterious "people like that."

I seldom use the word *truth*, because it's a strong word with a lot of promises behind it. But in this instance, I'm going to use it because, out of all the things I've learned in the past decade, the one concept that I believe has the biggest potential for helping us overcome shame is this: We are "those people." The truth is . . . we are the others.

Most of us are one paycheck, one divorce, one drug-addicted kid, one mental health diagnosis, one serious illness, one sexual assault, one drinking binge, one night of unprotected sex, or one affair away from being "those people"—the ones we don't trust, the ones we pity, the ones we don't let our children play with, the ones bad things happen to, the ones we don't want living next door.

In fact, let me prove my point. If you or your family members have NEVER experienced any one of the following issues, you should just skip the remainder of this chapter:

- Addiction (alcohol, drug, food, sex, relationships, etc.)
- Any mental health diagnosis (depression, anxiety, eating disorders, bipolar, attention-deficit, etc.)

- Any stigmatized illness (sexually transmitted diseases, obesity, HIV/Aids, etc.)
- Domestic violence (physical, emotional, verbal, etc.)
- Sexual assault (rape, marital rape, date rape, etc.)
- Child abuse (physical, sexual, incest, neglect, emotional, etc.)
- Suicide
- Violent death
- Criminal activity or incarceration
- Serious debt or bankruptcy
- Abortion
- Nonmainstream religious beliefs
- Poverty (including class issues)
- Low educational attainment (lacking basic literacy skills, dropout, etc.)
- Divorce

OK, statistically, everyone should still be reading. This is the list of "otherness," and like it or not, we are on the list—some of us multiple times. You may read this list and think, "She's got to be kidding. Just because I'm divorced doesn't mean people think of me like they think of someone who's gone to jail or someone who's on drugs?" Not true. For some people, divorcing may be worse than drug addiction. In fact, I interviewed a woman in her early sixties who told me that she often felt ashamed of her kids. Specifically, the most shame she felt was about her daughter. Her son-in-law caught the daughter having an affair and divorced her. This same woman had a son who spent several months in jail after getting his second DUI at college. She compared the two by saying, "Boys will be boys. I can live with that. But, having a trashy daughter is something I'll never get over."

The point of this list is not to rank or compare the issues. As I've mentioned before, I don't think that gets us anywhere. It's about understanding that we are all vulnerable to being judged and feeling shame about our experiences. And equally important, we are all vulnerable to judging and shaming others about their experiences.

I've interviewed recovering drug addicts who have high levels of resilience about the stigma attached to their addiction, and I've interviewed women who are envied by their friends, but can barely function under the shame of coming from "the wrong side of the tracks." Every single one of us is someone else's other.

Jennifer and Tiffany are the perfect examples. Jennifer's family history of addiction, Amber's marital history and the woman who passed out in the carpool line were all "others" for Tiffany. They were "those people." Remember how she told Jennifer, "Carly doesn't look like an alcoholic," and how she kept repeating how upset she was that the carpool incident happened in "our neighborhood" and at "our school"?

Tiffany couldn't accept "the other" in her friends, because she denied it so fiercely in her own life—with Andy's encouragement, she tried to pretend that her mother and the poverty she grew up in didn't exist. She had worked so hard to create a world where she could never be perceived as the other, that she couldn't accept otherness in Jennifer or Amber.

We use the concept of otherness to insulate ourselves and to disconnect. This is why it is such a serious barrier to reaching out as a method of shame resilience. Reaching out in either direction is tough—practicing courage is as difficult as practicing compassion. They both require us to lean into our discomfort. It was hard for Tiffany to tell Jennifer the truth about her life and it was also painful for Jennifer to listen. But she forced herself to do it because Tiffany and her relationship with Tiffany were important to her.

Sharing our shame with someone is painful, and just sitting with someone who is sharing his or her shame story with us can be equally painful. The natural tendency to avoid or reduce this pain is often why we start to judge and insulate ourselves using otherness. We basically blame them for their experience. We unconsciously divide people into two camps: worthy of our support and unworthy. When someone is feeling shame over one of these otherness issues, we don't feel that compelled to reach out. Likewise, when we are feeling shame because we are experiencing one of these stigmatized issues, it is difficult to reach out for support. It's easier to believe we deserve our shame.

The concept of labeling people worthy or unworthy is not new. If you look at the history of charity and philanthropy, going as far back as written history, those needing help have always been separated into the deserving poor or the undeserving poor. This thinking has become part of our culture. You can see it in our public policy, our neighborhoods and in our families. It plays out on an individual level exactly like it plays out at the community level.

Let's go back to the carpool story. Let's say the woman who was slumped over her steering wheel had suffered a major heart attack and was hospitalized. How many casseroles do you think her family would have received? While she recovered, how many neighborhood moms would have offered to drive her children to and from school? Given the reality that she was passed out drunk in her car in the carpool line, how many casseroles do you think her family received? If she was admitted into a rehabilitation facility, what's your guess on how many neighborhood moms offered to drive the kids or set up play dates while she was recovering? My guess is not many.

The story is very similar for Bette, a woman I interviewed a couple of years ago. Her teenage son committed suicide. Even though she had a large network of friends and colleagues, very few of them attended his funeral. She vacillated from tears to anger as she told me, "Just six months before my son died, my co-worker's daughter was killed in a car accident. She was the same age as my son. The funeral was standing room only. You couldn't move. Scott had as many friends as this young girl. He was on the yearbook staff and active in school. I'm as close to my co-workers as this girl's mother. But because Scott committed suicide, no one came."

Bette said, "I was so hurt and so furious that I finally asked one of the women at work why so few people came. Why only three co-workers sent cards. She told me they thought I needed my privacy. They didn't want to make it harder on me." Bette drew a deep breath and said, "Let me tell you what that means. A lot of them think it must somehow be my fault. They didn't know what to say. They didn't want to deal with it."

Just Too Scary

Fear is another reason we insulate. As my husband, Steve, read through this "other list," he shook his head and said, "Yep, these are the issues that we judge and blame people for." Then he thought for a minute, and asked, "What about those issues that we don't really blame people for, but scare us and send us running in the other direction?" I knew exactly what he meant.

Sometimes we don't turn away from people because their experiences are so stigmatized and socially unacceptable, but simply because they're too scary. My story about the NICU is a good example. I first became aware of my own fear-based insulating when my husband was in his residency. Steve was spending the month in the neonatal intensive care unit (NICU). On the nights he came home he would tell me stories from the NICU. I found the courage to listen only because I knew he needed a safe place to process his grief and celebrate his successes. After a couple of weeks of stories about dangerous deliveries, dying babies and grieving families, I became less empathic and more freaked out. It didn't help that I was six months pregnant with my first baby.

I started asking him questions about each family—mostly questions about their race, income and medical history. Fearing I would seem insensitive, I would disguise the questions as concern and interest. "I want to picture them. Do they look like anyone we know? Are they our age? It must be expensive—do they have insurance? Is there a medical reason this happened?" One day, sensing Steve's frustration with my litany of bullshit questions, I did away with the niceties and cut straight to demographics—What race? Poor? Drug users? Prenatal care? Genetic problems?

Steve looked at me and said, "No, Brené, they look just like us. This happens to all types of people, even people just like us."

I started crying. "No! It can't." I didn't want to believe it. I wanted to use every existing system of difference to separate me from "those people" and if, by some strange chance, they matched us on all the descriptors I would move to the next step—"Well, then, what did they do wrong?"

After Steve confronted me about my efforts to separate myself from "those people" in the NICU, I realized that I often rely on that technique when I watch the evening news. If I'm in the kitchen, cooking and listening to the news on the TV in the living room, and a horrible story about rape, murder or child abduction comes on, I often fly into the living room, whisk in hand, to see what the victim looks like and where it happened. The second I spot someone "different" from me or a neighborhood far from mine, I feel a little less fearful.

One day when I was discussing sexual assault with my students, we started talking about how often victims of sexual assault are re-victimized during court proceedings. I told the students, "The defense attorneys don't want the jurors to relate to the victim—what she looks like, her age, her race, where she was when the assault happened, et cetera. Fearing the jurors may relate to her, the defense attorneys attack her character so that no one would want to relate to her." I continued, "I'm sure that's easy to do—I wouldn't want to relate to her, because that would mean it could happen to me too."

As the discussion progressed, I shared how much I rely on this technique to protect myself. One by one, the students acknowledged doing the same thing—sharing their own stories of how and when they insulated themselves in the face of fear.

While sitting in a classroom, it is easy to be outraged about sexual assault survivors, even children, being blamed and ostracized when they are abused, yet the practice of separating ourselves from others is something most of us do on a daily basis. Unfortunately, as we recognized in finding ourselves on the otherness list, most of us will experience a loss or trauma that others will find difficult and scary.

If we've spent our lives continually insulating ourselves from the people who are suffering and surviving great losses, what happens when something happens to us? I think most of us turn on ourselves. What did I do to deserve this? Why me? This happened because I did something bad or wrong.

Once we've convinced ourselves that "things like this don't happen to people like me," then when it does happen it means we've done something terribly wrong. We've been kicked out of the group that kept us safe—that mythical group that always escapes tragedy. That's why people who survive cancer, women who survive sexual assault, adults who were once homeless, parents who have lost children and families who have been affected by acts of violence often tell me two things: "Before it happened I never believed it could happen to me—it only happened to other people," and "You never know—it can happen to anyone. I just want to be there for others who are going through the same thing."

It's hard. We don't want to connect with people who are in pain, especially if we believe they deserve their pain or if their pain is too scary for us. We don't want to reach out. It feels risky. Just by associating with them, we could either end up in the same "other" pile or be forced to acknowledge that bad things happen to people like us. I hear the same thing again and again from the women who are willing to connect: It's not easy. The women who take the casseroles when people are gossiping and judging or the women who walk through their own fear to comfort someone else aren't superheroes. They are ordinary women who sometimes have to force themselves to do it. It doesn't always come naturally, but they all say it gets easier with practice.

My mom is one of those women. I have very vivid memories

of my mom being the one sitting next to the neighbor who was in crisis. Not just the "acceptable crises" either. I grew up in the suburbs—trust me, there were some very traumatic events that didn't fit that cookie cutter life that we were all supposed to be living.

I even remember being embarrassed sometimes because my mother was the one taking the casserole to the person who everyone was talking about. Or she would invite the family who was swirling in horrible rumors to our house for dinner. I didn't understand it then, but now I get it.

My mom grew up with several boxes checked on the "other" list. As I noted earlier, my grandmother was an alcoholic. She was an incredibly generous and compassionate person who struggled for years with addiction. Back then, alcoholism was misunderstood and a source of even more shame than it is today—especially for women. On top of that, my grandparents divorced when my mom was in the third grade.

My mom has talked openly to us about the difficulty of reconciling her life with the social-community expectations that defined the 1950s. However, somewhere along the line, she found the courage to talk openly about her experiences. By doing this, she realized that she was not alone in this struggle and made the decision to get out from under the shame that was heaped on her by the *Ozzie and Harriet* culture and its followers. In doing so, she charted a new course for my siblings and me.

Even now, as I get older and the "hard things" seem to be happening to the people around me more often, I sometimes still struggle. And, predictably, I call my mom. She still tells my brother, my sisters and me the same thing every time, "You just go to the funeral. You just take the casserole when the neighbors are gossiping and peeking out of their blinds. Put yourself in a trance if you need to, but get in the car and drive over there. Write down exactly what you want to say, but pick up the phone and make the call."

I think the most important thing she has told me about reaching out to others in crisis is this: "You do it because that's the person you want to be. You do it because that could have been me and one day it could just as easily be you."

Your Connection Network

If we want to develop shame resilience, we must learn how to reach out. We must take what we know about courage, compassion and connection and put it into practice. It's not easy to ask someone to listen and it's not easy to be the one who listens. In the workshops, I have participants look at their shame triggers and try to identify the people with whom they can reach out. It's important to realize that, often, the person we can turn to regarding one issue is not the best person to talk to about other issues.

For example, Susan's sister (from the Introduction) made a shaming comment about Susan's putting her child in Mother's Day Out. Susan said, "When it comes to parenting, my mom and my sister are definitely in my shame web. But, when it comes to religion and faith, they are the strongest members of my connection network." This is why it is important to think about specific issues when we try to identify the people with whom we can reach out. Sometimes these "reaching out" questions help when you look at them by shame categories:

- Who are the individuals and groups who form your connection network?
- Who reaches out to you with empathy and support?
- Who are the individuals and groups who form the shame web around these issues?
- When you see people who are struggling with these issues, do you reach out with empathy or do you insulate yourself?

Here is how Susan, Kayla, Theresa and Sondra answered these questions.

Susan: When it comes to parenting and motherhood, my mom and sister are more a part of my shame web than my connection network. They're too close—they have too much riding on my decisions. My connection network includes my husband, my best friend and my moms' group from church.

Kayla: Well, naming the shame web for my professional life is easy. It's Nancy and the work environment. My connection network is probably my cousin and Cathryn, one of my friends. She used to work in this industry, but now she's home with kids. She understands. I'm afraid I'm a member of my own shame web around this issue too.

Theresa: I think my husband and my best friend are really the only people I can talk to about it, but they're both tired of hearing me complain. My husband is really fed up. I'm seeing a therapist and I think it helps. She's helping me make the connections between my expectations and my family growing up. It's painful, but worth it if I can get to a better place. My shame web is me, my mother and several of the women I hang around. They're what my therapist calls my constant critics. Even if they don't see what's going on in my house or with my kids, I always wonder what they would think.

Sondra: This is hard. My best connection is my husband. We can talk about anything except this issue. We really struggle about this. I think he's on my web and my connection network. I'm also on both. Sometimes I'm too hard on myself and sometimes I'm my best friend. I'd definitely put my in-laws, my teachers growing up, my pastor and other powerful people from my childhood on my web. My connectors are my students, my friends and, of course, my parents.

SIX

The Fourth Element: Speaking Shame

There is nothing more frustrating, and sometimes frightening, than feeling pain and not being able to describe or explain it to someone. It doesn't matter if it's physical pain or emotional pain. When we can't find the right words to explain our painful experiences to others, we often feel alone and scared. Some of us may even feel anger or rage and act out. Eventually, many of us shut down and either live silently with the pain or, in cases where we can't, accept someone else's definition of what we are feeling simply out of the desperate need to find some remedy.

Shame is a type of pain that often defies definition. As discussed throughout this book, shame unconsciously drives thoughts, feelings and behaviors. Its survival depends on remaining undetected; therefore, it seeks silence and secrecy. If we recognize and understand our triggers, practice critical awareness and reach out to others, we can increase our resilience by building connection networks. These networks are sources for the empathy, connection and power we need to free ourselves from the shame web. But to tap into these sources, we need communication skills.

We need to be able to identify and communicate what we are feeling and why we are feeling it.

Most of us don't naturally acquire the vocabulary we need to identify, describe and discuss the actual process of experiencing shame or increasing shame resilience. Shame is a complex language—learning it requires practice and skill. Speaking shame requires us to develop names and terms to describe some of the most painful and abstract concepts that we, as humans, have to confront.

For example, how do we describe the overwhelming physical and emotional responses that most of us experience when we are in shame? Barbara, whose letter you read in the last chapter, does it beautifully. She speaks shame. She said she knows that when she's in shame, her face flushes, her stomach tightens and she replays the incident over and over in her head. This is very different from many of the participants who described their responses to shame as "freaking out, losing it or dying inside." When people gave me these loose descriptions, I would sometimes ask them if they could give me any specifics. Often, they would just get increasingly frustrated as they tried to tie words to their experiences.

When we speak shame, we learn to speak our pain. As I wrote earlier, we are wired for connection, and this makes us wired for story. More than any other method, storytelling is how we communicate who we are, how we feel, what's important to us and what we need from others. Without language, we cannot speak our stories. Narrative therapists Jill Friedman and Gene Combs write, "Speaking isn't neutral or passive. Every time we speak, we bring forth a reality. . . . If the realities we inhabit are brought forth in the language we use, they are then kept alive and passed along in the stories that we live and tell."

Throughout the interviews, women identified "not having a way to explain shame" and "not knowing how to talk about shaming experiences" as major factors contributing to feelings of fear, blame and disconnection. The women who demonstrated high levels of shame resilience were able to express how they felt when they experienced shame *and* they could ask for the support they needed from

others. In the following sections, we'll look at the specific tools related to speaking shame.

Translating Shame

We've all been shamed by someone. As I wrote in the Introduction, every one of us has been wounded by subtle, and sometimes downright mean, comments about the way we look, our work, our parenting, how we spend our money, our families or even the life experiences over which we had no control. Shaming comments can be direct, indirect, manipulative, intentional and even, I believe, unintentional. What they all share in common is how much they hurt and how they send us reeling and desperately searching for protection.

Of course, when we're reeling and desperate, we rarely find effective methods for protecting ourselves. In fact, many of the coping skills we use to deal with shame only magnify our feelings of powerlessness and cause us to sink even deeper in shame (like shame screens). In this chapter, I'll discuss how speaking shame allows us to express how we feel and ask for what we need so we can more effectively build shame resilience. Let's start by examining the shame trap.

The Shame Trap

The shame trap is one of the most difficult forms of shame to recognize, process and speak. The shame trap is often so hidden or camouflaged that we unknowingly walk right into it—often over and over and over. When we get caught, we come up shaken and asking, "What just happened? Why am I bleeding?" The shame trapper often replies, "What do you mean? I didn't see anything. Maybe you're seeing things? Are you OK?" We are often so taken by surprise that we repeat the experience to make sure it didn't just happen in our imagination.

I've had experiences in the past, one in the recent past, where I had to get snared several times before I understood what was happening. Here's my shame trap story.

Right after I had Ellen, I was very excited to meet other mothers with newborns. One night, at a work function, I was introduced to Phyllis, another new mother. She was also taking time off from work and I insisted that we go to lunch and maybe even plan a couple of play dates.

I was so excited to have someone to talk to about my new motherhood journey, that the very first time we went to lunch I did the "too much connection too soon" thing. Anxious to share my new experiences, I said, "I wasn't prepared to be this tired. Sometimes I just crave a short break from being a mom so I can get some sleep or take a long shower." She replied, "Really, I've never regretted having my baby."

Of course, I was shocked. I quickly responded, "My God, I don't regret having Ellen, I didn't mean that. I'm just tired."

Without missing a beat, she said, "It's OK, some new mothers have a very difficult time with motherhood—it's not for everyone."

At this point, I started getting increasingly upset. "Listen, Phyllis, I love being a mother and I love Ellen. I don't have any regrets. It's great."

She looked at me like I was pathetic and said, "It's OK, don't get hysterical. Maybe it will get better when she gets older."

OK—at this point in the conversation I was looking for Allen Funt and the *Candid Camera* crew. I was literally looking around the restaurant hoping that someone had overheard this insane conversation and could bear witness to both my sanity and my love of motherhood. I started crying.

Phyllis said, "Look, I didn't know this was such a sensitive issue for you. Let's talk about something else." I went home dazed and confused.

When I told my friend Dawn about this story, she was shocked. She wasn't shocked about the "shame trap." She was shocked to learn that I had already made plans to have lunch with Phyllis again.

Dawn kept saying, "That is crazy-making stuff—why are you subjecting yourself to that?" I couldn't answer her then, but in hindsight, I think I needed another shot at proving that I was a normal and worthy friend and mother. I also think that it was just so bizarre, I couldn't help but believe that maybe I had imagined the whole thing.

For about two months, every time I was around Phyllis I came home feeling angry, depressed and weirdly competitive. It got to the point that I would spend a tremendous amount of time and energy trying to anticipate what she might say the next time we were together so I could craft ruthless responses and comebacks to put her in her place.

I specifically remember one morning when I was getting ready to meet her for lunch; I opened a new bottle of lotion that someone had given to me as a shower gift. It was green tea, basil and patchouli "organic" cream. As I started putting it on I realized it was a little too "earthy" for me. It smelled like mulch.

As I was rubbing it off with a damp washcloth, I started thinking, "Boy, I bet Phyllis would say something rude about this. She always smells like the Estée Lauder counter." So, instead of continuing to take it off, I put more on and got dressed.

On the way to lunch I started planning my comebacks. I think the best one was "Oh, you don't like it? It's organic. I try to keep the baby away from strong, chemical perfumes. What about you?"

Of course, she never said a word about my mulch lotion. She found other targets. I sat at the table nauseated, disappointed and wondering how I could get my forearm under her nose without making it look obvious. It would be too sad to say, "Hey, smell my arm. You hate it, don't you?"

This was the last story Dawn volunteered to listen to. She said, "You need to figure out what's going on. This is getting ridiculous." I remember replying, "I know. I'm trying to figure her out." Dawn sighed. "Figure her out? I don't care what's going on with her. What in the hell is going on with you?"

About one month later, I unexpectedly ran into Phyllis at the drugstore and she said, "Wow, you look really bad. Have you put on some weight?" Luckily, I had the flu. I felt so bad and so exhausted that I couldn't even muster up the energy to "engage." I just looked at her, shrugged and kept looking for my medicine. When she walked away I thought, "Wow, that was mean and it really hurt my feelings."

When I stopped trying to beat her at her own game and instead focused on how I felt, I recognized my vulnerability with her. Rather than staying in combat mode, I recognized how badly she hurt my feelings, how frequently she said mean and shaming things and, most importantly, that I needed to alter my relationship with her.

I had always felt bad about myself after our lunches, but it wasn't until I actually spoke the words, "That hurt my feelings. That was really mean," that I decided to end that relationship and spend some time examining my own role in the whole destructive mess.

Speaking shame allows us to translate our experiences so we can learn from them—which are the goals of shame resilience. We can't stop shame from happening, but we can learn to recognize it early enough to move through it constructively, rather than destructively.

When I apply the four elements of shame resilience, here's what I learned from this experience:

First, I was feeling very alone and desperate for connection around my new role as a mother. I was very vulnerable, and I would soon learn what a major trigger motherhood could be for me. While I was aware that our relationship had become less about meeting for lunch and more about preparing for battle, I did not recognize the warning signs that I now associate with "crafting ruthless responses and comebacks."

I've come to realize that planning ways to get back at people usually means I've missed a shame trigger. When I'm preparing shaming comebacks and gearing up to be hurtful, I'm often knee-deep in an area of serious vulnerability. I also now know that when I use shame to "fight back" it compounds my shame rather than alleviating it. That's not who I want to be.

Second, because I was a new mother, I had not developed the critical awareness skills I needed to know what a powerful shame trigger motherhood is for most mothers. I definitely individualized *(This is about me)* and pathologized *(I'm crazy)* this experience. Critical awareness about motherhood took time to learn and put into practice.

Third, when I reached out to Dawn to tell her about the lunch conversation and she tried to support me, I should have listened. I hadn't fully processed the fact that Dawn is big in my connection network around motherhood. I wish could have heard what she was saying, rather than shrugging off her concerns.

Fourth, during our lunch, when I said that motherhood was sometimes tiring and Phyllis responded by saying, "Really, I've never regretted having my baby," I might have used my speaking shame skills to say something like "Wow. How did you get from me being tired to regretting having children?" If the conversation continued to nosedive, I might have just said something like "We don't seem to be able to understand each other, let's change the subject." And, of course, not pursued that friendship.

Lastly, I learned how to translate my experience in a way that allows me to recognize the ineffective patterns that keep me in shame—my shame screens. This story is a great example of how the four elements of shame resilience work together (and not always in a linear fashion). When I really started thinking about my behavior with Phyllis, I came to realize that I had been using (and can sometimes still use) an interesting combination of disconnection strategies, especially around the issue of motherhood.

I have a tendency to use the *moving toward* and *moving against* combo. I either shut down or try to people-please when I'm actually with that person, then I turn into the angry, plotting shamer when I get home. In this case, I kept trying to convince her that we were the same and that I was a good mother, until I got home. Then I would act out my anger as I tried to figure out how to verbally skewer her.

I think I also displaced some of feelings of anger toward Dawn by thinking, "She just doesn't want me to have a new friend." Protecting ourselves by redirecting our feelings at another human target (displacing) is a common defense strategy when we feel shame. Many of the participants spoke about getting angry or raging at their kids, partners and friends rather than dealing with the person or issue triggering the shame.

My daughter is seven years old, so this story happened about that many years ago. I've told this story many times and thought about it even more. It's taken me a long time to get clear about what happened and why it happened. This is not an instant process. It develops slowly.

In the following section, we'll talk about shame as intentional or unintentional. As I discuss it, I think it's important to point out that the motivations behind shame don't buffer us from the pain. Unintentional shame is still painful.

What Are Your Intentions?

Identifying shame as intentional or unintentional is very difficult. It assumes we know the motivation of the person who has made the comment or triggered the shame. Sometimes the motivation is clear and sometimes it isn't. In the examples below, the research participants believed the remarks were meant to hurt and be shaming, but each gave a different reason for the motivation behind the shame. (I've labeled each quote with the motivation identified by the research participant.) Under the quote is an example of how we might address the motivation while expressing how hurt we feel by the shaming remark.

- Every time I go home to visit my mom, the first thing she says is "My God, you're still fat!" and the last thing she says when I walk out the door is "Hopefully you can lose some weight." (Shame as motivation)
  - I feel so ashamed when you say hurtful things about my weight. It's so painful for me. It's like all you care about is how I look. If you're trying to make me feel bad so I'll change, that doesn't work. It makes me feel worse about myself and our relationship. You really hurt me when you do that.
- Shame is when my husband left me for another woman and my son told me it was because I was a "fat-ass." (Shame as anger)
  - When you call me names, especially hurtful names like "fat-ass," it is really devastating to me. If you're angry with me or your father, we can talk about it. But we can't talk to each other if we are attacking each other.
- The very first time my son got an ear infection, my pediatrician said, "Well, what's it going to be? Your career or your son's hearing?" (Shame as judgment)
  - When you say, "What's it going to be? Your career or your son's hearing?" I don't know how to respond. I want your medical advice, but when you shame me like that, it's hard for me to hear what you're saying.

In the following examples of unintended shame, the participants made comments like "I really don't think s/he meant to shame me" or "I honestly don't think they know better." But again, it's important to note that the participants also pointed out that, regardless of the "intention," the experiences were still shaming and very painful, and their relationships with the "shamers" were threatened by these experiences. Again, I've labeled each quote with the motivation identified by the participant.

- Shame is becoming the cancer survivor. Everyone at work thought, "She can't do this anymore." Everyone at home thought, "She can't do this anymore." Everyone treated me like I was completely incapable of anything. (Uncomfortable, sympathy)
  - Since I've returned to work, I feel that you're treating me differently because of my cancer. Even if you are trying to help me or support me, treating me differently makes me feel alone and like an outsider. I want and need to know that I am the same person and that people will treat me that way.
- When I told my friends about my miscarriage, they completely invalidated my feelings. They said things like "At least you know you can get pregnant" or "At least you weren't too far along." (Uncomfortable, sympathy—trying to make it better)
  - I feel really sad and lonely about my miscarriage. I know women experience that in different ways, but for me it is a big deal. I need you to listen to how I'm feeling. It's not helpful when you try to make it better. I just need to talk about it with people who care about me.

Working our way out of the shame web can be very difficult because, like most traps, it entangles you the more you struggle and fight. To free ourselves, we need to move slowly, deliberately and with a tremendous amount of awareness about what we are doing and why.

In that first example, many of us might have reacted by saying,

"Get off my back. I'm sick of you saying shit about my weight. I'm sick of it." That just doesn't get us anywhere. In many ways, it is actually a way of protecting the person who is shaming us from hearing "You are hurting me," and protecting ourselves from having to say "I'm hurt." It seems counterintuitive, but telling someone how we feel takes more courage and is often more powerful than verbally attacking them.

The same type of honest focus on feelings also works when it comes to addressing unintentional shame. Unintentional shame often happens when people are trying to be helpful but end up either giving unsolicited advice, judging or shutting down the conversation out of their own discomfort. One topic that seems to elicit unintentional shame is infertility. Because it's a topic that touches many of our lives, I'm going to use it as the example in this section on unintentional shame. For those of you who have struggled with getting pregnant, you have a better understanding of how this works than most of us will ever have.

Most of us who have not struggled with infertility have had a friend or family member who has. And most of us have had the experience of having someone tell us, "We're trying to get pregnant; I'm having fertility issues." And then what? This is when it happens. We get nervous and uncomfortable and say things like "It will happen, you'll see," or "Have you thought about adopting?"

When we talk about infertility in workshops, it's always very emotional. I've been so moved by the depth of this struggle and my personal feelings of inadequacy about addressing it that I started looking for resources. I came across the following guide and found it to be very powerful. I asked a close friend who has struggled with infertility and is also a social worker to review it personally and professionally. She thought it could be an incredibly powerful example of how to express your feelings and ask for what you need.

Speaking shame allows us to tell others how we feel and to ask for what we need. These are the basic requirements of resilience and connection. I encourage you to use this guide as a model (the abridged version appears below—the full version is available online at www.infertilityeducation.org.) Maybe your issue is unemployment or obesity or recovery from addiction. We can all learn something from this guide and use it to think about how we might give voice to our feelings and needs. As you read each of the sections, think about your own issues and how this might serve as a helpful resource. Speaking shame is a very personal and individual experience. It doesn't work to use someone else's words; however, I find it helpful to learn by example.

The author, Jody Earle, frequently felt the need for a brochure like this one during her own eleven-year infertility struggle. She experienced three pregnancy losses, one in each trimester, and eventually, the premature births of her two sons. She continues to be a peer counselor for those working through infertility. The guide was prepared by Ms. Earle and the Educational Materials Advisory Committee of the Ferre Institute.

Infertility: A Guide for Family and Friends

I want to share my feelings about infertility with you, because I want you to understand my struggle. I know that understanding infertility is difficult; there are times when it seems even I don't understand. This struggle has provoked intense and unfamiliar feelings in me and I fear that my reactions to these feelings might be misunderstood. I hope my ability to cope and your ability to understand will improve as I share my feelings with you. I want you to understand.

You may describe me this way: obsessed, moody, helpless, depressed, envious, too serious, obnoxious, aggressive, antagonistic, and cynical. These aren't very admirable traits; no wonder your understanding of my infertility is difficult. I prefer to describe myself this way: confused, rushed and impatient, afraid, isolated and alone, guilty and ashamed, angry, sad and hopeless, and unsettled.

My infertility makes me feel **confused**. I always assumed I was fertile. I've spent years avoiding pregnancy and now it seems ironic that I can't conceive.

My infertility makes me feel **rushed and impatient**. I learned of my infertility only after I'd been trying to become pregnant for some time. My life plan suddenly is behind schedule. I waited to become a parent and now I must wait again.

My infertility makes me feel **afraid**. Infertility is full of unknowns, and I'm frightened because I need some definite answers. How long will this last?

My infertility makes me feel **isolated and alone**. Reminders of babies are everywhere. I must be the only one enduring this invisible curse. I stay away from others, because everything makes me hurt.

My infertility makes me feel **guilty and ashamed**. Frequently I forget that infertility is a medical problem and should be treated as one. Infertility destroys my self-esteem and I feel like a failure. Why am I being punished? What did I do to deserve this? Am I not worthy of a baby?

My infertility makes me feel **angry**. Everything makes me angry, and I know much of my anger is misdirected. I'm angry at my body because it has betrayed me even though I've always taken care of it. I'm angry at my partner because we can't seem to feel the same about infertility at the same time.

My financial resources may determine my family size. My insurance company isn't cooperative, and I must make so many sacrifices to pay the medical bills. I can't miss any more work, or I'll lose my job. I can't go to a specialist, because it means more travel time, more missed work, and greater expenses. Finally, I'm angry at everyone else. Everyone has opinions about my inability to become a parent. Everyone has easy solutions. Everyone seems to know too little and say too much.

My infertility makes me feel **sad and hopeless**. Infertility feels like I've lost my future, and no one knows of my sadness. I feel hopeless; infertility robs me of my energy. I've never cried so much nor so easily. I'm sad that my infertility places my marriage under so much strain.

My infertility makes me feel **unsettled**. My life is on hold. Making decisions about my immediate and my long-term future seems impossible. I can't decide about education, career, purchasing a home, pursuing a hobby, getting a pet, vacations, business trips and houseguests. The more I struggle with my infertility, the less control I have.

Occasionally I feel my panic subside. I'm learning some helpful ways to cope; I'm now convinced I'm not crazy, and I believe I'll survive. I'm learning to listen to my body and to be assertive, not aggressive, about my needs. I'm realizing that good medical care and good emotional care are not necessarily found in the same place. I'm trying to be more than an infertile person gaining enthusiasm, joyfulness, and zest for life.

You can help me. I know you care about me and I know my infertility affects our relationship. My sadness causes you sadness; what hurts me, hurts you, too. I believe we can help each other through this sadness. Individually we both seem quite powerless, but together we can be stronger. Maybe some of these hints will help us to better understand infertility.

I need you to **be a listener**. Talking about my struggle helps me to make decisions. Let me know you are available for me. It's difficult for me to expose my private thoughts if you are rushed or have a deadline for the end of our conversation. Please don't tell me of all the worse things that have happened to others or how easily someone else's infertility was solved.

I need you to **be supportive**. Understand that my decisions aren't made casually, I've agonized over them. Remind me that you respect these decisions even if you disagree with them, because you know they are made carefully.

I need you to **be comfortable** with me, and then I also will feel more comfortable. Talking about infertility sometimes feels awkward. Are you worried you might say the wrong thing? Share those feelings with me. Ask me if I want to talk. Sometimes I will want to, and sometimes I won't, but it will remind me that you care.

I need you to **be sensitive**. Although I may joke about infertility to help myself cope, it doesn't seem as funny when others joke about it. Please don't tease me with remarks like "You don't seem to know how to do it." Don't trivialize my struggle by saying, "I'd be glad to give you one of my kids." It's no comfort to hear empty reassurances like "You'll be a parent by this time next year."

I need you to **be honest** with me. Let me know that you may need time to adjust to some of my decisions. I also needed adjustment time. If there are things you don't understand, say so.

I need you to **be informed**. Your advice and suggestions are only frustrating to me if they aren't based on fact. Be well informed so you can educate others when they make remarks based on myths. Don't let anyone tell you that my infertility will be cured if I relax and adopt. Don't tell me this is God's will. Don't ask me to justify my need to parent.

I need you to **be patient**. Remember that working through infertility is a process. It takes time. There are no guarantees, no package deals, no complete kits, no one right answer, and no "quickie" choices.

I need you to **be strengthening** by boosting my self-esteem. My sense of worthlessness hampers my ability to take charge.

Encourage me to maintain my sense of humor; guide me to find joys. Celebrate with me my successes, even ones as small as making it through a medical appointment without crying. Remind me that I am more than an infertile person. Help me by sharing your strength.

Eventually I will be beyond the struggle of infertility. I know my infertility will never completely go away because it will change my life. I won't be able to return to the person I was before infertility, but I also will no longer be controlled by this struggle. I will leave the struggle behind me, and from that I will have improved my skills for empathy, patience, resilience, forgiveness, decision making and self-assessment. I feel grateful that you are trying to ease my journey through this infertility struggle by giving me your understanding.

———

I know this feels risky. I'm a social worker and a shame researcher and putting my emotional needs on the table still feels scary to me. We feel vulnerable and exposed. And, sometimes, sharing doesn't work. It can overwhelm people and they can throw up their own shame screens and that will be painful.

When you learn to speak shame, it allows you to pick up on some of the subtle language of the shame web. This is language that is used to shame and language that is used to defend shaming when we're trying to explain how we feel and what we need. I'm now very cautious when I hear things like:

- You're so sensitive.
- I didn't realize you were so fragile.
- I didn't realize that was such an issue for you.
- You're so defensive.
- I guess I'll have to watch what I say around you.
- It's all in your head.

And last, but certainly not least, I don't like anything that's brutal, including honesty. Honesty is the best policy, but honesty that's motivated by shame, anger, fear or hurt is not "honesty." It's shame, anger, fear or hurt disguised as honesty.

Just because something is accurate or factual doesn't mean it can't be used in a destructive manner. The shame web is often baited with honesty. It gives the shamer an easy comeback—"Well, I'm just telling you the truth. These are just the facts."

When we talk about the crazy-making aspects of shame, including shame disguised as honesty, it's important to understand that "crazy-making" runs the continuum from what I experienced with Phyllis to very serious forms of emotional abuse.

In the domestic violence arena, we sometimes use the term *gaslighted*. This is a reference to the classic Ingrid Bergman film *Gaslight*. In the film Bergman's character is slowly driven crazy by some of the "shame trap" techniques discussed in this chapter. I make this point because it is critical that our fluency in shame includes the understanding that shame can be a real and dangerous form of abuse.

Again, the interview participants who demonstrated high levels of shame resilience depended heavily on the members of their connection network to practice courage and compassion. Their ability to articulate their feelings and needs made that possible.

As you've read through each of these chapters, you've started building an understanding of shame and shame resilience. Some of you are following along, doing the exercises with your own issues, and others are reading and soaking it all in. Either way, you are learning to speak shame by simply reading and thinking.

Exploring the Issues

As the previous chapters have demonstrated, shame is a highly individualized experience. Each of us must examine our own triggers and the messages behind them and develop our own paths to resilience. But as we've seen throughout the book, there are also some universal patterns that run through our experiences. For example, women's shame experiences fall broadly into the twelve shame categories—appearance and body image, motherhood, family, parenting, money and work, mental and physical health, sex, aging, religion, being stereotyped and labeled, speaking out and surviving trauma. In addition to the shame categories, we also share culture. In our culture today, the fear of disconnection feels very real. Most of us have to constantly work to feel grounded and stay connected. As we start to develop shame resilience, we will find that many of the expectations and messages producing shame are driven by fear, blame and disconnection—the culture of shame.

In these next three chapters we'll explore how the culture of shame influences our lives, especially around the issues of perfectionism, stereotyping, invisibility and addiction. We'll also look at how, despite our culture's emphasis on being perfect and being liked, we can develop and maintain the authenticity and strength we need to practice courage, compassion and connection.

SEVEN

*Practicing Courage in
a Culture of Fear*

There may be no more powerful relationship than the one that exists between fear and shame. These two emotions often work together to create the perfect emotional storm—shame leads to fear and fear leads to shame. They work together so furiously that it's often hard to tell where one stops and the other begins.

Shame, or our fear of disconnection, causes us to be afraid of many things. The issues that I see affecting women the most are our fears of being imperfect, ordinary and uncool and vulnerable. In the following sections we'll explore these struggles and how the elements of shame resilience can help us practice courage and compassion in the face of fear.

PERFECTIONISM IS THE VOICE OF THE OPPRESSOR.

Anne Lamott, *Bird by Bird* (1994)

Shame and Perfectionism

I think I've seen the movie *Flashdance* at least twenty times. In the 1980s, I wanted to be just like Jennifer Beals's character, Alex. She was the tough construction worker by day and talented, ambitious dancer by night. Of course, my favorite part of the movie is the dance scene in which Alex auditions for the hoity-toity ballet school.

I'm too embarrassed to tell you how many sweatshirts I ruined and how many leg warmers I bought. Of course, I wasn't alone. Nothing took the mystique out of my secret *Flashdance* fantasy like showing up to meet friends for dinner and realizing that all six of us had permed hair, headbands and ripped sweatshirts.

We all wanted to be Alex in *Flashdance*. She was perfect—ripped clothing looked sexy; welding looked exciting; ballet looked cool and break dancing looked easy. But alas, the perfection was only an illusion. I was disappointed to learn that the film director used four different people to create that audition sequence: Jennifer Beals's beautiful face, a professional dancer for the ballet scenes, a champion gymnast for the leaping and jumping and a male street performer for the break dancing. All those bad perms and all that money for leg warmers . . . for what? To try and achieve some level of perfection that doesn't exist.

If most of us stopped to examine the expectations we set for ourselves, we would discover that, like the scene in *Flashdance*, our concept of perfection is so unrealistic that it can't exist in one person. Instead, it's a combination of pieces or snippets of what's perceived as perfect. We don't just want to be good at what we do, we want to be perfect—we want to edit together all the best clips of what we see to form our lives.

So, where does this idea of "editing for perfection" come from? The answer is right in front of us—it's the shame web. If we look at all of the people in the shame web—family, partners, friends, self, colleagues, group members, etc.—most of us can identify the expectations these people have of us. This is especially true around some of the shame categories like appearance, motherhood, parenting, work and family.

The primary reason the expectations around these issues are so influential is related to how quickly they are imposed on our lives. On the day that we are born, there are immediate expectations that we will be cute and attractive, we will grow up, get married, be successful, become mothers, have natural parenting skills and be loving members of sane and well-balanced families. Complicating matters, we have the media, which makes perfection appear attainable by inundating us with images that are, quite literally, edited for perfection. We stare down at our newborns and fast forward through their lives, thinking and dreaming about their potential. As parents, we even think, "I haven't screwed anything up yet—they could have it all."

In some families, these expectations are spoken loud and clear. In other families, they are more latent. But regardless of how they are articulated at home, girls and women have these messages reinforced on a daily basis by what we see on television, the books we read, the toys we are given to play with, the conversations we overhear and what we are taught by educators and peer groups. The powerful effect of these expectations can easily be seen around the issues of body image, caregiving and motherhood—three of the biggest "perfectionism" struggles that emerged from the research. Let's look at these issues, starting with body image.

Body Image
When I first identified the shame categories, appearance stood alone and was meant to capture all parts of how we look—including body image. But as I continued to collect data, I realized that the specific topic of body image has more than earned its place on the list of shame categories.

While appearance is a broad category that covers everything from body image to clothing, fitness and style, body image is the driving force behind appearance shame. In fact, body image is the one issue that comes closest to being a "universal trigger," with more than ninety percent of the participants experiencing shame about their bodies. Body shame is so powerful and often so deeply rooted in our psyches that it actually affects why and how we feel shame in many of the other categories, including sexuality, motherhood, parenting, health, aging and a woman's ability to speak out with confidence.

Our body image is how we think and feel about our bodies. It is the mental picture we have of our physical bodies. Unfortunately, our pictures, thoughts and feelings may have little to do with our actual appearance. It is our image of what our bodies are, often held up to our image of what they should be.

While we normally talk about body image as a general reflection of what we look like, we can't ignore the specifics—the body parts that come together to create this image. If we work from the understanding that women most often experience shame when we become trapped in a web of layered, conflicting and competing expectations of who, what and how we should be, we can't ignore that there are social-community expectations for every single, tiny part of us—literally from our heads to our toes.

I'm going to list our body parts because I think they are important: head, hair, neck, face, ears, skin, nose, eyes, lips, chin, teeth, shoulders, back, breasts, waist, hips, stomach, abdomen, buttocks, vulva, anus, arms, wrists, hands, fingers, fingernails, thighs, knees, calves, ankles, feet, toes, body hair, body fluids, pimples, scars, freckles, stretch marks and moles.

Again, I bet if you look at each of these areas, you have specific body part images for each one—not to mention a mental list of what you'd like it to look like and the unwanted identities that you want to avoid.

When our very own bodies fill us with disgust and feelings of worthlessness, shame can fundamentally change who we are and how we approach the world. Consider the woman who stays quiet in public out of the fear that her stained and crooked teeth will make people question the value of her contributions. Or the women who told me that "the one thing she hates about being fat" is the constant pressure to be nice to people. She explained, "If you're bitchy, they might make a cruel remark about your weight."

The research participants also spoke often about how body shame either kept them from enjoying sex or pushed them into having it when they didn't really want to but were desperate for some type of physical validation of worthiness.

There were also many women who talked about the shame of having their bodies betray them. These were women who spoke about physical illness, mental illness and infertility. We often conceptualize "body image" too narrowly—it's about more than wanting to be thin and attractive. When we begin to blame and hate our bodies for failing to live up to our expectations, we start splitting ourselves in parts and move away from our wholeness—our authentic selves.

We can't talk about shame and body image without talking about the pregnant body. I think there are stages to the pregnant body—each susceptible to shame in its own way. First there is the woman who wants to become pregnant. I heard story after story about the pressure to be thin and in top shape before becoming pregnant. As we saw from the quote earlier in the book, one woman took her own health and her prenatal care into her hands to avoid being shamed by the doctor because she feared she was "too fat" to be pregnant.

Next there is the pregnant body. Has any body image been more exploited in the past few years? Don't get me wrong. I'm all for exploring the wonders of the pregnant body and removing the stigma and shame of the pregnant belly. But let's not replace that with one more airbrushed, computer-generated, shame-inducing image for women to not be able to live up to. Movie stars who gain fifteen pounds and have their stretch marks airbrushed for their "Look! I'm human too!" portraits do not represent the realities that most of us face while pregnant.

Last there is the postpregnant-mother body. When women spoke to me about their postbaby body-image struggles, I heard more than experiences of shame. I heard grief, loss, anger and fear. In addition to the weight gain, hemorrhoids and stretch marks, women struggle with the very real and permanent changes that we often experience after pregnancy and delivery. Again, the media is a very strong force in the expectation-setting done around postpregnancy body images. Within a week we're expected to be back in our low-rise jeans, midriff-baring T-shirts, sporting a five-hundred-dollar diaper bag and carrying our children around like the year's hottest accessory.

Parenting is also a shame category affected by body image. As an admittedly vulnerable, imperfect parent, I'm not one to jump on the "blame parents for everything—especially the mothers" bandwagon. Having said that, I will tell you what I found in my research. Shame creates shame. Parents have a tremendous amount of influence on their children's body image development, and girls are still being shamed by their parents—primarily their mothers—about their weight.

When it comes to parenting and body image, I find that parents fall along a continuum. On one side of the continuum, there are parents who are keenly aware that they are the most influential role models in their children's lives. They work diligently to model positive body image behaviors (self-acceptance, acceptance of others, no emphasis placed on the unattainable or ideal, focusing on health rather than weight, deconstructing media messages, etc.).

On the other side of the continuum are parents who love their children just as much as their counterparts, but are so determined to spare their daughters the pain of being overweight or unattractive (and their sons the pain of being weak) that they will do anything to steer their children toward achievement of the ideal—including belittling and shaming them. Many of these parents struggle with their own body images and process their shame by shaming.

Last, there are the folks in the middle, who really do nothing to counter the negative body-image issues but also don't shame their children. Unfortunately, due to societal pressures and the media, most of these kids do not appear to develop strong shame resilience skills around body image. There just doesn't appear to be any room for neutrality on this issue—you are either actively working to help your children develop a positive self-concept or, by default, you are sacrificing them to the media- and society-driven expectations.

As you can see, what we think, hate, loathe and question about our bodies reaches much further and affects far more than our appearance alone. The long reach of body shame can impact how we live and love. The same can be said for caregiving and motherhood.

Caregiving

I was not surprised to hear painful story after painful story about caregiving—especially stories about the struggle to take care of a sick partner or an aging family member. The most difficult experiences centered on taking care of sick or aging parents.

In the mental health field, we recognize caregiving as one of the most stressful life events people face. When women talked about the anxiety, fear, stress and shame of being a caregiver, I could hear the demons of perfectionism in their stories. Regardless of the words spoken, I could hear them comparing the hard realities of their day-to-day responsibilities to their idealized images of stress-free, dutiful and rewarding caregiving.

I'm afraid any image of stress-free, dutiful and rewarding caregiving is a luxury available only to those who have yet to fully engage in this process. When most of us think about the eventuality of taking care of an elderly parent or partner, we get anxious, sad and fearful. In order to quash those uncomfortable emotions we sometimes convince ourselves that it will be different for us— it won't be as horrible as it is for the woman who sits next to us at work or our good friend whose mother is "a tough case." We try to escape reality by dwelling in the possibilities of perfection: It will work out just fine. It will be a great chance for us to spend some more time together.

So when we find ourselves actually caregiving, we are not at all prepared for the first time our feelings of "I love you and it's a privilege to take care of you" turn into "I hate you and I'm ready for you to die because I need my life back." The stress, anxiety, fear and grief are magnified as shame and self-loathing set in. Are we monsters? How can we feel like this?

We're not monsters and we feel like this because we are human beings trying to manage a major life event with very little of the support and resources typically offered to people in crisis.

During the interviews, women in caregiving roles were incredibly hard on themselves. They often sounded disappointed, and sometimes even disgusted, by their lack of natural caregiving skills. As I probed deeper about this disappointment, many of them compared their caregiving experiences to parenting. They saw themselves as good, kind people whose nurturing skills had somehow failed them.

People often make the mistake of comparing caregiving with parenting. On the face of it, this might make sense. But if we really examine the differences, we can see how absolutely different they are and how believing they are the same sets us up for shame.

First, and most importantly, we don't have the same relationship with our parents or partner as we do with our children. We don't have to bite through our lips not to cry when we are bathing our children. But that's exactly what I did the first time I bathed my grandmother. And I wasn't even her primary caregiver. My mom was shouldering the burden of taking care of her and her sister at the same time.

The energy we need to take care of children is fueled by promise. Taking care of another adult is often steeped in fear and grief—especially if this person is at the end of his life or facing an unknown future. Fear and grief don't fuel us—they usually drain us.

Second, we live in a society that has put systems in place specifically to support parents and children. Schools and child-care facilities are the easy ones. But it's more than that. Tables, houses, cars, restaurants—they're all built for families that are defined as parents and children. There are thousands of parenting books and magazines. There are play groups and organized activities. As parents, we are given lots of opportunities to fit in and build connection.

When we are caregiving for another adult—parent or otherwise—nothing fits. Our jobs are on the line because we constantly need to leave work for appointments and medical emergencies. Our partners can no longer make it down the stairs in our house, or our parent absolutely refuses to move in with us (if that's even a possibility). And worst of all, we feel absolutely disconnected. In order to maintain the energy we need to caregive, we unhook ourselves from our lives and plug into the person who needs our time and attention.

There is one thing that parenting and caregiving have in common, and it's not a positive thing: When it comes to these two issues, everyone is a critic. Chelsea, a woman in her late fifties, spoke powerfully about the scrutiny of caregiving:

• My dad died two years ago. It was sudden and unexpected. My family was heartbroken, especially my mom. She has been sick for what feels like forever and he was the one who took care of her. Now we take care of my mom. Or, I should say, I take care of my mom. My older brother is far too busy with his important life. My older sister's role is to observe and critique my every move. About six months ago, my husband and I realized we could no longer do it—neither physically nor emotionally. We decided to put Mom in an assisted-living facility close to our house. Well, my brother and sister were appalled. My sister actually said, "I can't believe you're going to put her in a prison like a criminal." My brother just said, "Absolutely not," in this very matter-of-fact tone. Of course, both of them said, due to their hectic lives, they couldn't do any more than what they were doing. When I told them we had no choice, they said it was cruel and they wouldn't help pay for it. She's still living in her house. I still go over there every day on my lunch break or after work. My brother and sister choose to think everything is just perfect, even though my mom is getting worse and it's getting more dangerous for her to live by herself. And me, my marriage is on the rocks, my boss is always pissed and I'm at my personal breaking point.

Chelsea's story captures many of the complexities of caregiving. After we look at motherhood and a few of the shared triggers around perfectionism, we'll examine the resilience strategies that can help us reality-check the expectations that make this complicated issue even more difficult.

Motherhood

While motherhood and parenting are certainly related, they emerged as two distinct shame areas. Mother shame is about our identity as mothers or our identity as women who are not mothers. Parenting shame is focused on how we raise and interact with our children.

Mother shame is an overwhelming issue for women. Every single participant in a mother role identified mother shame as an issue. And, because motherhood is an identity that is so closely tied to being a woman, it became clear that you don't have to be a mother for motherhood to be a shame issue. As we learned in the powerful guide on understanding infertility, women struggling with infertility talked passionately about the mother shame in their lives. So did women who have chosen to delay having children or not to have children.

Society views womanhood and motherhood as inextricably bound; therefore, our value as women is often evaluated by where we are in relation to our roles as potential mothers. In some communities, the expectation of motherhood has many layers, including norms of what's too young, what's too old and what gender babies should be (as if mothers controlled this). Once women hit "the age" set by their community, they begin to feel the need to defend themselves against expectations of motherhood. Women are constantly asked why they haven't married or, if they're married, why they haven't had children. Even women who are married and have one child are often asked why they haven't had a second child. Women who have four or five kids are expected to explain why they had so many.

Mother shame seems to be a birthright for girls and women. On top of the societal expectation that motherhood defines womanhood, there are some very rigid expectations about what the good mother looks like. There are some very desirable qualities associated with motherhood, and there are some characteristics that are universally unwanted. Interestingly, to be perceived as "trying too hard" was identified as an unwanted characteristic, not only for motherhood but also for all the areas in this category. We want perfection, but we don't want to look like we're working for it—we want it to just materialize somehow.

Poof! There It Is

"You don't have the time or talent to look that messy." Even though I hear this every time I bring my stack of Meg Ryan pictures to my hairstylist, I still don't believe her. All I want is Meg Ryan hair. This last time I asked, "I want to look like I just rolled out of bed. How hard can that be?" She spit back, "It takes two hours and ten people to get that 'natural' look—get over it."

We want to be natural beauties, natural mothers, naturally good parents, and we want to belong to naturally fabulous families. Think about how much money has been made selling products that promise "the natural look." And, when it comes to work, we love to hear "She makes it look so easy," or "She's a natural."

The research participants really exposed an interesting perfection paradox: Imperfection brings shame, and working too hard for perfection brings shame. In this age of instant gratification and celebrity for celebrity's sake, it is easy to understand how we've fallen for the idea that we can just want something bad enough and . . . Poof! There it is. How many of us have fallen prey to that saying, "It shouldn't be this much work," or "It just doesn't come naturally to me; it must not be my thing."

Yes, there are naturally talented people. But for most of us, including the celebrities and superstars, achievement is about hard work and commitment. Ninety-five percent of the people who are in great shape and have healthy bodies work at it . . . a lot.

I know several people who possess parenting skills that I really respect—they work at it. They talk about parenting as a skills-based job that requires training, practice and a significant time investment. They read, they take classes, they practice and they evaluate their techniques and strategies.

The same applies to family and motherhood. There is a direct correlation between input and output. The areas in this category are like other skills-based endeavors: If you have reasonable goals, the more you invest your time and resources and the more you practice, the more likely you are to reach those goals.

A couple of years ago, a doctoral student told me, "I'd love to write a book. I've been collecting material for several years. I just don't think I can do it." When I asked her what was stopping her, she stared down at the ground between us and said, "It's not easy for me. Writing is so stressful. I'm not like you—it just doesn't pour out of me. Plus I'm not very thick-skinned and they say writers need to be able to laugh off criticism."

I could sense that she felt some shame as she explained this— part of me felt real empathy for her. The other part of me was a little pissed off. I stood there thinking, "Writing doesn't pour out of me. I tweeze it out one word at a time. Sometimes it's not too bad and other days it's excruciating. And criticism . . . every writer I know struggles with criticism." You work at becoming better at hearing it, but it's painful—especially when it's personal.

When we believe that success should be effortless, we simultaneously set ourselves up for shame and diminish the efforts of people who are working on their issues around perfectionism; we become part of our own shame web and other women's shame webs.

How many times have we dismissed someone's efforts because we have bought into the expectation that "family" or "motherhood" shouldn't be that hard? Marriage, parenting, health, careers, motherhood—each of these requires a tremendous amount of work. And trying to balance the demands of these five areas might be the defining challenge of our lives.

We need to reality-check our expectations. Just because we don't sit down and channel the great American novel in one week doesn't mean we won't be good writers. And we need to remember that behind every "naturally gifted" person is normally a huge amount of work, dedication and commitment.

Defending Our Lives

When I spoke with women about the pressures of perfection, they were quick to explain that failing to look, love and work perfectly was only part of the problem. Of equal importance is the shame that stems from what we are willing to do to appear perfect or hide our imperfections. When perfection is the expectation and/or the goal, we are willing to put a lot on the line to maintain and protect our image. Here are some women's stories.

- Shame is being married for twenty years and never walking around naked in front of your husband—not even once.
- I lie to people all the time. I tell them that my father lives in New Jersey. He's been in prison for six years. I'm more ashamed of myself for lying than I am of my dad for being in jail. It's one thing if your family is different because your parents are divorced or something. It's different if your dad is a felon.
- My husband had an affair last year. I haven't even told my best friend. Everyone loves my husband and thinks we are a great

couple. I know if I told her she would think less of both of us—not just him.

- I want to go back to school and finish my degree. But with my kids and my part-time job I just can't imagine being able to do it like I want to. I'm afraid I'll get a B or C. I don't want to do it unless I can do it one hundred percent, so I don't go.

- I just tell people my parents travel a lot. Last year I was the only freshman in my dorm whose parents didn't come up for parents' weekend. I didn't invite them. They are racist and hateful and they think the whole world is out to get them. My dad thinks everybody owes him. When I was growing up I was always embarrassed for anyone to come to my house. It's like they're from a different planet.

- I filter everything I tell my parents. They don't know I'm gay and they don't know I have a partner. There's a lot of pressure in the gay and lesbian community to "come out." I know it's important, but you have to be prepared for your parents to walk out of your life. Not many people have to face that reality.

- People at work always say, "Everything she touches turns to gold." Sometimes it's true, but lately my projections have been way off. The first time I packaged a deal that lost money, everyone in my office freaked out. They blamed everyone but me, when, in fact, it was my fault—I made a bad call. The second time it happened, my co-workers did the same thing. That's when I realized that I'd become poster child for the department—they couldn't stand the thought of me making a bad call. In this business, we just need to make more than we lose. No one makes money on every deal, but I'm expected to. My boss told me, "We need you to show people how it's done—we need you to set the bar." Now I dread work. I've started lying about my numbers and blaming losses on other people.

We are also more willing to use shame, fear and judgment with people who threaten our pursuit of perfection. We can feel threatened when people challenge or criticize us, or we can feel threatened simply because someone is making different choices than we would make.

This came up a lot around parenting, which is a particularly complex issue because we base our level of perfection both on how we are perceived as parents and how our children are perceived. As the examples throughout the book—and certainly several of the ones below—demonstrate, we are very susceptible to using shame, fear and judgment against our children when they engage in behaviors that damage the "parenting image" we are trying to create.

- When my husband and I told my parents that we had decided not to have children, they fell apart. They kept asking, "What's wrong with you?" and "How could you do this to us?" My mom actually said, "It's a disgrace to the family—everyone will think something's wrong." I had known it would be hard, but it was far worse than I imagined.

- My partner's dad was on one of his regular tirades, yelling at her about being lesbian. He was calling her "a butch" and telling her she was an embarrassment to their "well-respected" family. Then, right in front of me, he says, "And of all things, you have to be a butch with a colored girlfriend." I remember just standing there thinking, "He did not just say that." We're not talking about Archie Bunker here; we're talking about a fifty-year-old, overeducated oil-and-gas executive. Shame really causes people to act crazy.

- My husband is very tough on our son. He puts a lot of pressure on him. He wants him to get perfect grades and be the best baseball player at the school. I try to soften my husband up, but it never works. I see my son's stress. I used to talk about it with the other baseball moms, but I've stopped. They started giving me a really hard time. They said the other kids think my husband is cruel and unfair. The other mothers think my husband and I are ruining my son's life. I have no idea what to do. I just stay quiet.

In more extreme cases, our inability to expose imperfections can mean putting ourselves and/or the people we care about in real danger:

• When I was pregnant all my girlfriends said, "Oh, just wait, just wait, you're going to feel a love that you've never felt before, it's amazing." They'd go on and on, and after my first child was born, my son, I got really depressed and I actually didn't feel anything toward him. I just felt sad and overwhelmed and really wanted to go back in my life to a time before I was even pregnant. To feel like that when you look at your new baby, I was so ashamed, I thought, "My God, I'm going to be one of those mothers that you know . . . my son's going to turn out to be a crazy person and I'm a crazy person." My husband was so freaked out. I think he thought he was married to a monster. I don't think he knew what to say, and my mother-in-law just kept saying, "Something is wrong, she's not normal, something is wrong, she's not normal." For two months my life was a living hell. I wouldn't go to the doctor because I was too ashamed. Finally, when it got so bad I could barely function and I was afraid my family was going to put me away, I forced myself to go to the doctor. The doctor explained that some women experience depression after having a baby and it could be based on my hormones. She said it could happen to me even if I'm normally a loving person. I got on medication, which that's pretty bad itself, but it's not as bad as feeling nothing toward your child. Within two months, I felt normal again. I just look back at that time and know that was the darkest place I've ever been.

• I'm ashamed at how much I absolutely hate my body. I mean, I hate my body sometimes so much that I wish I'd get sick, I mean really sick. So sick that I lose thirty or forty pounds. I don't want to die, but if I could just be sick enough, I don't even care how miserable I'd be, but if I could be sick enough to lose thirty or forty pounds and then be well, it'd be worth it. I mean, can you imagine hating your body that much? It's like I'm ashamed of my body and I'm ashamed of how much I hate it.

- My daughter is on drugs and my son in junior high is failing school. When your only job is raising your kids and they're both failures, then you're a failure. My friends keep telling me I need to get help for my daughter, but I don't know what to do. I can't tell my husband; he'd go nuts. I know she drinks and drives, but if I take her car away, he'd want to know why.

- At some point I realized that refusing to see a doctor because I was ashamed of my body and being overweight was tantamount to suicide. It had to get that bad before I could force myself to go to the doctor.

- Sometimes I have unprotected sex. I know it's stupid, but it's such a turnoff to guys. It's hard enough being thirty and single; I don't want to be the safe-sex police on top of that. If I ask and they pretend like they don't hear or say they don't want to—I'm not comfortable making it an issue.

As these quotes demonstrate, pursuing perfection can be as dangerous as it is unfulfilling. Sometimes, the risks we take are not as obvious as the ones above. One example of this is my own struggle with being perceived as an overprotective and uptight mother.

Between my experiences as a social worker and Steve's experiences in pediatrics, I've seen a disproportionate number of bad things happen to children. Sometimes it's difficult for me to tease out the fear from the reality-based concerns. Two issues that are particularly important to me are gun safety and seat belts.

If Ellen is invited to play at someone's house, I want to make sure there aren't loaded guns in the house. And I want to make sure that she's properly restrained in a car seat if she's going to be in a car. For the past few years she's been young enough that we accompany her to play dates. But as she gets older, that's changing.

Sometimes I find myself silenced by the shame of appearing obsessively worried. I don't want to be perceived as that "hysterical, hovering mom." I've had to really reach out to my connection network for support and help reframing the issues.

A friend of mine who works in a teen-pregnancy prevention program told me what she tells the kids: "If you aren't comfortable enough to talk about condoms with someone, that means you don't know them well enough to have sex." Now, rather than thinking, "I hope they don't think I'm crazy," I think, "If I'm too ashamed to talk about these issues, I'm probably not comfortable enough with these folks to let Ellen go to their house unsupervised."

Perfectionism and Shame Resilience

To better understand how each of the four elements of shame resilience can help us overcome perfectionism, I'll share another story about one of my personal struggles with perfectionism.

When I was pregnant with Ellen, several companies, including a computer manufacturer, had advertising campaigns that featured young mothers working from home. Invariably, the ads portrayed the mother, in her bunny slippers, working away at the computer while her child gazed lovingly at her from the play mat situated right next to the desk. The commercials would always end with the mother simultaneously receiving praise and validation from her child and from her professional colleagues.

I thought about that image every day. I wanted to be just like the commercial. I would picture myself in a cool T-shirt and size-eight yoga pants (I've never been a size eight), with a loose pony-tail (I've had short hair for the past decade), a laptop, a cooperative baby smiling from the play mat, exciting work and loads of personal and professional validation. Suffice it to say that someone at that marketing agency did their homework—I'm sure I was the targeted demographic and I fell for it, hook, line and laptop.

One day, when Ellen was about two months old, my vision was realized. I was one of three researchers being considered for a community evaluation project. I had a phone interview with two community leaders scheduled for 1:00 P.M. I had everything scheduled down to the minute. Ellen nursed at noon and was sound asleep by 12:55 P.M. The call came in promptly at 1:00 P.M. I had all my questions prepared, a cell phone with a mute button and a headset ready just in case. It was perfect . . . until 1:05 P.M.

About five minutes into the interview, Ellen started crying. Not screaming, but crying. At 1:06 P.M. she stopped crying and started screaming. She screamed so loudly that both of the interviewers asked if everything was OK. I quickly replied, "Everything's great—please continue." As they explained the project, I went into Ellen's room, holding down the mute button and periodically testing its power by repeatedly asking, "Can you hear me? Can you hear me?"

By the time I got to her crib, the front of my T-shirt was soaking wet with breast milk. Ellen had a certain "call of the wild" that would immediately send my milk making into overdrive. Ellen was screaming because she'd had one of those explosive poops that shoot up the back of the diaper and don't stop until the entire back of the onesie is covered.

All of a sudden, as I'm evaluating the crib damage, I hear the dreaded "Ms. Brown, are you there?" "Yes, I'm here. I'm just taking notes so I can more thoroughly think through the project. Can you tell me about the project funding?"

Whew. It worked. As they started explaining important things that I should have been writing down, I kept one hand on the mute button, pushed Ellen against the crib bumper and slid her into my arm. Poop was everywhere. I managed to get her undressed, clean her off with a dozen wet wipes and carry her, naked, back to my room.

She was still crying and at this point milk was literally dripping off my shirt. I laid her on my bed long enough to get one arm out of the T-shirt, pulled my drenched bra down around my waist, pulled the nursing pillow around me and started feeding her. As soon as she was quiet, I came back to the call. I managed to make a few coherent statements before all hell broke loose.

The stress of the situation was too much for my body to take. Within seconds I was riding the wave of a serious diarrhea attack. At this point, I was standing up with the nursing pillow around my waist, tears pouring down my face, my T-shirt hanging down my back and trying to do the pressed-cheek penguin walk around the room.

As gracefully as possible, I took myself out of the running for the position and thanked the interviewers for their time. I just sat there, holding Ellen and crying. I felt ashamed about my inability to pull off my vision of working-mother perfection. It was one thing to take myself out of the running for the research position, but it was even worse to look down at little, naked poop-smeared Ellen, and feel like I had let her down too.

A few weeks later, Steve and Dawn suggested that I apply what I was learning about shame to this situation (I'm no stranger to the "shame researcher, heal thyself" comment). As I thought about it, my shame turned into disappointment followed by disillusionment, followed by a healthy dose of "I'm never going to fall for that smiling-baby-laptop-bunny-slipper bullshit again."

Now when my first-time-mom friends tell me how they are going to work at home with their newborns, I'm quick to share my story. They often respond by asking, "Can't you just plan your work around the baby's schedule?" or "Can't you just make sure she goes potty before the call?" I lovingly tell them, "Only in the commercials."

When I applied the four elements of shame resilience to this situation, here's what I learned:

Recognizing Our Shame Triggers: I did not want to be perceived as incapable of balancing motherhood and work. I did not want to be perceived as needing help. I wanted to be perceived as one of those "laid-back, balance everything, don't need help" working mothers. I'm still not sure about the origin of the messages that fueled that identity. I know some of them came from what I saw growing up in my family.

My mom didn't work outside the home until I was in my late teens. She was the room parent, the Girl Scout leader, the swim-team mom, the carpool coordinator, etc. . . . That's the picture I had in my head for me, but with work somehow added to the vision. I'd just do what she did, plus work full time and finish graduate school.

The whole idea that "something would have to give" wasn't for me. That was for the other mothers—the ones who couldn't do it all. I figured that I belonged to a different group of moms—you know, the ones in the commercials. I liked their messages better:

- Buy this laptop and working from home with a newborn will be easy and you'll be hip, cool and funky.
- Start your busy "work from home" morning with our coffee and you'll live in a cool loft in SoHo and have great clothes.
- If you buy our detergent, you'll find yourself walking on the beach with your baby in one hand and your promotion letter in the other.

Practicing Critical Awareness: There are expectations that women can do it all—the superwoman syndrome. Despite my best efforts and the lessons I've learned, I sometimes still think I can do it all, and all at the same time. I think the expectation exists as a result of women striving for equality in the workforce, yet not getting the support and help that is necessary for real equality.

I also think the need to do it all at the same time, especially work and mothering, is related to the fact that we view motherhood as unpaid, unimportant, easy work. The reality is that raising children is more difficult (and rewarding) than any job I've ever had. You just don't get formally evaluated, validated or paid.

Lastly, the entire debate over "going back to work versus staying at home" is reserved for women who have the resources to think of work as an option. We often blame women for taking on too much—for choosing the superwoman lifestyle. Many women have to "do it all" or their kids don't eat.

For me, part of practicing critical awareness is constantly decoding messages. Sometimes when people make comments about our choices, it feels shaming and we don't know why. Here are some of the conflicting underlying messages that fuel our shame and self-doubt:

- You are what you earn.
- Motherhood is easy—what else do you do?
- You should have a real job. You need your own money and identity.
- You should be at home. That's your job.
- If you were a better mother or better professional, you could do both easily.

Reaching Out: When it comes to my personal struggles with appearance, family, parenting, motherhood and work, I'm one hundred percent dependent on my connection network. I depend on them for advice, guidance, support, feedback, validation, praise and sometimes I need them for plain old handholding or babysitting.

I've worked very hard to build this network—it's now big and strong. I also depend on these people to lean on me. I know it sounds funny, but I want to be in relationships that work both ways. Receiving empathy is a wonderful gift, but so is offering it. Both giving and receiving make me a better person and help increase my shame resilience.

My shame web around these issues is primarily the media and myself. I constantly work on it, but I'm still vulnerable to magazines and movies. I have to be vigilant about practicing critical awareness and talking to my connection network about these topics. There are also friends and family members who can push buttons—especially about parenting and work.

Speaking Shame: If the goal of speaking shame is learning how to express how we feel and ask for what we need, then I'd say I'm getting better. I'm definitely better at the former. Like many women, I often find it difficult to ask for what I need—especially if I need help or support.

During the interviews, an interesting pattern emerged around help seeking. It seems that many women struggle to ask for help or support. So often, we are the caregivers and helpers. We convince ourselves that we shouldn't need help so we don't ask for it. Then, we get angry or hurt because no one offers. We think, "Doesn't he see me drowning?" or "Why won't she do something?" This can quickly escalate into a blame-and-shame situation: We need help, but we don't ask for it. We get angry because we don't get it. We feel ashamed for even thinking someone would help us when we knew they wouldn't.

For me, asking for help is a work in progress.

Growth and Goal-Setting

As we become more fluent in speaking shame, the power and meaning behind words become more apparent. Women with high levels of shame resilience use very different language from women who are struggling with shame in the same area. For example, when I spoke to women about appearance, motherhood, parenting, work and family, women who demonstrated high levels of shame resilience spoke less about perfection and more about growth. Some of the language patterns I heard include:

- "I want to work on getting better at . . ."
- "I'd like to improve the way I . . ."
- "I'd like to do a little less of this and a little more of . . ."
- "These are my goals. . . ."
- "I want to be perceived as doing my best at . . ."
- "I want to be perceived as trying . . ."

When we choose growth over perfection, we immediately increase our shame resilience. Improvement is a far more realistic goal than perfection. Merely letting go of unattainable goals makes us less susceptible to shame. When we believe "we must be this" we ignore who or what we actually are, our capacity and our limitations. We start from the image of perfection, and of course, from perfection there is nowhere to go but down.

When we think, "I want my parents to see me as the perfect daughter," all we can do is fail. First, perfection is unattainable. Second, we can't control how people perceive us. Lastly, there is no way that we can do every single thing that is expected of us or that we expect of ourselves.

When our goal is growth and we say, "I'd like to improve this," we start from where and who we are. "I'd like to work on my relationship with my parents" is a completely different goal from "I want my parents to see me as the perfect daughter."

To illustrate how different these statements are, many of the women I interviewed described how their relationships with their parents improved after they stopped trying to be the "perfect daughter." This also holds true for appearance, motherhood and parenting.

When we give ourselves permission to be imperfect, when we find self-worth despite our imperfections, when we build connection networks that affirm and value us as imperfect beings, we are much more capable of change.

This goes back to the sentence that launched this entire journey for me: You cannot shame or belittle people into changing. This means we can't use self-hate to lose weight, we can't shame ourselves into becoming better parents and we can't belittle ourselves or our families into becoming who we need them to be. Putting people on the "loser board" doesn't work. *Shame corrodes the very part of us that believes we are capable of change.*

Goal-setting: Women with high levels of shame resilience did not trade perfection for goals of "working toward perfection." Building shame resilience requires realistic goal-setting. Saying, "I don't ever want to be perceived as impatient," is the same as saying, "I want to work on becoming more patient so I never get angry." Ultimately, the goal of both approaches is still perfection.

When I asked women about "growth goals," like "I want to be more patient," I asked them how they saw that happening. Based on their answers, I saw a direct connection between their level of shame resilience and their ability to identify specific objectives related to their goals.

For example, Cheryl, a good friend and colleague, told me her parenting goals are to be "fun, strong, kind, knowledgeable, patient and loving." She specifically said that these were her goals and she knew it was unrealistic to be all these things all the time.

When I asked what she did to meet these goals, she very confidently started listing simple, measurable (they happen or they don't), tangible objectives. She said: "I get sleep—I'm a better parent when I'm well rested. Even though it's difficult, I keep my sons on schedules so they feel good. I read a lot of parenting books—when they're good I use the advice, when they aren't, I don't. When I see another parent doing something well, I ask him or her about it. My husband and I go to parenting workshops. I stay connected with my mothers' group. I changed pediatricians several times until I found one who shares my values and gives me the guidance I want and need. I set boundaries with my work. When someone criticizes my parenting, I have a support system of friends to talk to about it. I try to practice self-care by taking the time I need to replenish my own well. When my well is dry, I don't have anything to give to anyone else."

Oddly, growth and goal-setting can feel like more work than dreaming of perfection. When we try to be perfect, we fail so often that we almost get used to it. After a while, we trick ourselves into believing that forecasting perfection is nobler than working toward goals. It is much easier to say, "I'll be thin by December," rather than "I'll start eating healthy and exercising today." Or "Things will be great when we get out of debt," rather than "I won't buy anything on the credit card this week."

When we set realistic objectives for meeting "growth goals," we hold ourselves accountable for today, tomorrow and the day after tomorrow rather than postponing accountability until six months down the road.

Women with what I would consider the highest levels of shame resilience around the perfection issues had very realistic goals and concrete, measurable strategies for meeting those goals. One example was a woman who struggled with an eating disorder for more than ten years. She said that she overcame her eating disorder and the shame around being bulimic by setting realistic, written "health goals" for every week rather than universal "thinness goals." She said she no longer wants to be perceived as "thin" but as "healthy," and she works toward that by exercising for thirty minutes five times a week and eating at least three healthy meals per day.

One of the benefits of growth through goal setting is that it is not an all-or-nothing proposition—success or failure is not the only possible outcome. If our goal is to be a better parent and we set two reasonable objectives of reading one parenting article per month and talking to parents who demonstrate skills we respect, we can still learn and grow even if we don't meet all the objectives.

If we don't read the article, but we learn a lot from another parent, that is still growth. And maybe we learn that reading articles is not our strength. Maybe it would be more helpful to spend even more time around other parents. When we set improvement goals and set measurable objectives to meet those goals, we can learn and grow from both missed and met objectives. If our goal is perfection, we will inevitably fail and that failure offers us nothing in terms of learning and change; it only makes us vulnerable to shame.

Going Back

The ability to learn from our mistakes rather than seeing them as failed attempts at perfection is the essence of "going back." Going back emerged as an extremely important concept in this research. Women with high levels of shame resilience in the areas of appearance, motherhood, parenting, work and family spoke passionately about the value of believing that it's never too late to grow and change. They resisted being defined by mistakes and viewed "imperfection" as a necessary part of growth rather than a barrier. Furthermore, many of these same women emphasized the value of having members of their connection network who modeled "going back" as a powerful strategy for growth and change. Women were especially influenced by their parents' willingness to change and grow as parents.

In contrast, women who spoke of ongoing shame struggles in these same areas perceived past mistakes and failed attempts at perfection as enduring and permanently altering their levels of connection and power. Like the women who demonstrated high levels of shame resilience, they were equally influenced by outside forces; however, in these cases, those forces were mostly members of their shame webs rather than their connection networks. When women spoke about the permanency of mistakes and the inability to move away from perfection and toward growth, at least eighty percent of them described this attribute as something they learned from their parents and/or families.

So, the first reason that going back is an important concept in shame resilience relates to our ability to move past mistakes and failures toward change and growth. The second reason is its influence on our efforts to build empathy through connection networks—not only do we need to be willing to go back and learn from our mistakes, we need people in our lives who are willing to do the same.

Of all the insights that emerged from this study, none was more powerful to me than the influence parents have on their children. It didn't matter if I was talking to an eighteen-year-old or a sixty-eight-year-old, women were greatly affected by their parents' willingness to go back and continually try to improve their relationships with their children. This was clear in all areas, but especially in the areas that fall into the "perfection" category. Of all the voices shouting expectations or whispering quiet affirmations, the voices of parents were consistently reported to be among the most influential.

When parents instill expectations of perfection in their children, it is very difficult for children to exchange that goal for growth and improvement. This is especially true when parents use shame as a tool to enforce expectations. Women whose parents demonstrated their own commitment to going back by encouraging them to strive for growth rather than perfection felt great connection and empathy from their parents.

It is difficult for me to capture in writing the emotion conveyed by participants when they explained what it meant to hear their parents say, "I'm sorry," or "I understand how that made you feel." When parents acknowledge the pain felt by their children—really show empathy without explaining or defending—amazing healing can happen.

Conversely, women whose parents continued to enforce expectations of perfection into adulthood either continued to struggle with shame or had to work diligently to develop resilience in the face of their parents' ongoing expectations.

Remember the example from the last chapter where the mother told her daughter, "My God! You're still fat." What if, after listening to her daughter explain how shaming that was for her, the mother had responded by saying, "I don't want to shame you or hurt you. I'm sorry that I've done that. I want us to be close. I love you."

This wouldn't automatically repair their relationship, but what a powerful start toward healing. Yes, I'm sure at some point this mother would want to explain or defend her motivation by saying, "I'm just so worried about your health." But to really go back, it's important that we start by first just acknowledging the pain we've caused and our desire to rebuild connection.

In my own life I've experienced the power of having parents who are willing to go back. Before I became a parent I wanted to do everything that I thought they did "wrong" perfectly. Now that I am a parent, I only hope that I'm as willing to go back as my parents are. I was recently talking to my dad about parenting and he told me, "You can't parent perfectly; your only measure of success is your children's ability to parent even better than you and your willingness to support them in that process."

I thought about that statement for a long time. It's powerful to observe your parents' willingness to reexamine their choices; it's even more powerful when you think about how your children will one day ask the same of you.

One of the greatest barriers to going back is related to empathy. If our goal is perfection rather than growth, it is unlikely that we are willing to go back, because it requires a level of self-empathy—the ability to look at our own actions with understanding and compassion; to understand our experiences in the context in which they happened and to do all this without judgment. I call this ability to reflect on our own actions with empathy "grounding."

Grounding

When we choose growth over perfection, we choose empathy and connection. I use the term *grounding* because in order to examine where we are, where we want to go and how we want to get there, we must have a level of self-acceptance about who we are. Grounding gives us the stability we need to reach out and examine who we are and who we want to be. The more grounded we are, the less we feel compelled to defend our decisions and protect ourselves. We can look at ourselves with compassion rather than self-loathing. Grounding also prevents us from chasing acceptance and belonging by attempting to become whatever people need us to be.

During the interviews I met two women who had similar stories regarding their appearance. Both women had been very overweight during their teens and early twenties. Both women were in their mid-thirties, very slim, and had young daughters at the time of the interviews.

The first woman had great contempt for the person she used to be. She told me, "I was fat and disgusting. I can't believe I ever looked like that." She went on to tell me how much she disliked overweight women. She told me that her mother was very slim and was constantly "on her" about her weight. She said that she has two daughters and she watches everything they eat. She said that her oldest daughter (who was seven at the time of the interview) was already on a diet. She told me that it was better that she told her daughter that she was looking fat rather than her school peers. I sensed that this woman, despite having lost weight, still had a great amount of shame attached to her weight issues. She appeared more rooted in shame than grounded in self-acceptance.

The second told me that she had struggled with her weight for twenty-five years. She said she was an overweight child and didn't get into shape until she turned thirty. When I asked her how she felt when she thought back to her life when she was overweight, she said, "It's just part of who I am. I got married and had my children during that period of time, I lost my mom during my twenties—just like everyone else I had good times and bad times." She said that her daughter and son were too young to really remember her being that heavy, so when they see old movies and pictures they sometimes make comments. She said, "I explained that it hurts my feelings when they make fun of my old pictures. I also used that as an example of why you shouldn't judge people based on how they look. They love me and think I'm a great mom. I told them if all you saw was a fat woman, you'd miss all the good stuff. They have become very sensitive about that issue with their friends." This woman said she felt great power and freedom about her appearance. She said she had a huge support system of friends and family. She seemed securely grounded in self-acceptance.

Celebrating the Ordinary and Uncool

One destructive obsession related to perfectionism is the fascination with celebrity culture. We desperately flip through magazines to find out all of the intimate details about the stars we love and the ones we hate. We want to know who has lost weight, how they decorate their houses, what they eat, what they feed their dogs . . . you name it. If they eat it, wear it, own it or lose it—we want to do the same!

We want to share in their lives because we believe it's the way to bring us closer to the perfection we seek. Celebrities also bring us closer to another highly coveted asset—coolness. The importance of being cool should not be underestimated. We know that teenagers will often take terrible physical and psychological risks to maintain their coolness among their peers. Unfortunately, in our culture, the value of cool doesn't decline after high school. Women from age eighteen to eighty spoke to me about the emotional pain of being perceived as "uncool" or "unhip." They spoke as candidly about some of the life-altering consequences they faced as a result of trying to maintain a perception of being "with it." Unfortunately, in a culture driven by profit, there are multibillion-dollar industries making sure that perfection and coolness stay as elusive as they are seductive. There is no such thing as perfect enough or cool enough.

In her book *The Shelter of Each Other: Rebuilding Our Families*,

Mary Pipher speaks wisely about the real threat that the media poses to our families. She explains that the media forms our new community—a community far less diverse than real life. "We 'know' celebrities but they don't know us. The new community is not a reciprocal neighborhood like earlier ones. David Letterman won't be helping out if our car battery dies on a winter morning. Donald Trump won't bring groceries over if Dad loses his job. These vicarious relationships create a new kind of loneliness—the loneliness of people whose relationships are with personae instead of persons."

In addition to fostering perfectionism and loneliness (which are often connected), there is the issue of comparing our lives with the lives of celebrities. We watch hours of shows that do nothing more than detail their comings and goings. And consciously or un-consciously, we compare our lives to theirs.

In my research with both women and men, many participants talked about feeling ashamed of their "small, boring lives." With very few exceptions, these participants were comparing their lives to what they saw on television or read about in magazines. Dr. Pipher also explains this phenomenon in the context of the new media community. She writes, "The electronic community is less diverse than real life. The problems it deals with are not the prob-lems real people face. Certain situations, such as young starlets be-ing threatened or handsome men fighting crime, are overexplored. Other stories, much more common, such as school board meet-ings, poetry writing, trips to museums, piano practice or the deliv-ery of Meals on Wheels, are virtually ignored. People who are not visually interesting, which is most of us, are underrepresented. The stories that are selected are those that make money. A rich-ness and complexity of real life disappears."

In our culture, the fear and shame of being ordinary is very real. In fact, many of the older women I interviewed spoke about looking back on their lives and grieving for the extraordinary things that would never come to pass. We seem to measure the value of people's contributions (and sometimes their entire lives) by their level of public recognition. In other words, worth is measured by fame and fortune.

Our culture is quick to dismiss quiet, ordinary, hardworking men and women. In many instances, we equate *ordinary* with *boring* or, even more dangerous, *ordinary* has become synonymous with *meaningless*. One of the greatest cultural consequences of devaluing our own lives has been our tolerance for what people do to achieve their "extraordinary" status.

Baseball players who pump themselves full of steroids and hormones are heroes. Corporate leaders with billion-dollar salary packages are envied, even if their employees are losing their pensions and benefits at the same time. Young girls are starting Web sites and chat rooms to talk about the tricks that celebrities use to hide their eating disorders in order to stay thin and beautiful. Young children are overstressed and suffering from high rates of anxiety due to the overscheduling of extracurricular activities and the emphasis on standardized testing scores.

These examples beg the question, what are we willing to sacrifice in our pursuit of the extraordinary? We can use the shame resilience tools to learn more about our fears and our vulnerabilities to cultural pressures. Practicing critical awareness is especially important if we want to better understand the media community that has become part of our lives.

Fearing Vulnerability

If we are going to recognize and accept what makes us human, including our imperfections and less-than-extraordinary lives, we must embrace our vulnerabilities. This is extremely difficult, because we are afraid to be vulnerable. As I wrote in Chapter 1, we equate vulnerability with weakness, and in our culture, there are very few things we abhor more than weakness.

When I listened to women talk about their fear of being vulnerable, I heard the same thing over and over: "I don't want to share information with someone, then have them use it against me." It is extremely painful to share a vulnerability or fear with someone, only to have them use it against us as an insult, as leverage in an argument or as a fodder for gossip.

One concept that emerged across the interviews is what I call the *vulnerability hangover*. The vulnerability hangover directly relates to our fear of vulnerability, and unfortunately, most of us have experienced it. We have all been in situations where we're with a friend, colleague or family member and we feel that deep yearning to connect. Despite the fear, we feel that push or need to share something meaningful, and before you know it, we've let it all out. We've told them everything; shared our deepest vulnerabilities.

The next hour, day or week that feeling of regret comes over us like a warm wave of nausea: "Oh, my God, why did I tell her that? What's she going to think about my family? Who's she going to tell?" That's the vulnerability hangover.

When we begin to work on our shame resilience, the need to reach out and talk about our experiences can be a very strong force. So strong, in fact, that it sometimes leads us to purging with people with whom we have not developed the kind of relationship that can absorb that information.

The good thing about the vulnerability hangover is that it's universal. When I talk about this concept in my lectures I usually see a room of nodding heads and expressions that convey, "Oh yeah—been there—hated it." When it comes to sharing information, it would be nice to believe that most of us have the ability to recognize the right people, the right times and the right ways to share. But alas, the reality is that most of us have turned to people we barely know and thrown up vulnerability all over them.

Harriet Lerner offers some wonderful advice on this topic. She writes, "When it comes to sharing vulnerability, it's wise to take time to test whether the other person is worthy of hearing our stories and to assess our own level of safety and comfort in sharing sensitive material. We want to trust that the other person isn't going to deny and minimize our pain, or alternatively, overfocus on our problem in an unhelpful way. We don't want to be put down, pitied, or gossiped about, nor do we want to have sensitive information used against us."

Fear, Vulnerability and Expectations

We also fear vulnerability because it is often related to our expectations and the pain of disappointment. Elizabeth, a woman I interviewed several years ago, talked about the shame she felt when she wasn't offered a promotion she was expecting. She said, "I was most ashamed because I told everyone how much it meant to me. I talked about it with everyone—my husband, my kids, my neighbors, my mom and my colleagues. It's not that I told everyone I was going to get it; I was just honest about how much I wanted it. Instead of just feeling sad and disappointed, I felt sad, disappointed and ashamed."

When someone has the courage to share their hopes with us, we are given an important opportunity to practice compassion and connection. Think how powerful it might have been for Elizabeth to hear, "You had such courage to apply for that promotion and then to be honest about how much you wanted it. I'm so proud to be your daughter/friend/mother."

As Elizabeth's example demonstrates, there is a complex relationship between our expectations, vulnerabilities and fears. When we develop expectations we paint a picture in our head of how things are going to be and how they're going to look. Sometimes we go so far as to imagine what they're going to feel like, taste like and smell like. We put a picture in our head that holds great value for us.

We set expectations based not only on how we fit in that picture, but also on what those around us are doing in that picture. And often, the failure we feel when these expectations do not come to pass results in shame. When I lose thirty pounds, this is what it's going to be like . . . if I get accepted into graduate school, this is what it's going to feel like . . . if we can buy this house, all of this will change . . . if I tell my father how I feel, he will understand . . . if I do this for my children, they will be very grateful. Sometimes broken expectations lead only to mild disappointment, but in many cases they lead to shame, especially if vulnerability and fear are at work.

Kelli, one of the participants I interviewed, spoke very candidly about how her expectations and fears consistently set her up for shame whenever she was around her mother-in-law. Kelli described her mother-in-law as very critical of the way she parented, very critical of the fact that she stayed at home with her kids and very critical of the way she treated her husband (this woman's son). When we talked about her mother-in-law's visits, she described how she planned for weeks, sometimes even months, for the visits. She would go to great lengths to engineer situations that would allow her to demonstrate the kind of parenting and partnering skills she thought would please her mother-in-law.

Without fail, every time her mother-in-law visited, nothing worked as planned. Not only did her mother-in-law remain critical, she also saw right through Kelli's transparent efforts to manufacture situations that made her look good.

Regardless of what we do, we can't control how people are going to respond or react. If we lose thirty pounds so we can see the looks on our friends' faces at the class reunion, what happens when there's no look? We can experience anything from mild disappointment to major shame.

Kelli told me that she eventually stopped trying to predict and control her visits with her mother-in-law. When Kelli and her husband finally shared their feelings with Kelli's mother-in-law, she was somewhat unresponsive. Kelli finally developed other strategies for dealing with the visits. She limited the duration of the visits and she prepared for them in a much different way. Rather than trying to control the visits, she surrounded herself with support from her family and her girlfriends.

Kelli actually shared this story with me as an example of developing shame resilience. She said that she never expected it to change because she changed; she thought it would change because her mother-in-law would eventually change. I think that's the trouble with expectations: They're often unrealistic and placed on the wrong people. In the next section we'll discuss an interesting exercise that can help us recognize our fears and reality-check our expectations.

The Life Shuffle

The pregnancy shuffle is a very powerful exercise that many hospitals use in their childbirth preparation classes. Expectant parents are given ten notecards and asked to write one important expectation for their labor and delivery on each card. There's an assumption that families are hoping for healthy outcomes for mother and child, so they're asked not to include those. Women typically write things like vaginal delivery, no epidural, no inducements, no episiotomy, family arrives on time, no forceps, latches to breast immediately, formula feed and nice nurses. Their cards describe the picture that they've painted in their minds about their labor and delivery.

When they're finished and proudly gazing at their cards, they're asked to flip the cards over so they can't see what's on them, shuffle them and pick five from the ten. At this point they're told that these five work out and the other five do not. Then they're asked, "Do you feel prepared if five out of ten happen rather than ten out of ten?"

I think this is a very profound exercise, and not just for labor and delivery. We should expand the exercise to the "life shuffle." When we develop expectations in our minds that have our entire self-worth riding on their realization, we set ourselves up for shame. Using the life shuffle to acknowledge our vulnerabilities and fears is a powerful way to reality-check some of these expectations.

The Magnification Principle

The life shuffle can help us better understand how much emotion we've attached to specific expectations. But if we're going to address expectations and the fear of vulnerability, we have to talk about how most women are socialized to believe that certain life events are lifesavers. No matter how bad things are, if we find a boyfriend things will be better. If we get married, they'll be even better. If we have children, they'll be so much better we won't be able to stand it.

Through the research process I have come to believe that whatever problems you take into a life event will become instantly magnified the moment the hoopla surrounding that life event comes to a close. If you're single and struggling with identity issues, finding a partner will magnify your issues. Again, the magnification may not show up until the shine of "new love" is over, but it will show up.

Whatever problems you and your partner take into a marriage get magnified. The same thing applies to having children. Not only are the issues staying, they're going to get more complicated and complex. If your parents' approval is very important to you, having a child will not change that. You'll just have many more items to submit for approval.

I interviewed a woman in her late fifties who told me that she married her physically abusive boyfriend despite warnings from her friends and family. At the time she believed his promises to work on his anger once they got married. After the birth of her first son, her husband became more violent. She felt totally isolated. She said, "I didn't listen to anyone. I really believed getting married or having kids would change him. It was so bad, but there was no way I could go to my parents or friends. They warned me.

I stayed until he broke my nose and my arm. I couldn't hide that from my family."

Change can happen and there's always the potential for growth; however, a life event will not provide the change or growth we're seeking. If we get married, the jealous partner becomes more fearful because the stakes are higher. The mother who expects us to do everything perfectly has even higher expectations because the stakes are higher. Strained sibling relationships become even more strained in the face of family caretaking challenges. In this way, the magnification principle serves as a catalyst for exposing the failed expectations tied to a major life event. When we have our self-worth riding on the realization of something that we can't control, we put our self-worth in jeopardy. When we say, "This relationship will get better, we just need to get married," and things get worse after you get married, that can become a tremendous source of shame.

Again, if we are going to recognize and accept what makes us human, including our imperfections and less-than-extraordinary lives, we must embrace our fears and vulnerabilities. Understanding our fear is part of the shame resilience process. It's also an important piece in building the kind of relationships that we need to have full and connected lives.

EIGHT

Practicing Compassion in
a Culture of Blame

This is YOUR fault! This is all MY fault! You're to blame. I'm to blame. We are a culture obsessed with finding fault and assigning blame. Holding ourselves or others accountable is a good thing, but blame and accountability are very different. I think the difference between accountability and blame is very similar to the relationship between guilt and shame. Like guilt, accountability is most often motivated by the desire to repair and renew—it is holding someone responsible for his actions and the consequences of his actions.

On the other hand, we often use blame to discharge overwhelming feelings of fear and shame: "This is painful—who can I blame? I'll blame you! You are bad and this is your fault." Inherent in holding ourselves or others accountable for our behavior is expecting change or resolution. Like shame, blame shuts us down and is not an effective tool for change.

If I experience shame because I lose my patience with my child and I blame myself for being a bad mother, I'm more likely to get pulled even further into my shame. If, on the other hand, I lose my patience with my child, experience shame, then hold myself accountable for my behavior, I'm more likely to apologize to my child and figure out how to move through the shame so I can be the parent I want to be.

The same ideas apply to blaming others. Maggie, a mother in her twenties, told me that one of her worst shame experiences happened when her six-year-old son fell off their trampoline and broke his wrist. When her best friend, Dana, arrived at the emergency room, Maggie fell apart and started crying. She told Dana, "I feel like such a horrible mother! I can't believe Matthew broke his little wrist. I should have been watching him more closely." Dana replied, "No. You should have bought that fence I told you about. I told you something like this would happen." Maggie sank deeper into shame. Dana didn't feel the need to practice compassion with Maggie because she blamed Maggie for her son's injury.

The blame I'm talking about in Maggie and Dana's story is very overt, but this is not always the case. Often, blame is subtle and insidious—we don't even know that we're doing it or why we're doing it. For example, if we're driving down the street and get a flat tire, we wind up berating ourselves because we're fat and ugly. We convince ourselves that flat tires don't happen to thin, beautiful women—just bad people like us. Or, we bounce a check and all of a sudden, rather than thinking, "I need to watch that account a little closer," we're thinking, "I'm stupid. This happened because I never finished college."

The culture of blame permeates our lives. We are constantly blaming and shaming ourselves and others. In earlier chapters we talked about separating and insulating. Both of these are the byproducts of a blaming culture. In this chapter, we'll explore four more concepts related to blame: anger; invisibility; stereotypes and labeling; and exclusion. I'll also discuss how women use the four elements of shame resilience to move from blame to compassion.

Anger

The emotion that underlies our obsession with blaming and finding fault is anger. In our shame-and-blame culture, visible anger is everywhere. Political talk shows have become screaming matches. A short drive to the grocery store becomes an obstacle course of raging, finger-flipping drivers. Angry public outbursts directed at strangers and customer service people are becoming more commonplace.

Anger can be motivated by many different experiences and feelings—shame, humiliation, stress, anxiety, fear and grief are several of the most common triggers. The relationship between shame and anger is about using blame and anger to protect us from the pain caused by shame.

Shame researchers June Tangney and Ronda Dearing explain that one strategy for protecting ourselves during a shaming experience is to "turn the tables" and shift blame outward. In their research, they found that when we blame others we often experience *self-righteous anger*. Because anger is an emotion of potency and authority, being angry can help us regain a sense of control. Regaining control is important because shame leaves us feeling worthless, paralyzed and ineffective. The shame/blame/anger response described by Tangney and Dearing is very similar to *moving against*—the strategy of disconnection we talked about in Chapter 3. Moving against is the strategy of trying to gain power over others, being aggressive and using shame to fight shame.

I interviewed many women who talked about using anger and blame to cope with their overwhelming feelings of shame. What I heard from these women was a profound sense of regret and sadness about their misuse of anger. Turning to rage and anger as a solution for shame only increases our sense of feeling flawed and unworthy of connection.

Tangney and Dearing write, "It almost goes without saying that such shame-based anger can pose serious problems for our interpersonal relationships. The recipients of shame-motivated anger are apt to experience such anger as erupting 'out of the blue.' Feeling that it makes little rational sense, the hapless observing other is often left wondering, 'Where did *that* come from?'" Tangney and Dearing go on to say, "Thus, although defensive anger may represent a short-term gain in lessening the pain of shame in the moment, on balance this sort of shame-blame sequence is likely to be destructive for interpersonal relationships—both in the moment and in the long run. Defensive shame-based blame and anger may subsequently lead either to withdrawal (by either party or both parties) or to escalating antagonism, blame and counterblame. In either case, the end result is likely to be a rift in the interpersonal relationship."

Anger is not a "bad" emotion. In fact, feeling anger and appropriately expressing anger are vital to relationship building. Lashing out at others when we are in shame is not about "feeling anger." When we are doing this, we feel shame and mask it with anger. Furthermore, shame-motivated anger and blame are rarely expressed in a constructive way. Shame floods us with emotion and pain and the shame/blame/anger instinct is to pour it all over someone else. If one of our primary shame screens is anger and blame, it is essential that we understand and acknowledge this coping strategy. Next, we need to find out how, when we recognize that we are in shame, to calm down and stay mindful.

Many of the women I spoke with talked about the value of deep breathing. I know that staying quiet and taking deep breaths helps me get back on my emotional feet when I feel shame. Some women talked about excusing themselves from situations and literally walking away. We all need to find how to get the "time out" we need to feel our way through the shame so we make conscious decisions about our reactions and responses. In my research and in my personal life, I've found this takes a lot of practice. It also takes the courage to go back and make amends when our anger/blame responses get the best of us.

Invisibility

Using anger and blame as protection from shame makes sense when you think about shame as "being exposed." For many of us, shame is about exposure or the fear of exposure. This is why we work so hard to hide the flawed parts of ourselves that leave us open to being ridiculed or judged. Our fear of being put down keeps us from speaking out. Our need to look or act perfect keeps us at home, under the covers.

But, in addition to feeling shame about what we see in ourselves or what others see, we can also feel shame about what we don't see. This other side of shame is sometimes more difficult to identify and name—it's the shame of invisibility.

For several years I taught a graduate social-work course on women's issues. During each semester, I would dedicate one class to "magazine day." Students would bring copies of their favorite fashion magazines to class—we'd always end up with at least 150 diverse magazines spread across the floor. I'd give the students scissors, glue and construction paper. Their first assignment was to spend one hour flipping through the magazines and cutting out images to make a collage of their ideal looks—the clothes, jewelry, hair, makeup, arms, legs, feet, shoes, etc., that inspired them.

By the end of that first hour of class, each student would have a completed collage—many of them very detailed. One of the most significant consciousness-raising issues that emerged from this exercise is how quickly we cut women up to piece together our ideal images. We want her eyes, her nose, these lips, this hair but in this color. Her arms are too skinny but I like her thighs. We basically dismember women to carve out perfection.

Their next assignment was to find and cut out images from the magazines that actually looked like them—pictures that closely represented the way they really look, their actual body size and shape (arms, legs, butts), what they were wearing that day, their hair, etc. After about fifteen minutes, students often became frustrated and stopped searching. When they held up these collages, some had a pair of shoes or a similar hairstyle, but that was it. I asked the class one simple question in relation to this exercise: "Where are you? You pay for this magazine. You love it. Where are you?"

The answer is simple, yet potentially shaming. We're not there, because we don't matter in that culture. And the further you get away from the ideal (young, beautiful, white, fine features, sexual, thin and looking childlike/wealthy/seductive/needing to be rescued/confused/in danger) the less you matter.

The last step in the magazine exercise is answering the question "How does being invisible make you feel?" The vast majority of the women told me that they immediately felt self-blame: *I'm invisible because I'm not good enough* or *I'm invisible because I don't matter*. It was not until we started talking about the critical awareness questions that women realized that blaming themselves was shaming and destructive.

Invisibility is about disconnection and powerlessness. When we don't see ourselves reflected back in our culture, we feel reduced to something so small and insignificant that we're easily erased from the world of important things. Both the process of being reduced and the final product of that process—invisibility—can be incredibly shaming.

In the interviews that focused on aging, trauma issues and stereotyping, there was a strong connection to this issue of invisibility. This was also true for participants who spoke about identity issues like race and sexual orientation. In sharing their experiences and insights with me, the research participants helped me discover the primary mechanism used to reduce and erase us: stereotypes.

Stereotypes and Labels

Even though we all use stereotypes every day, I think starting with a definition is helpful. Here's the clearest one I have found: "A stereotype is an overgeneralized and rigid definition of group characteristics that is assigned to people based on their membership in a group." Sometimes we feel OK about using stereotypes, because we're not using them to be malicious or enforce prejudice; we're just using them to give someone a quick picture:

- She won't do it. She's really granola.
- I'm not sure what she'll think. She's pretty Red State.
- Don't ask her. She's the total soccer mom.

The ones I catch myself using most often are shoe-related: She wears clogs, she's more "flip-flops" than "loafers."

One the face (or foot) of it, these seem pretty harmless. But it's a quick trip from benign to shaming. Take a look at these statements from the interviews:

- "She's Chinese or something—you know, she's smart."
- "She's Indian. They're super rude like that."
- "She's so closed-minded—I can't stand old people."
- "I think she's like that because she was raped a couple of years ago."
- "It won't hurt her feelings—she's the real sweet grandma type."
- "I don't think she's mad, she's just got that whole angry black thing going on."
- "Her boyfriend is from Pakistan—she's probably not allowed to go out."

These are not harmless—they are hurtful and shaming. And, while we might wince when we read them, most of us do this type of stereotyping on a regular basis. Stereotyping gives us a way to file people into predetermined categories that we understand and that make sense to us. It also gives us permission to blame people for their struggles so we are excused from our responsibility to practice compassion—"I don't need to sit with you in your pain—you brought it on yourself."

Positive or negative, stereotypes hurt people—individually

and collectively. According to researchers, positive stereotypes produce sanitized and idealized images, while negative stereotypes produce demeaning and ridiculing portraits. Either way—we've reduced you to something we can fit in our mental drawer.

Here's what Michelle Hunt, an organizational development and diversity expert, writes about stereotyping: "I don't want to be categorized. I can't afford it. I have spent my whole life building up who I am with all my multidimensions and complexities, and I get offended when I'm put into a category as (for example) a feminist or an African-American. It's saying that I walk, talk and think like one whole group of people. That's the danger of some of the ways in which diversity is addressed today. The discussion threatens to increase categorization, not diminish it. At the same time, my uniqueness—which includes being a woman and an African-American, and everything else I am—is what I want to have valued. I need to be allowed to bring my uniqueness to the table."

When women spoke about being stereotyped and feeling invisible, I heard two different issues emerge. I call the first one "whispered-labels." I named it this because that's how the participants described them—quiet whisperings behind their backs; pieces of their lives used to label who or what they are. For example: *She's just a mom. She's a cancer survivor. She was abused growing up. She's bipolar. She's a recovering alcoholic. Her husband committed suicide. She's old and senile. She's a feminist. Her husband beats her. She lives in a trailer. She's an only child. She's on welfare. She's a lesbian. She's Mexican. She was raped a couple of years ago.*

If you say, "She's an only child," as a point of fact, that's not hurtful. However, if you say, "She's an only child," as a way to explain why someone acts a certain way—"She's really self-centered. You know, she's an only child"—then it becomes a label. Likewise, if you describe someone's ethnicity by saying, "She's Mexican," that's great. If you use it to explain why someone is behaving a certain way or to set up expectations for a person, that's a hurtful stereotype.

Stereotyping and labeling limit our ability to build connection. When we think we know someone because of her membership in a particular group, we build relationships on assumptions. We miss the opportunity to know others and to be known. For many women, labels are about engaging in a "fixed" fight against preconceived social-community expectations and ultimately turning ourselves over to invisibility. Here's how one participant explained her experiences:

- The most difficult thing about people finding out I'm a lesbian is the assumptions they make. People automatically assume they know everything about me. Once they know you're gay, people think they can fill in the blanks for the rest of your life. They assume you've probably been abused by a man at some point in your life; they assume you hate men; they assume you're masculine and like sports; they expect you to act, dress, vote and spend money a certain way. Most people outside the gay and lesbian community don't understand that there is as much diversity in our community as there is in the straight community. You never hear people saying, "Oh, you're straight, say no more—I know everything about you." Sexual orientation doesn't dictate your politics, your religion, your beliefs, your values, what you like and who you are. I don't assume to know you when I find out you're straight. Don't assume to know me when you find out I'm a lesbian.

The second issue related to stereotyping is name-calling, and it is almost always driven by social-community stereotypes. Examples of name-calling include hurtful labels like slut, whore, trash, loudmouth, ballbuster, bitch, crazy, drama queen, neurotic, dyke and pushy broad. When used as put-downs, terms like *gay* or *queer* are equally offensive. Many of these names are premanufactured and ready to apply the second women break from social-community expectations. They are used so frequently that it is easy for us to forget how hurtful they can be. It is also easy to overlook the fact that name-calling is one of the most powerful ways to reinforce a stereotype. Using identities as insults demeans individuals and entire groups of people.

Always the Exception to the Rule

If we're honest with ourselves, I think most of us would admit that we are very susceptible to relying on stereotyping, labeling and name-calling. One mechanism that helps to keep stereotypes alive and strong is "the exception factor." Many of us find ourselves supporting stereotypes for the population at large, yet dismissing the same stereotype when it doesn't fit with our personal experiences. We may make broad generalizations about feminists, but when someone challenges us by saying, "I'm a feminist and I'm not like that," we automatically grant her special immunity. We will say something like "Oh, not you. I'm talking about the other feminists," or "C'mon—you're different."

Here are some examples of how the "exception factor" really works against our efforts to build connection and resilience:

- I'm a thirty-two-year-old mother of two. I'm very involved in the community and I'm vice-president of the neighborhood association. When I was in college I was in a sorority and I drank a lot. I realized after graduation that I had a problem and I went to Alcoholics Anonymous. I'm a recovering alcoholic with eight years' sobriety. People want so badly to believe that all alcoholics are old, smarmy, unscrupulous businessmen that they always tell me what an odd alcoholic I am or they ask me questions like "Are you sure you're an alcoholic?" When I explain that there are a lot of people in recovery that look just like me, they absolutely refuse to believe it. They think that making me the exception is a compliment when it's really shaming and hurtful. It's those kinds of uneducated, narrow-minded people that make talking about addiction so difficult.

• One day I was talking with my best friend about my boyfriend, Matt. Things were starting to get serious and she was asking all about our relationship. My friend asked me if I was going to tell Matt that my father had sexually abused me. I told her that we had kind of talked about it but I would probably tell him everything eventually. She freaked out. She told me, "You better not—it will change things." When I asked her what she meant she warned me that he might not enjoy sex with me anymore or he might think that I will cheat on him or, worse, that he might not want to get married because he'll be scared I'll do it to my kids. I was shocked and totally hurt. I asked her if she thought being abused made me weird, promiscuous or more likely to abuse my children. She said, "I don't think that about you neces-sarily, but probably it might be true of other people who've been abused." She'll never know how much that hurt me or how much it changed my feelings for her.

In schools of social work, we spend a considerable amount of time studying stereotyping and labeling. As I mentioned previously, we don't believe in the concept of pure objectivity, so in order to maintain meaningful, ethical relationships with our clients, we have to explore our beliefs, values and stereotypes. If we don't, we are likely to jump to conclusions about our clients, their problems and our work.

Over the years I've realized how important it is for us to under-stand that we are not immune to applying stereotypes to ourselves and other people who share specific identities. The stereotypes that are among the most difficult to unearth and discuss are the ones that we believe we are allowed to express because they are aimed at our own group. Somehow, we've come to believe that being a woman gives us permission to stereotype and label other women; being a lesbian gives us the right to stereotype and label other les-bians, etc.

About five years ago, I developed an exercise to help social workers identify these "permitted stereotypes." To complete the exercise I ask them to make a list of three identity groups to which they belong. Then I ask them to identify some of the stereotypes and labels associated with each identity group. Last, I ask them to identify stereotypes they use to characterize various members of their identity group.

Our students are predominately female, so most of the students identify "women" as a group that they belong to. When they identify stereotypes associated with women they use labels like gossips, liars, backstabbers, manipulative, hysterical and neurotic. Many of the students are quick to admit to using those terms to describe other women. This always sparks great conversation because I normally respond by saying, "I don't think I am a gossip, a liar or backstabber. I don't think I'm manipulative or neurotic or hysterical. I haven't experienced any of you in these ways. I'm curious, if these are the terms we use to describe women, yet we are not any of these things, who are we? Where are all these gossiping, backstabbing, lying, alliance-making, neurotic, crazy women?"

This is when people say, "Well, we're the exception." They also make the case that if they're in the group, they can use these labels to describe other group members. If I'm overweight, I'm allowed to call you a fat-ass. If we share a racial or cultural identity, I'm allowed to use terms that people outside of this group can't use. I think giving ourselves permission to stereotype and label our own group members becomes a slippery shame slope. We often fail to realize that we abandon ourselves and other group members when we turn against our own groups.

Aging

During a recent workshop, I asked if anyone wanted to share his or her experience of completing the shame trigger exercise. A woman raised her hand and said, "I looked at these triggers and perceptions and realized that it's not getting older that hurts—it's the fact that I actually believe all the myths about myself, my abilities and my body. I don't think my body has betrayed me—my stereotypes are betraying me."

When it comes to aging, participants explained that the power of aging stereotypes is far more painful than the actual aging process. This is partly due to the fact that aging stereotypes pervade every aspect of American life. Marty Kaplan, media analyst and associate dean at the University of Southern California Annenberg School for Communication, states that advertisers and television programmers have no interest in men and women over fifty. He explains, "In fact, some programmers are positively fifty-plus averse. If there are statistics that show you are watched by that demographic, it's like kryptonite to advertisers."

These were Dr. Kaplan's comments during a segment on *CBS Sunday Morning*. The show was doing a story on the coveted eighteen–to–forty-nine demographic—America's most valued marketing and advertising demographic. The segment also highlighted an AARP ad that reads "These days doctors don't pronounce you dead, marketers do."

Let's look at some of the negative aging stereotypes and corresponding traits found by researchers:

- Despondent—afraid, depressed, hopeless, lonely, neglected
- Recluse—naïve, quiet, timid
- Shrew/Curmudgeon—bitter, complaining, demanding, inflexible, prejudiced, nosy, stubborn
- Mildly impaired—dependent, fragile, slow-moving, tired
- Severely impaired—feeble, inarticulate, incoherent, senile
- Vulnerable—afraid, bored, emotionless, hypochondriacal, miserly, wary, victimized

Now let's look at four of the positive stereotypes that emerged from the same research:

- Golden Ager—active, alert, capable, lively, sociable, healthy
- Perfect Grandparent—fun-loving, grateful, happy, loving, wise
- Small-Town Neighbor—frugal, old-fashioned, tough
- John Wayne Conservative—emotional, nostalgic, patriotic, religious

As we look at these, it's hard to deny the way they might ring true for some of the people we know. That's what makes stereotypes so dangerous. The stereotype fits so closely that we give ourselves permission to dismiss anything that deviates from that image. When we see the woman across the street as "the perfect grandmother," we are less likely to notice her bruises or other signs that she's being battered; moreover, she might become so committed to living up to that expectation that she would never tell us. When we need our "John Wayne" father to live up to his tough-guy image, he may be too ashamed to share his fears or vulnerabilities with us. Or, as seen in this example from the interviews, we might buy into the stereotype that our Golden Ager grandmother is so happy that she doesn't mind being reduced to a source of entertainment:

- My children and my grandchildren will say things to me like "Dance for us, Grandma, dance!" Not because I used to be a wonderful dancer, but because they watch me and they laugh at me. Sometimes if I'm dancing around they'll say, "Go, Grandma, go!" It's hurtful. I feel shame because they enjoy laughing at me. They see me as an old person who is entertaining. I'm their grandmother, not a real woman with feelings—not a talented, interesting person. I'm ashamed that it bothers me so much. I know they love me very much; it's just that they can be very insensitive at times.

Stereotyping is a form of blaming and reducing—two of the primary ingredients for creating shame. If we want to move from blame to connection and compassion, we must work to become mindful of how, when and why we stereotype.

Surviving Trauma

As we learned in the previous chapter, many of the messages that drive shame are about perfection, but when it comes to surviving trauma, the stereotypes are based on *imperfection*, that stigma of being damaged or permanently wounded, and *blame*, or somehow being responsible for your trauma.

When I spoke with women about surviving and healing from trauma, I learned that social-community expectations and stereotypes around trauma force women to deal with two separate issues: surviving the event itself and surviving the shame we heap upon them when we use stereotypes to question their experiences and define who they are as survivors. When I say, "questioning their experiences," this can range from using stereotypes about women to asking questions like "Was it really that bad?" or "What were you doing with him?" Rather than listening and trying to understand, we invalidate and diminish their experiences.

In addition to questioning, stereotypes are used to frame someone's identity after the trauma. Most of us have internalized very strong ideas about how people can or *cannot* survive traumas. I recently gave a lecture at a women's professional organization. During the book signing that followed, a woman brought four books to the table.

As tears rolled down her face, she said, "One book is for me, the others are for my sister and her two daughters. My niece was raped at college several months ago." She took a deep breath and said, "She was a beautiful, smart girl. She had her whole life in front of her."

At first, it caught me off-guard and I thought, "Oh my God! She was killed." Then I realized I was signing a book for her. Her aunt meant that she was beautiful and smart before she was raped. I seriously doubt that this woman, standing in front of me crying in public about her niece, realized what she was saying or how it could shame her niece.

We are all vulnerable to making these kinds of assumptions or judgments. How many times have we heard or thought, "She'll never be the same," or "She's screwed up forever now"? We can also use the knowledge of someone's trauma to explain his or her behavior. Alicia's story is an excellent example.

Alicia and Tom had been dating for almost two years when I interviewed her. She described their relationship as "coming to a sad end." When I asked why, she said that several months earlier she had confided in Tom that she had been physically abused by her mother and stepfather growing up and that was why her grandmother had raised her. She said that Tom was very compassionate and supportive, but now, every time she got angry or upset, Tom attributed it to the fact that she had been "an abused child."

Alicia explained that, in Tom's eyes, this was her new identity and the basis for all of her behavior. She said, "He even went back to when we first started dating and said things like 'Oh it makes so much sense now—that's why you hated that movie.'" Just a couple of days before the interview, Alicia said she came home from work and started crying. Her boss had given her a really hard time in front of one of her colleagues. Tom's response was "You have such a hard time dealing with criticism at work because you were abused by your parents." Alicia explained to Tom that it was normal not to want to be criticized in front of her peers and asked him, "Can't I be like everyone else?" Tom didn't get it and she asked him to move out. Alicia said, "I was abused growing up. It was shameful and I couldn't do anything about it because I was a kid. I won't continue to be defined that way in my thirties. I have the right to be someone besides that kid."

When women talk about the shame of being sexually abused or raped, they associate most of the shame with the pain of being defined by their trauma. The events are, of course, horrific and can have a lasting effect. But the social-community reaction to their experience—and the attendant loss of identity and the right to "be normal"—is just as painful, and often produces the more enduring shame.

- If she has a father who could do that do her, what does that mean about her?
- She'll never be the same—she's damaged.
- She'll never be whole after that.
- I don't see how she'll ever be a good_____(fill in the blank: mother, partner, vice president).

There are times when our feelings, thoughts and actions relate directly to our past or current struggles. But there are certainly times when they don't. The problem arises because, at some point, most of us begin to believe the expectations about who we're supposed to be, what we're supposed to look like, what we're supposed to do, how much we're supposed to be and how *little* we're supposed to be.

We also develop a fear of rejecting those expectations. We constantly see evidence that if we do reject these expectations, we will experience very painful disconnections and rejection. So we internalize these expectations and they become an emotional prison. Shame stands guard.

Exclusion

I think it is impossible to talk to women about shame and blame without hearing stories about the pain of not fitting in or of feeling excluded. Throughout the interviews, women talked about "gossiping," "excluding" and "backstabbing" as tremendous sources of shame:

- I hate working with other women. They're so petty and jealous. They take things so personally and all they do is talk bad about each other.

- On the outside I'm just like everyone else in our neighborhood. On the inside, I'm struggling to keep a marriage together that's falling apart right in front of my very eyes. My kids have problems. Shame is what happens deep on the inside, and the worse it is on the inside, the harder you have to work to make it look good on the outside. Sometimes I wish we could just show our insides so it wouldn't be so hard. But trust me, I'd never do that because I know how women talk about each other—they're brutal.

- Shame is when I grab my child by the top of the arm and my teeth are clenched and pure rage is coming out of my eyes and I'm getting ready to just lay into him and I look up and another mother is watching me. That's not the kind of mother I want to be. Sometimes I just feel so pushed to the edge, I can't help it. I feel so ashamed when other mothers catch me in those moments because I want to scream and yell to them, "This is really not who I am. I'm really a good mother; I'm not like this all the time." You know they tell everyone you're a nut case—what else do they have to talk about?

- I went to a party a couple of months ago and a woman came up to me and asked me what I did for a living, and I told her I stay home with my three kids. Immediately she got this kind of disappointed look on her face like "Oh, you poor thing," and said, "Oh, well, good for you," and walked away. About twenty minutes later I saw her talking to another woman and I thought to myself, "I'm not interesting anymore; nothing matters about my life anymore that doesn't have to do with my kids." I wanted to start screaming at the top of my lungs in the middle of this party, "I used to be an engineer, I used to be someone, I swear, I promise, I used to be important, like you!"

- At work, the guys dangle this carrot in front of the women. You can hang out with them if you sell enough . . . if you work more . . . if you give up your family. On one hand, I desperately want to be in the boys' club. They have more fun, get better clients, make more money and have more freedom. On the other hand, I hate them. I don't want to be like them or do what they do; I just want to enjoy the perks. And, when it comes to the women in that group—they are even more disgusting than the men. They'll really treat you like shit.

• Before I got promoted I had lots of friends in my department. We even hung out after work and on the weekends. When I got promoted I became "the bitch that fucked her way to the top." I've never dated or slept with someone from work and they know that. I don't know about men, but when they promote women, they need to move them to another department.

• I told one of the women in my son's play group that we spank with the belt. Within one week, every single person in that group asked me about it. They were shocked and disgusted. A couple of them told me it was child abuse. I was completely taken by surprise. They acted like I was a monster. They even felt sorry for my kids. Not one of them invited me back to their house for play group. They didn't even invite my son to birthday parties.

While some people propose that parts of "excluding" behavior are genetically predetermined, I don't believe that is true. I don't believe women have a natural tendency to be mean, manipulative gossips. Nor do I believe that all women are naturally kind, nurturing caregivers. I don't think either one of these stereotypes fits, and I don't think subscribing to sweeping generalizations helps us to understand or change some of the behaviors that we would indeed like to change.

As I read over the interviews and tried to get a handle on this issue of gossiping and exclusion, I started to see parallels between these behaviors and my daughter's experiences in elementary school. Not because women are infantile and immature in their behaviors, but because observing young children can teach us a lot about ourselves. Most young children are truly authentic—what you see is definitely what you get. They have yet to learn how to hide, filter and manipulate their experiences to fit what others are expecting. Their motivations are out in the open and studying these motivations can sometimes help us better understand our own motivations—those that are hidden under layers of pretending and protection.

The major connection I see is between gossiping and bullying—two painful forms of exclusion. In many bullying situations, kids taunt kids, not out of hatred or meanness, but out of the need to belong. Of course, there are children who, for varying reasons, have serious problems and are "lone bullies," but most bullying is done by groups of kids. When you talk to the individual child, he or she often admits to participating in the bullying only as a way to maintain a connection and sense of belonging. This is also true of gang mentality; hurting or excluding others is often a way members demonstrate their loyalty and increase group acceptance.

I think these same dynamics often apply to us as adults when we are in group situations. It's hard to admit, but picking someone apart or judging her is frequently used as a tool to connect and gain acceptance with other women. Think about how easy it is to forge an instant connection by talking about someone or saying something cutting about a mutual acquaintance. It's almost a rite of passage among new friends—if you can't think of something to say, talk bad about someone.

We might go along with the water-cooler gossip, not because we believe it, but because it's how we connect with the co-workers who are standing there with us. We huddle close together and share secret information. We form a cohesive jury and pass judgment together. And when we walk away from the cooler, we have a little bounce in our step as we think, "These are my friends. They like me and I like them."

Of course, as the day wears on, we might get that sinking feeling when we wonder, "Do they talk like that about me?" When the woman who we earlier tried and convicted walks over and says something friendly, or just asks a question about the project we're working on, we wonder if she knows. We try to imagine how she'd feel if she had any clue about what we had said. We feel bad for a second, then we push that feeling away.

But for most of us, that bad feeling creeps back up. We get angry with ourselves. "Why did I do that? I hate it when I gossip like that." Now the bounce in our step is gone and we're on shaky ground. We've lost touch with our courage and compassion. We've also forged a slippery bond with our co-workers. We know what happens at the water cooler. We feel like we have two choices: join them in the gossip or risk being the next target.

I'm often asked if gossiping is really a serious form of exclusion—is it a shame issue or just something that makes us feel mildly guilty? I think there are several answers to this question. First, we have to clarify—there's the issue of doing the gossiping and then there's the issue of being the target of gossip. I can't tell you if gossiping about people is shaming. That's a very personal issue. For many of the women I interviewed, gossiping was described as shaming because it was often motivated by their need to belong. It also moved them away from being compassionate people. For others, it was more of a guilt issue. These women described it as more of a habit that made them feel bad. I can feel shame or guilt about gossiping. It depends on why I'm doing it, what I'm saying and how I'm feeling.

Being the target of gossip, however, is usually very shaming and extremely painful. What people say behind our backs can mirror our list of unwanted identities. It's our greatest fear—we walk out of the room and people start using our most hated identities to describe us. This happened to one of the research participants—let's look at her story.

I met Lori through her best friend, Melanie. Melanie participated in an early round of interviews, then again last year. During my second interview with Melanie, she suggested that I call Lori, who, as she explained, had experienced "one of the worst shaming events you could imagine." Lori and I ended up connecting over the phone.

Lori and Melanie had been friends since high school. Now in their thirties, they live in different states but manage to stay connected through e-mail and occasional visits. Lori lives in a large suburban neighborhood and has many friends. She works part-time for her husband's company and is very involved in neighborhood activities. Melanie described her as the kind of person who knows all the neighbors and everyone at her kids' schools. Both Lori and Melanie pointed out how Lori is very committed to being a good mother and parent.

Every month, Lori and eight other families in her neighborhood take turns hosting a family potluck dinner. Lori was at one of these potluck dinners with her family when this "hard to imagine" shame story unfolded.

Lori explained that she was in the kitchen with five or six other mothers; the men were outside and the kids were playing in the den and the bedrooms. Lori said, "My youngest daughter came in and told me that her sister, Callie, didn't eat any of her pizza but was eating her second cupcake. I got frustrated and followed my daughter out of the kitchen to find Callie. I found her, talked to her about skipping dinner and was heading back into the kitchen when I stopped to scoop up a bunch of cupcake crumbs on the floor, right outside the kitchen."

Lori continued describing the scene. "As I'm cleaning up the floor, I hear my friends whispering. One said, 'She's so hard on those girls.'"

Another agreed, "Yeah. She gets so mad when they don't eat, but look at her. She's skin and bones. What does she expect?"

Another friend said, "I know. She's such a perfectionist. Do you think she's anorexic?"

Lori explained that it didn't even cross her mind that they could have been talking about her. But when she walked into the kitchen, it became clear right away, just from the looks on their faces, that Lori was the subject of these comments.

Lori told me, "I just stood there with my mouth open. I didn't know if I should scream and run out of the house or just start crying." She said finally one of the women said, "I'm so sorry, Lori; we were just talking." Another jumped in and said, "Really. We're sorry. We just get worried a little. You know we love you to death."

Lori said she just looked at them and said, "It's OK. I need to go." Lori gathered up her kids and her husband and went straight home.

Lori didn't leave the house all weekend. Sheila, one of women in that kitchen, left two messages asking Lori to call her. Lori didn't return the calls. On Monday morning, she had her husband drop the kids off at school. Early Monday afternoon, three of the women came to her house. She reluctantly opened the door but didn't invite them into the house. They stood on her porch and apologized. Lori said, "They were sorry that I overheard them and that it hurt my feelings, but they didn't apologize for what they said."

About two weeks later, Lori finally told Melanie what had happened. Lori said, "It was even shaming to tell her about it. It's degrading for Melanie to know my friends think that of me." Lori told her about the three women coming to apologize and that one woman had left five messages on her answering machine.

Melanie listened and offered her support. Melanie also suggested that Lori return Sheila's calls. A couple of days later, Sheila called again and Lori, checking the caller ID, decided to answer.

Sheila was profoundly sorry. She apologized for not speaking up and putting the gossiping to an end. She told Lori, "We are your friends. We should either tell you that we're worried about your health or we shouldn't say anything at all. We definitely shouldn't talk behind your back. I'm so sorry I didn't say anything when they were doing it or when you walked in."

Lori and Sheila talked for an hour. Lori said, "I was crying. I just kept asking her how I could face everyone and act normal again." Lori also asked Sheila why she hadn't come with the group of women or left an apology on the answering machine. Sheila explained that she needed to do this by herself. She told Lori, "Trying to fit in with this group is what got me into this nightmare in the first place." Sheila also told Lori, "I didn't say anything on the recorder because I didn't know if you had told your husband or not. I'd probably be too embarrassed to tell anyone."

Both of these answers made Lori feel better. Sheila was being honest. It stung a bit when she told Lori why she hadn't apologized on the answering machine, but it also made Lori believe that Sheila understood how shaming this experience was for her.

Sheila and Lori decided that they would go together to pick up the kids and that Sheila would help Lori ease back into the group. Sheila also volunteered to call a meeting of the friends if Lori wanted to discuss it. Lori didn't want to do that.

Lori told me, "Things are about as back to normal as I think they can be. I don't know if it will ever be the same. Sheila and I are much closer, but the group seems to be split a little more. I, for sure, will not be the same. That was a moment of shattering pain for me. I never knew gossiping and talking about people could be so damaging."

If there is any question about how hurtful or shaming gossiping can be, this story should provide a good answer. Most of us can't bear to consider what might be said about us by a gossiping group of neighbors.

Resilience and Exclusion

The greatest challenge for many of us is finding a way out of the excluding and gossiping when it's actually happening. If we are with friends or colleagues who start talking bad about or ganging up on someone, how do we decline to participate? Again, this is a difficult situation because our connection is in danger.

For a couple of years I experimented with various techniques for staying connected to women without relying on exclusion and competition as the catalysts for connection. I found that some techniques are very effective and others leave you very vulnerable to attack. Often, we use the default technique of moving the target from one person to another. Unfortunately, this technique still leaves someone with a bull's-eye on her back.

For example, suppose someone says, "She's such a bitch. I can't believe she got promoted. Who do you think she slept with to get that?" We might try to shame the shamer: *"I can't believe you are buying into that idea that women who succeed are bitches that sleep their way to the top! That is such a demeaning stereotype. You are just feeding it and making us all look bad!"*

When I first came into my critical awareness, I felt the need to publicly hold people accountable for their shaming. I soon realized that it's not a good idea to back people into a corner. Even making a valid point doesn't warrant using shame or intentionally putting someone on the spot in front of other people.

Next I tried the "teach/preach" approach. Although it's a little less drastic than shaming, it doesn't work well either. In this example we might respond to the same comment by saying, *"I'm not going to talk badly about her. It hurts all women. We need to support one another."* But when we teach/preach, we are likely to find the target stuck to our backsides as we swagger away from the group.

I've come to the point in my life where I often express my feelings about statements I perceive as hurtful and/or hateful. But, for me, that's best accomplished by talking with someone one-on-one and focusing on how a comment or discussion made me feel. When I'm in the gang-think situation, I've found two techniques that work without relying on "moving the target." Reflecting and/or redirecting are very effective ways to "not participate" and provoke thought.

Reflecting is a way to infuse a conversation with a probing question or statement. Redirecting is moving the conversation away from blaming and toward empathy.

> "She's such a bitch. I can't believe she got promoted. Who do you think she slept with to get that?"
> *Reflect: "I don't really know her."*
> This poses the question: How much do we know about someone? Many times it forces people to realize that they don't know much about the person they're targeting or, at the very least, it points out that their style of bad-mouthing doesn't require fact.

> "Can you believe she slapped that toy right out of her daughter's hand?"
> *Reflect:"I didn't see the whole thing—I don't really know what happened."*
> This poses the question: How much do we know about a situation? Given a choice, most of us would think it unfair to have our entire parenting approach defined by one or two bad moments.

> "She's so mean. I'm not surprised that he's leaving her."
> *Reflect and Redirect: "I really don't know a lot about him or their marriage. I really like her. I wonder if there is something we can do for her?"*
> This says we don't know what's going on and we should lend support rather than gossip.

"Susie is such a raving lunatic. Have you ever worked with her?"

Reflect: "Yeah, a couple of times. I don't really experience her that way."

This says you are entitled to your opinion, but I don't agree.

"I heard Bonnie is still trying to get pregnant. She's obsessed—it's ridiculous."

Reflect and Redirect: "I can't imagine what that's like. It sounds like she's really struggling."

This also says we should be trying to help, not judge.

In this next section we'll examine some of the broader strategies for building compassion in a culture of shame.

Resilience and Blame

The participants with high levels of shame resilience around blame relied heavily on their connection networks to understand and combat invisibility and stereotyping. While we might be erased, reduced or rejected based on a given group we belong to, those groups can also be tremendous sources of strength and support. Women consistently described the power of connection-network members who shared identity characteristics like race, ethnicity, physical ability, work status, religion, sexual orientation, class, appearance, age, gender or other life experiences.

Most of us have witnessed the power of groups who come together to work for increased visibility and their basic human rights. We can see that in organized senior-citizen groups, racial identity groups, professional groups, women's groups and groups that have worked to fight against the stigma of physical and mental illness, addiction and trauma. Most of us have also experienced the support of belonging to informal identity groups, whether community, civic or parenting. Building connection with identity groups is a great way to turn the tables on invisibility and stereotypes.

On the personal level, there are a couple of ways we can become more mindful about invisibility, stereotyping and labeling. The first strategy involves completing the exercise I hand out to my students. It's important that we recognize how we view our own identities and that we acknowledge our susceptibility to stereotyping members of our own group. Next, we can identify the stereotypes to which we are sometimes subjected and examine them in light of a problem-posing dialogue developed by researcher and educator Mary Bricker-Jenkins. Dr. Bricker-Jenkins suggests we ask ourselves:

1. Who am I?
2. Who says?
3. Who benefits from these labels?
4. If these labels don't benefit me, what must change and how?

The participants with high levels of shame resilience really emphasized the importance of change. Invisibility is insidious and stereotyping is a default way of thinking. If we don't recognize or admit our parts in these processes, then we can't change them.

One woman who spoke about aging said, "I'd rather spend my time, energy and money working to redefine what it means to be old. Spending your resources trying to stay young is a tiresome and impossible battle. At least when you're fighting against ageism, you can make a difference for more than just yourself."

I'll close this chapter by sharing some of Annie's writings. Annie is of one of the research participants. She was raped in her apartment during her junior year in college. As you can see by her answers to the shame resilience exercises, she has found tremendous resilience by reaching out to other young women about date rape on college campuses.

Annie's Exercises

Triggers: I want to be perceived as normal, healthy, the same person I was before the assault and not to blame.

Critical Awareness: No one can turn back time and make it go away, but the people around me can make it better by not whispering behind my back or assuming that I can't ever be happy again. I know it's a lot to ask, because I need them to validate the difficulties but at the same time not define me by them.

Connection Network: My counselor, my support group, talking to college girls about sexual assault, my mom and dad, my sister and brother, my boyfriend and my best friend.

Unwanted Identities/Triggers: I do not want to be perceived as damaged, never be the same, screwed up mentally, always on the verge of going crazy.

Critical Awareness: I'm not denying that I'm different in some ways—I am and that's normal. I had a lot taken away and I'm working on that. I just don't want my friends to take even more away by changing their relationships with me or treating me different. If you make everything I do or say about the assault, then you are taking more away from me.

Shame Web: My friends, the stereotypes about assault survivors, my mother's friends, my aunt and cousins.

NINE

Practicing Connection in
a Culture of Disconnection

I sometimes explain my shame research as a study on the *power of connection* and the *dangers of disconnection*. Disconnection is both the source and consequence of shame, fear and blame. Insulating, judging others, blaming, raging, stereotyping, labeling—these are all forms of disconnection. But there is another form of disconnection, one that is often more painful and confusing than all of these other forms: It is the feeling of being disconnected from ourselves. We are often so influenced by what other people think and so overwhelmed with trying to be who other people need us to be, that we actually lose touch with our sense of self. We lose our grounding. We lose our authenticity. The reason this is so painful is because our authenticity is the very foundation from which all meaningful change occurs.

In this chapter we will examine the concept of authenticity and why we must be authentic if we want to practice courage, compassion and connection. We'll also explore how shame resilience relates to addiction, speaking out, spirituality and our need to feel "normal."

Authenticity

What is authenticity? We may not know how to define it, but we certainly know it when we see it. In fact, when we are in the presence of an authentic person, many of us can even feel it in our bones. We gravitate toward people whom we perceive as honest, real and sincere. We love women who radiate warmth and that "down to earth" feeling. We gather around the people who can "tell it like it is" and laugh at themselves in the process.

Authenticity is something we revere in others and strive to maintain in our own lives. We don't feel good about half-truths, disingenuous connection and fearful silence. We all want to have a clear sense of who we are and what we believe and to feel confident enough to share that with others. I've always liked the saying "We want to feel comfortable in our own skin."

Shame often prevents us from presenting our real selves to the people around us—it sabotages our efforts to be authentic. How can we be genuine when we are desperately trying to manage and control how others perceive us? How can we be honest with people about our beliefs and, at the same time, tell them what we think they want to hear? How do we stand up for what we believe in when we are trying to make everyone around us feel comfortable so they won't get angry and put us down?

Social work educators Dean H. Hepworth, Ronald H. Rooney and Jane Lawson define *authenticity* as "the sharing of self by relating in a natural, sincere, spontaneous, open and genuine manner." We *cannot* share ourselves with others when we see ourselves as flawed and unworthy of connection. It's impossible to be "real" when we are ashamed of who we are or what we believe.

Shame begets shame. When we sacrifice authenticity in an effort to manage how we are being perceived by others, we often get caught in a dangerous and debilitating cycle: Shame, or the fear of being shamed, moves us away from our authentic selves. We tell people what they want to hear, or we don't speak out when we should. In turn, we feel shame for being dishonest, misrepresenting our beliefs or not taking an important stand. You can see the cycle in these quotes:

- I sometimes say whatever people need me to say. If I'm with my liberal friends I act liberal. If I'm with my conservative friends, I act conservative. I guess I'm so afraid that I'll say something that upsets someone that I just go with the flow. It makes me feel very shallow and dishonest.

- My faith is a very important part of my life. I want to feel free to talk about my spiritual beliefs just like people talk about their politics or their social beliefs. But I can't. If I even mention the word *church*, people get offended. They look at me like I'm crazy and I'm trying to convert them. I used to have a voice mail message at work that said, "Thanks for calling, have a blessed day." My boss made me erase it because it was "offensive." The people in my office use the "*f*-word" all day, but they try to make me feel like I'm the outcast because I say "blessed."

- As a Japanese-American woman I constantly hear people make sweeping assumptions about Asian women. Some of them portray us as perfect minorities—smart, hardworking and overachieving. Some of the stereotypes are sexual in nature—Asian women are often portrayed as both permissive and submissive. All of these assumptions and stereotypes diminish our humanity. I often want to say something, but I feel too much shame. It's partly because of my culture and partly because I'm a woman. I'd like to speak out more often, but it is very difficult and makes me feel very vulnerable.

- I work with a group of men and women who are absolute bigots. They always say demeaning stuff about minorities. They tell horrible jokes and send around racist e-mail messages. I'd report it to the human resources manager, but he's the worst of the bunch. One day I was in the break room and a small group of these people told a horrible joke about the gay man, Matthew Shepard, who was beaten to death in Laramie, Wyoming. I didn't laugh, but I didn't say anything either. I just looked down. I felt horrible. When I watched *The Laramie Project* on television I cried the entire time. I kept thinking, "Why didn't I say something? Why didn't I tell them how hurtful they were being?" I was really ashamed of myself.

- I watch the news and read the newspaper. I'm very interested in politics and what's going on in the world. I try to think through my opinions and my positions before I talk about them, but invariably, I screw up. I get nervous when someone disagrees with me or challenges my facts. Sometimes I react by shutting down and sometimes, if I really feel backed into a corner, I get louder and more emotional. Either way, I look stupid. I hate it. Why do I have to practice? Why can't I just say what's on my mind?

- Over the past two years I've become trilingual. When I'm at work I use "white language." When I'm at home I speak naturally, like we did growing up. I recently met new friends at church and they shunned me at first because my natural speech was not "black enough." I quickly started speaking a third language so they wouldn't think I was trying to act white. It is one thing to not feel "real" in the white world, but it feels far more dishonest to change who you are to feel accepted by members of your own community.

Below is a list of the messages and expectations that women described in relation to speaking out. If we look at the characteristics of authenticity—natural, sincere, spontaneous, open and genuine—we can start to see how difficult authenticity can be if we try to filter our actions and thoughts through these narrow expectations.

- Don't make people feel uncomfortable, but be honest.
- Don't sound self-righteous, but sound confident.
- Don't upset anyone or hurt anyone's feelings, but say what's on your mind.
- Don't be offensive, but be straightforward.
- Sound informed and educated, but not like a know-it-all.
- Sound committed, but not too reactionary.
- Don't say anything unpopular or controversial, but have the courage to disagree with the crowd.
- Don't seem too passionate, but don't come off as too dispassionate.
- Don't get too emotional, but don't be too detached.
- You don't have to quote facts and figures, but don't be wrong.

One the face of it, they seem ridiculous—they are completely contradictory and totally subjective. Who gets to define *offensive* or *emotional*? What is too passionate and what is too dispassionate?

These "rules" are built around rigid gender roles that leave women with very little room to navigate expectations while maintaining authenticity. If we break one of these rules, we are automatically labeled and stereotyped. If we assert ourselves, we become the pushy, loudmouthed bitch who everyone loves to hate. If we clarify or correct, we become the arrogant know-it-all who no one can stand to be around. If we're honest about something that is taboo or makes other people feel uncomfortable, we're labeled as a weirdo or freak. If two women get into a heated political debate on television, it's a "catfight." Whereas, if two men get into the same debate, it's a lively discussion on important issues. When we start to examine the messages and expectations that fuel our unwanted identities, it's easy to understand how shame can undermine our authenticity. We simply can't speak our truths when we are held hostage by what other people think. In the next section, we'll take a look at the concept of normalcy. Sometimes our need to feel normal or be perceived as normal overrides our commitment to authenticity. This is especially true around the shame triggers that leave us feeling alone and like an outsider.

Shame and Normalcy

Shame makes us feel like we are different—like we are the only ones. During the interview process, I can't tell you how many times I heard women say, "I just want to feel normal." As women, we are absolutely bombarded with media-driven messages about normalcy—especially about sex and physical and mental wellness. A great example of this is a recent *Glamour* magazine cover that read "Are You Normal About Sex? Intimate Details on What Everyone Is Doing." To overcome these feelings of shame about being strange and abnormal, we seek normalcy. Being real, genuine or sincere can feel secondary to fitting in.

During the interviews, I realized that sometimes the quest for normalcy comes down to numbers. How many times per week do my husband and I need to have sex to be normal? How many sexual partners am I allowed to have if I'm twenty-five and single? On a scale from one to ten, how weird is it if my husband likes to do this? How many couples try this? How many women do you know who are willing to do that? How many women my age are on this medication? What are my odds if I get off the hormones? How many women have this diagnosis? How many times have you seen a case like mine? How long will it take for my sex drive to come back? How much weight do I need to lose to avoid a lecture at my next weigh-in at the doctor's office? Somebody, please just give me a number!

When we can't get good information because it's either tainted by marketing spin or the topics are too taboo for public discussion, we become desperate for a measure of normalcy. We want to know what's normal because "being normal" affords us a greater opportunity for acceptance and belonging.

When I spoke to women about sex and health, many participants asked me how their responses compared to the responses from other participants. It was only during discussions about these topics that women asked questions like "What are other women saying?" or "Does this fit with what you're hearing from other people?"

What makes these media-driven expectations so dangerous is their ability to exploit our need to feel normal by showing us images of reality and labeling them "abnormal." Think about all those ads that say, "If you are feeling tired and overwhelmed . . ." or "If you aren't having sex this much . . ." or "If you are too anxious about the safety of your children . . ." or "If your skin looks like this. . . ."

Clearly, some interventions and medications are very useful and appropriate. Many advertisements, however, prey on the vulnerabilities of women by exploiting our need to feel normal. They also exploit our very human need for acceptance and belonging by showing images of so-called "undersexed" or "unhealthy" people alone and sad. Of course, the final shots of the commercial show the once-distraught person, having tried their pill or used their lotion, surrounded by friends and family and full of slow-motion laughter.

The money and marketing behind these advertisements result in more than the overprescribing and overuse of medicines and "remedies." In a market-driven medical environment that values expediency and profit, many women who could benefit from drug therapy are denied services because they lack the resources to cover medical expenses. Additionally, as a result of U.S. insurance companies' stripping mental health coverage from most plans, women who would benefit from a combination of medication and counseling (which research shows is far more effective than medication alone) can only access medication.

I remember carefully watching the pharmaceutical television ads that aired the week after the events of 9/11. About three or four days after the attacks, an entire advertising campaign was launched that targeted women who worried too much about their children. The ads used lines like "You used to be more fun," or "You used to smile more." One minute I'd get really angry and think, "How sinister! There's not a mother in this country who's not worried about her kids right now." The next minute I'd think, "OK, I need those pills. I'm obsessing about safety. I think this is exactly what I need."

After about a week, I was afraid I was going crazy simply because I continually felt crazed about this situation. I finally called a friend who has young kids and is a family therapist. "Here's what I'm doing and here's what I'm thinking. Am I normal?" "Yes, very. You're normal and the other hundred women who have called me are normal. If you're so worried about Ellen that you aren't functioning, we should talk more about it. If you're mostly worried because you think you're crazy because you're so worried, you're normal. Worrying about our children and our safety is a very appropriate reaction right now. These are scary times."

This sentiment illustrates a pattern of vulnerability that I heard over and over during the conversations about health and sex. Here is how I summarize that pattern:

> I can't get to my real feelings about sex, my body, my physical health or my mental and emotional health because there are too many messages and expectations blocking my way. I'm so worried about what, who, and how I'm supposed to be that I can't figure out who I am and who I want to be. If I try to talk about it, I feel shut down because very few people are willing to have honest conversations about sex and health. Eventually, I give up on being authentic and just hope to be perceived as normal.

The deluge of messages and expectations combined with the stigma of talking about sex and health can leave women feeling overwhelmed with shame. When we feel like this, we are more likely to reinforce the messages and expectations, individualize the problems and feel like our inability to meet the expectations is about our own deficiencies or pathologies. When the code of silence prevents us from reaching out to others, we feel alone, we feed shame with secrecy and silence, and end up grasping for our shame screens:

- My husband likes to have sex all the time. I do it because I don't want him to cheat or do it with someone else. Sometimes I wonder if I'm the only person that feels like that, if there's something wrong with me or if other people have husbands that are like that too. The part that's so hard is you really can't talk to anybody about it, so I don't know what you really do.

- When I was in my twenties I loved sex, or at least I think I liked sex. Either way, I slept around a lot. Now that I'm married and I have children it's like a constant battle between me and my husband. I will do anything to avoid having sex. I will fake being sick; I'll pick a fight; I'll do anything. What I really want to do is just go into the bedroom and shut the door and be by myself. The last thing I want to do is have sex. My husband says something's wrong with me. Sometimes I think he's right and sometimes, when I hear other people talking about it, I think I'm OK.

- When I think about sex and shame, the first thing I think about are blow jobs. I don't think there's anything more shameful than that. It's degrading. Of course, now it's become popular. Now, if you say no, you feel like you're the only person not doing it and your boyfriend is the only one in the universe with a girlfriend who does not like it. Sometimes I do it because I feel like I'm supposed to. One time I almost started crying.

- No one knows I've been diagnosed with clinical depression. Not even my partner. She thinks I've been acting weird because

I'm going through menopause. Once you tell someone you have a mental health problem, they blame everything on you being "crazy." You automatically become untrustworthy and unstable. I don't want people to think I'm weak or I can't handle my life.

- I just can't do things like get pap smears and mammograms. I could never get a colonoscopy. I know it's horrible and I know that I need to, but I just can't do it. I always worry about what the nurses will think or what the doctor will think. What if I do something gross or what if they think I'm disgusting? I just can't bring myself to do it. My children ask me if I've gone and I lie and tell them yes. That makes me feel even worse.

- Sex is the most difficult issue in my marriage. We both know it's a problem, but it's the one issue we can't seem to talk about. It's helpful to know that other couples struggle, too, but it doesn't really make it better. I've almost given up on having a good sex life. Sometimes I just wish we could have sex enough so it didn't feel like the pink elephant in the room. I'm so uptight about it. I've lost touch with my physical and emotional feelings.

When we feel all of the painful and overwhelming feelings associated with shame, we are also not very good at assessing where we are or what we want. It presents a very difficult situation for women—how do I get out of shame about sex and health long enough to develop resilience to shame about sex and health? To answer this question, let's look at some of the strategies employed by women who have high levels of shame resilience around sex and health.

Resilience and Normalcy
The women who have developed shame resilience around sex and health issues work on all four elements, but they are particularly

aware of the vulnerabilities created by the secrecy and silence that shroud these issues. Through a variety of strategies that directly relate to each of the four continuums, these women have managed to hear their own voices over the competing and conflicting messages and expectations around them. They have managed to build enough empathy to think clearly, evaluate their own needs and determine what makes them feel connected, powerful and free.

When I first started talking to women about sex and health, I thought the difference between "wanting to be normal" and "not knowing or caring about normal" was about confidence level rather than shame resilience. However, the more I talked to women, the more I realized that the participants with high levels of shame resilience are not inherently more confident. Rather, they are committed to working on each of the four continuums in order to build resilience. Here is how I summarize the pattern that emerged across the interviews:

> *In order to get to my real feelings about sex, my body, my physical health or my mental and emotional health, I have to acknowledge and filter all of the messages and expectations that block my way. When I'm so worried about what I'm supposed to be, who I'm supposed to be and how I'm supposed to be, I can't figure out who I am and who I want to be. I must understand where those messages come from so I can address them and move on. I need to talk about it, and because so few people are willing to have honest conversations about sex and health, I have to build connections with people who I can reach out to. I need to talk about my feelings and my needs so I don't cut myself off from these important parts of my life. I don't know what's normal; I just want to be my authentic self.*

If you pull this pattern apart, you can see how the pieces fit with the continuums:

Recognizing Shame Triggers

- When I'm so worried about what I'm supposed to be, who I'm supposed to be and how I'm supposed to be, I can't figure out who I am and who I want to be. I must understand where those messages come from so I can address them and move on.

Practicing Critical Awareness

- In order to get to my real feelings about sex, my body, my physical health or my mental and emotional health, I have to acknowledge and filter all of the messages and expectations that block my way.

Reaching Out

- I need to talk about it, and because so few people are willing to have honest conversations about sex and health, I have to build connections with people who I can reach out to.

Speaking Shame

- I need to talk about my feelings and my needs so I don't cut myself off from these important parts of my life. I don't know what's normal; I just want to be my authentic self.

Next, we will look at the complex relationship between addiction and shame.

One way we ease the pain and discomfort of feeling inauthentic and different is substance abuse. We use food, alcohol, drugs, sex and relationships as relief. In this next section, we're going to take a closer look at the complex relationship between shame and addiction.

Addiction

"ADDICTIONS DO TO SHAME WHAT SALT WATER DOES TO THIRST."
Terrance Real, author of *I Don't Want to Talk About It:
Overcoming the Secret Legacy of Male Depression*

As you read through this book, you can see from the examples and stories that addiction and shame are inextricably connected. They are also very similar: Both leave us feeling disconnected and powerless. When we are in addiction, we have a tendency to either shut down or act out. Addiction can make us feel alone and on the outside. And lastly, there is often a sense of secrecy and silence about addiction.

Although many people think of addiction as a "guy's issue," that couldn't be further from the facts. Many of the most recent alcohol and drug studies show that teen girls are drinking more than boys and starting at an earlier age than their male peers. New research also shows that more college-age women are drinking, and drinking to get drunk. Researchers are finding that women often use alcohol to improve their mood, increase their confidence, reduce tension and feel less shy. Dr. Nora Volkow, director of the National Institute on Drug Abuse, calls alcohol a "social lubricant."

When I look back at my own history, the "social lubricant" idea certainly fits. Like many girls, I started drinking socially in high school. By college, I considered a cigarette and beer my social sword and shield. I'm not sure that I could have navigated a party or a bar without this armor. I never thought about my social dependence on drinking and smoking. Everyone I knew did it and everywhere I looked, the people I wanted to be did it. It was the 1980s—we were rebellious like the women in the Virginia Slims ads and we flocked to movies like *St. Elmo's Fire* and *About Last Night*.

It wasn't until I was in graduate school that I really learned about my family history of alcoholism. We never had much alcohol in our house and I didn't grow up around a lot of drinking. As I made my way through the personal work that most social work students do in conjunction with their studies, I learned that alcohol had ravaged the lives of many of my extended family members. I also started to get a clearer understanding of my own social dependence on alcohol. I quit drinking and smoking in 1996, the weekend I graduated with my master's degree in social work. I was lucky. I had the information and tools to make that choice and found the support I needed to put down the sword and shield. I consider my journey in recovery to be one of the greatest gifts in my life.

For many girls and women, their "bottoms" are much lower. They lose their partners, jobs, freedom or children. For many women, problematic alcohol use is connected to sexual assault, violence and/or dependence on other drugs. In a recent *Newsweek* article, studies are cited that show that young women who chronically abuse alcohol can get serious liver disease and ulcers and that all women who drink more than one drink a day are at higher risk for stroke, high blood pressure, suicide and breast cancer.

To better understand the role that shame plays in addiction (or perhaps the role addiction plays in shame), we need to understand how the two are connected. I intuitively knew there was a connection, but didn't really understand it. Shame and addiction feel so enmeshed in many ways that it's difficult to understand where one starts and the other ends. To get a better sense of how shame and addiction work together, I turned to the latest research examining their relationship.

In Chapter 2, I recommended the book *Shame and Guilt* by June Tangney and Ronda Dearing. In addition to their broader work on the topic, they also wrote an important article that recently appeared in the journal *Addictive Behaviors*. Ronda Dearing, who led the study, is a researcher at the Research Institute on Addictions, University of Buffalo, State University of New York. Rather than trying to translate the findings from their study, I thought it might be helpful for you to hear, firsthand, from the researcher. In an interview conducted specifically for this book, I asked Dr. Dearing to help us better understand the importance of her findings and how they might affect us. Here's what she had to say:

BB: I've read the book that you wrote with June Tangney and I think we agree that shame and guilt are two distinct emotions (Shame equals "I am bad" and Guilt equals "I did something bad"). What exactly do the terms *shame-proneness* and *guilt-proneness* mean?

RD: When we refer to shame-proneness and guilt-proneness, we are referring to any given individual's *tendency* to experience that emotion. In any given situation, some individuals are more likely to respond with an emotional reaction of shame, whereas others are less likely to experience shame, regardless of the situational triggers. We would refer to the individual who is likely to respond with shame as a shame-prone individual. To use a different example, some people may be "prone" to crying when they are feeling sad, whereas other individuals may feel sad equally often, but they are rather unlikely to cry in response to their sadness. We might refer to the tendency to cry as crying-proneness. Most individuals have a pretty good idea of whether they are prone to crying or not. Using measures such as the TOSCA [a research instrument], we present individuals with a variety of everyday situations and ask them to indicate their likelihood of responding in a variety of ways (some representing shame responses, others representing guilt responses). Using their responses, we can determine each person's tendency toward shame-proneness and guilt-proneness. Although it is possible to be both shame-prone *and* guilt-prone, it is more likely that a specific individual will respond with one emotion more than the other; thus, any given individual is more likely to be either shame-prone *or* guilt-prone, rather than both.

BB: In your article, you talk about the factors that lead to addiction. Specifically, you discuss the importance of understanding the difference between the "static" and "dynamic" factors associated with substance abuse. Can you help us understand what these terms mean?

RD: When I mention static factors, I am referring to things that really can't be changed. So, for example, although we know that genetic factors are related to one's likelihood of developing an addiction, a person really can't change the genes they were born with. Dynamic factors, on the other hand, are things that are constantly changing (or have the potential to change). Something like one's social network would be considered a dynamic factor. People have choices about who they socialize with, and any given individual can either choose to socialize with people who use drugs or people who don't (as just one example). We believe that shame-proneness and guilt-proneness are dynamic—they have the potential to be changed. Ideally, in a therapy setting, we'd like to help clients learn to become less shame-prone and more guilt-prone.

BB: In this study, you found a positive link between shame-proneness and problematic alcohol and drug use. What do you think is most important about this finding? What does it mean for people struggling with addiction?

RD: Well, first of all, I think that this finding is consistent with most of the other research on shame-proneness. Namely, the tendency to experience shame seems to be associated with negative life consequences, whether those consequences are difficulty managing anger, depressive symptoms, addictive problems, or anything else. So, I think that the most important thing about this finding is that it provides additional evidence that individuals who have a tendency to experience shame need to learn to derail this emotion in favor of the healthier emotional reaction, guilt. I think that many therapists try to help clients develop this skill, whether or not these therapists would specifically label their work as "shame reduction." However, there has been very little systematic research looking at ways to teach clients to reduce their tendency toward shame. Specific interventions of this type are much needed. And we need to test and validate these types of interventions using sound research methods, in order to provide therapists with specific tools to help their clients reduce shame.

BB: You also found that guilt-proneness may actually have a protective effect against the development of problematic alcoholic or substance abuse patterns. Can you help us understand what that means?

RD: People who are guilt-prone are likely to focus on the behavior in question. For example, a guilt-prone person who misses a day of work after a night of heavy drinking is likely to think, "If I keep missing work, I could lose my job." In contrast, a person who is shame-prone is much more likely to focus on what they view as a defective self ("I'm a complete failure because I keep missing work"). As you can imagine, it is much easier to change or fix any given behavior than it is to fix a defective self. So, as a result, the guilt-prone person in this situation will try to figure out what they can do differently. For instance, they might strategize about how it would be better not to drink on nights when they have to work the next day, or how it would be better not to drink to the point where they can't function effectively the next day. The shame-prone person, because he is overwhelmed by the emotion resulting from the realization that he is bad (defective, unworthy, etc.), can't problem-solve, and therefore can't make the same types of plans for how to do things differently (and hopefully better) the next time he finds himself in a similar situation. In essence, the shame-prone person gets stuck in the emotion, whereas the guilt-prone person is able to move on.

BB: I'm often asked if shame leads to addiction or if addiction leads to shame. What are your thoughts about this question?

RD: I don't think it is one or the other; I think it is both. I think that if a person has a shame-prone emotional style, he or she is at risk for developing an addiction. However, I think that once a person begins to struggle with issues related to their addition, shame is an inevitable consequence. So, for example, consider a person who has an addiction to alcohol. If that person is already shame-prone, his or her life problems that result from alcohol use (problems at work, problems at home, problems in relationships, et cetera) are likely to cause him or her to evaluate these shortcomings and react with feelings of shame and the accompanying interpretation that

"I must be a bad person." So, I think of the link between shame and addiction as a vicious cycle, and one that is difficult to change.

Resilience and Addiction

There are several issues that strike me as very important about this interview. The first is the cyclical relationship between shame and addiction. In the chapter on Speaking Shame, we talked about the three strategies of disconnection: moving away, moving toward and moving against. After years of using these strategies to fight shame, it is not easy to abandon them even when we know, at some level, that they are not effective. Many of us use these strategies to deal with unmet needs for empathy. Getting stuck in these disconnections not only moves us away from authenticity, but the "stuck" part also seems to play a central role in the relationships between shame and addiction.

The second issue, Dr. Dearing's references to therapists helping clients, is one that feels critically important to me. Throughout this book, as I've talked about the various ways that we build shame resilience, I've tried to emphasize, and I think it is worth repeating here, that, due to the complexities of shame, building resilience may require professional help from a therapist or counselor. If we are struggling with addiction, our family and friends are often negatively affected and truly incapable of helping. Dr. Abi Williams, director of the Center for Recovering Families, a division of the Council on Alcohol and Drugs in Houston, writes, "We estimate that three to four family members are directly affected to some degree when one of the members is making poor choices. These affected family members oftentimes believe that it is up to them to keep the family running smoothly; in truth, this belief might make matters even worse. The resulting behaviors in that family can become as destructive as the original problem the family was attempting to correct."

In this section on addiction, I want to clearly state that I believe we must seek outside help to overcome addiction. Help might come from a therapist, a recovery center or a twelve-step group, but we need to find outside help. Recovering from addiction requires guidance, support and information (and sometimes medical attention) beyond what we can get from even the most supportive connection networks.

Last, in Dr. Dearing's example, she said, "People have choices about who they socialize with, and any given individual can either choose to socialize with people who use drugs or people who don't." This is true. But one influence we need to examine in addition to our "social networks" is our culture.

We are members of a culture that fosters, then vilifies, addiction. Psychologist and activist Charlotte Sophia Kasl writes, "Patriarchy, hierarchy, and capitalism create, encourage, maintain and perpetuate addiction and dependency." As we've discussed throughout this book, the shame web is baited with expectations that are based on rigid gender prescriptions. If you combine the power of these expectations with the "us and them" mentality discussed in the section on *otherness* and the influence of the media culture, I believe she is right. We turn to food, drugs, alcohol, sex and dependent relationships to temporarily relieve the stress. And as expressed in the opening quote in this section, addiction doesn't relieve the stress, it only makes us more desperate for relief.

Additionally, we live in a shaming culture when it comes to addiction. On the one hand, we use negative stereotypes to characterize those struggling with addiction as smarmy, slippery, lying, cheating, untrustworthy and manipulative. On the other hand, we often use positive stereotypes to unrealistically describe men and women in recovery as pillars of spiritual strength who lead fearless and rigorously examined lives.

In supporting these cultural stereotypes, we often fail to acknowledge that all of us are, in some way, struggling, or connected to someone who is struggling, with addiction. And if we honestly reflect on our own lives, we know that stereotypes never capture the diversity, complexity and depth of real experiences.

Spirituality

The relationship between spirituality or faith and shame is a complex one. As you see in the illustrations of the shame web and the connection network, spirituality/faith/religion are sources of shame for some women and sources of resilience for others. I'm often asked if one religion was identified as "more shaming" than another. The answer is no. I saw no evidence of one religion or denomination being more shaming than another.

I did see important patterns and themes in terms of how women experienced their faith and spirituality. For example, the women who talked about feeling shame used the words *church* and *religion* more. The women who talked about resilience used the terms *faith*, *spirituality* and *beliefs* more. At first I wondered if there was a connection between "organized religion" and shame. I didn't find one. At least half of the women who used the terms *faith*, *spirituality* and *beliefs* attended church and were members of an organized religion.

What did become clear to me is this: It is the relationship that women have with God, their higher power or their spiritual world that often serves as a source of resilience. The essence of resilience, in a spiritual sense, is about relationship, spirit and faith. For many women, spiritual connection is essential to shame resilience. In fact, over half of the women who, as children, experienced deep shame around religion developed shame resilience by forging new spiritual paths. They may have changed churches or their beliefs, but spirituality and faith remain an important part of their lives. Another pattern that emerged is the belief that faith is about nurturing our best selves and shame moves us away from that purpose. The sources of shame seem much more connected to the earthly, man-made and interpreted rules and regulations and the social-community expectations around religion (Do you go to church regularly? Are you loyal to the family religion? Are you raising your kids a certain way? Are you breaking rules that might shame the family or community? Do you know your place as a woman?).

Just like in many other institutions (e.g., corporations, schools, medicine, government) individuals and groups in leadership positions can use shame as an instrument of control. When this happens in a repeated and systematic way, the entire organizational culture becomes shame-based. I don't believe, however, that any institution is inherently shaming—including those institutions that make up our faith communities.

For those of us who seek spiritual connection, understanding our faith history in relation to shame is very important. Many of the women who experienced religious-based shame as children found the greatest healing through faith and spirituality. Although they often changed churches, denominations and, sometimes, even beliefs, they healed shame-based religious wounds with spirituality.

My personal spiritual path has been changed by my work as a shame researcher. I now try to see my healthy experiences of guilt as a spiritual "checks and balances" system. When I do things or think things are inconsistent with who I want to be, I work on experiencing guilt as an opportunity for spiritual growth. On the other hand, when I experience shame, I now believe that it moves me away from the spiritual growth that is so important to me. There is a beautiful quote from spiritual teacher Marianne Williamson that really inspires me. As you read it, I invite you to think about what she has written in the context of experiencing shame:

> *Our deepest fear is not that we are inadequate. Our deepest fear is that we are powerful beyond measure. It is our Light, not our Darkness, that most frightens us. We ask ourselves, who am I to be brilliant, gorgeous, talented, fabulous? Actually, who are you NOT to be? You are a child of God. Your playing small does not serve the world. There is nothing enlightening about shrinking so that other people won't feel unsure around you. We were born to make manifest the glory of God that is within us. It is not just in some of us; it*

is in everyone. As we let our own Light shine, we unconsciously give other people permission to do the same. As we are liberated from our own fear, our presence automatically liberates others.

Given how important relationships are in our faith lives, you can see why it is so critical that we maintain our authenticity around our spiritual beliefs. In the next section, you will learn specific tools women are using to develop and maintain their authenticity in the face of shame and disconnection.

Authenticity and Resilience

We know from the beginning of this chapter that some of the qualities of authenticity include being natural, sincere, spontaneous, open and genuine. But what does authenticity look like in a person? When I think of authenticity, I think of Chaz, a very close friend of mine. I've known him for more than ten years and he is one of the most authentic people I know. He's the real deal.

Chaz certainly demonstrates all of the characteristics listed above, but I see his authenticity as something more. He is who he is, no matter who he's with and no matter what the circumstance. If you pulled people from all different parts of his life—people who don't know each other, but people who know him—they would probably all describe him in very similar ways. He is quite comfortable moving around and among many different types of people, but he articulates and acts on the same set of values and beliefs, regardless of who he is with or what they expect.

I saw this same quality in the women who clearly had high levels of shame resilience. To me, this quality of *being who you are regardless of who you are with* seems to be the very essence of authenticity—the result of being natural, sincere, spontaneous, open and genuine.

So how does authenticity relate to shame resilience? Based on the data, I would say that authenticity is difficult, if not impossible, to develop without some level of shame resilience. It is much easier to be authentic when we practice courage, compassion and connection. The participants spoke about the importance of building connections with people who support our goal of authenticity. Sometimes these people are also like-minded or like-spirited, but that's not the most important requirement—it's more important that they share our commitment to being authentic rather than just sharing our beliefs or values.

- During a very difficult conversation with my sister, she told me that she had trouble trusting me because I always tried to predict what people wanted and say whatever I thought they wanted to hear. She told me, "I don't care if we disagree. I just want to be able to count on you for the truth." I was ashamed that she perceived me that way, but it really helped me understand how I was being dishonest with everyone—especially myself. For the first few months after our conversation, I couldn't answer anyone's questions. I had totally lost track of what I really thought about issues. It's been about a year and I'm much more honest with myself and my family. My sister is so supportive and I feel like I have a lot more integrity.

- I used to feel like I had two choices with my parents—avoid conversations about religion or lie. Both options made me feel bad and caused huge problems between me and my husband. My parents are Catholic and they would always ask if we were going to Mass or if we were sending my son to catechism. I would tell them yes and try to end the conversation. My husband would tell them the truth—that we are Methodist—and they would go nuts. He told me that he felt abandoned when I lied to my parents to make them happy. I realized that I was being dishonest and hurting myself and him. I spoke with some friends from church who had similar experiences and they gave me great suggestions. I finally told my parents and explained that if they couldn't be supportive it would be best not to discuss it. They were mad but respectful . . . and that's OK.

Self-Empathy and the Strengths Perspective

One issue that is clear from the interviews is how incredibly hard we are on ourselves. More times than not, we are members of our own shame web. Even if we are only enforcing the expectations that we hear from others or from the media, we are still actively contributing to our own shame.

If we want to build shame resilience and cultivate our authenticity, we must learn how to become members of our own connection network. We must learn how to respond to ourselves with empathy and understanding. It takes a lot of work to stay out of judgment about others—it takes even more work to stay out of self-judgment. Our ability to be authentic and genuine often depends on our level of self-acceptance, our sense of belonging to ourselves and our ability to express self-empathy.

One way that we can increase our self-empathy and the connection to ourselves is to explore and acknowledge our strengths as well as our problems or limitations. As social workers, many of us do this using an approach called a "strengths perspective." According to social work educator Dennis Saleebey, the strengths perspective offers us the opportunity to examine our struggles in light of our capacities, talents, competencies, possibilities, visions, values and hopes. This perspective doesn't dismiss the pain and serious nature of our struggles; however, it does require us to consider our positive qualities as potential resources. Dr. Saleebey writes, "It is as wrong to deny the possible as it is to deny the problem."

One effective method for understanding our strengths is to examine the relationship between strengths and limitations. If we examine what we do best and what we want to change the most, we will often find that the two behaviors are varying degrees of the same core behavior. For example, I think about my own struggles of authenticity. Sometimes, when I'm feeling very critical of myself, I really question my authenticity. I judge myself for being too political and feeling chameleonlike in my behaviors. When I'm on my "work branch" I turn one color, when I'm at home I'm another color. When I'm with one set of colleagues I accent one hue and I turn on a completely different hue with a different set of colleagues. I can work myself into believing that I'm everything from slightly disingenuous to downright cheesy.

However, looking at those same behaviors from a strengths perspective, I could completely reframe my experiences. Rather than feeling inauthentic and chameleonlike, I can honestly say that I'm comfortable around many different people, in many different settings, and that I'm pretty comfortable discussing topics that range from economics to the latest Nick Jr. lineup on TV. I don't contradict myself, although I will avoid some subjects with some groups. I am often overwhelmed by how many different roles I play and how quickly I'm expected to switch gears; however, I think I do it pretty well and I would consider it a strength.

I can go through almost every one of my "faults" or "limitations" and find strengths. The purpose of doing this is not to dismiss the issues we'd like to change or invalidate our problems, but to allow us to work on those from a place of self-worth, empathy and connection. I think one of the most important things I learned from this research, and one of the key messages I hope I'm sending in this book, is this: *We cannot change and grow when we are in shame and we can't use shame to change ourselves or others.*

I can shame myself for being too controlling and uptight about my work, or I can recognize that I'm very responsible, dependable and committed to quality work. The issues at work don't go away, but from a strengths perspective I have the confidence to look at myself and assess the issues I'd like to change. It is important to understand that the strengths perspective is not a tool to simply allow us to put a positive spin on a problem and consider it solved, but rather to allow us to inventory our strengths so that we can use them to address the challenges.

I can shame myself for being too worried about my daughter all the time or I can reframe that using my strengths and focus on the fact that I'm trying to be a good parent and I'm a very thoughtful, involved and conscientious mother. From a place of self-worth it is easier for me to think about how I might be a better mom if I reality-check some of my fears and recognize that I'm doing plenty to keep her safe and happy. From a place of shame and disconnection, it would be very difficult for me to assess my behaviors, much less attempt to change them.

I often require my students to submit a "strengths assessment" at the beginning of the semester. I ask them to list ten to fifteen personal strengths. Be assured, I don't accept anything like "I'm a people person" or "I play well with others." They hate doing this exercise, which is ironic considering that this is something that social workers very often expect their clients to do. Not surprisingly, when I ask them to identify their limitations or opportunities for growth, they buzz right through it and normally list far more than the five examples I ask for. It's human nature. We focus on our shortcomings and ignore and take our strengths for granted.

It is critical that we catch ourselves doing things well. If we can acknowledge our strengths, they become tools that can help us meet our goals. For example, Natalie, a research participant, told me, "I can talk about my faith because I don't think there is one right answer—I'm not worried about sounding stupid. I don't care if people judge me, I just care about being honest. I freeze when people talk about politics or public issues. I feel so ashamed that I don't know more or I don't have the right information."

If Natalie wants to work on her authenticity around speaking out on political or social issues it would be very useful for her to assess the strengths that allow her to be authentic in her discussions about faith. What is she doing that makes her feel authentic? What tools is she using to be genuine in her discussions? Why is she comfortable talking about faith and not politics?

Based on my discussion with Natalie, I think it would be helpful for her to reframe her ideas about political and social issues' having only one right answer. She might also think about changing her goal from being right, having the right information and knowing more to being honest about her thoughts. She seems to do that really well.

Lastly, we can more readily identify our strengths and increase our resilience by adapting the reality-check questions to examine the expectations that attempt to govern how we articulate and act on our beliefs and values.

- How realistic are these expectations?
- Can I be all these things all of the time? Do I want to be?
- Can all of these characteristics exist in one authentic person?
- Does meeting the expectations make me more or less authentic?
- Am I describing my authentic self or who others want me to be?

When I asked participants how they determined who belongs in their connection network and who belongs in their shame web, about eighty percent of the women said something along the lines of "If I can always be myself with someone, they're in the connection network." I think the ability to "be ourselves" is both the heart of authenticity and the true benefit of building shame resilience.

Shame Resilience Theory

The information in this book is based on the theory of shame resilience that emerged from my research. I really like the definition of *theory* found in *The Fifth Discipline Fieldbook*—a wonderful book on building learning organizations. The authors define theory as a "fundamental set of propositions about how the world works, which has been subjected to repeated tests and in which we have gained some confidence. The English word 'theory' comes from the Greek root word *theo-rós*, meaning spectator. This derives from the same root as the word 'theater.' Human beings invent theories for the same basic reasons they invent theater—to bring out into a public space a play of ideas that might help us better understand our world."

My theory on shame is called the Shame Resilience Theory. It offers a set of propositions about how shame affects women. If we look at the continuums as distinct pieces of a larger puzzle, we can see how the theory comes together. The major propositions that explain how shame works are:

- Shame is best defined as the intensely painful feeling or experience of believing we are flawed and therefore unworthy of acceptance and belonging. Women often experience shame when they are entangled in a web of layered, conflicting and competing social-community expectations. Shame creates fear, blame and disconnection.

- The opposite of experiencing shame is experiencing empathy.

- Empathy requires that we practice ordinary courage, compassion and connection.

- We cannot become resistant to shame; however, we can develop shame resilience. Shame resilience is best conceptualized as a continuum, with shame anchoring one end and empathy anchoring the other end.

- Our level of shame resilience is determined by our combined ability to recognize shame and our specific triggers, our level of critical awareness, our willingness to reach out to others and our ability to speak shame. In other words, our position on the shame resilience continuum is actually the sum of our positions on these other four continuums.

- We must assess our shame resilience independently for each shame category. A high level of shame resilience in one area does not guarantee high shame resilience for all areas.

- Women with higher levels of shame resilience recognize shame when they are experiencing it and recognize their shame triggers. Understanding our triggers allows us to better recognize shame and reach out for support. When we don't know our vulnerabilities, we rely on ineffective methods to protect ourselves from the pain caused by shame. I call these "shame screens."

- Women who practice critical awareness have higher levels of shame resilience. Critical awareness helps us demystify, contextualize and normalize our shame experiences. A lack of critical awareness can result in our reinforcing, individualizing and pathologizing our shame experiences.

- Women who reach out to others who are experiencing shame have higher levels of shame resilience. Reaching out allows us to share our stories and create change. When we don't reach out to others, we often start separating and insulating ourselves from others.

- Women who speak shame have higher levels of shame resilience. Speaking shame gives us the tools we need to express how we feel and ask for what we need. When we don't speak shame, we often start to shut down or act out.

Shame Resilience Model

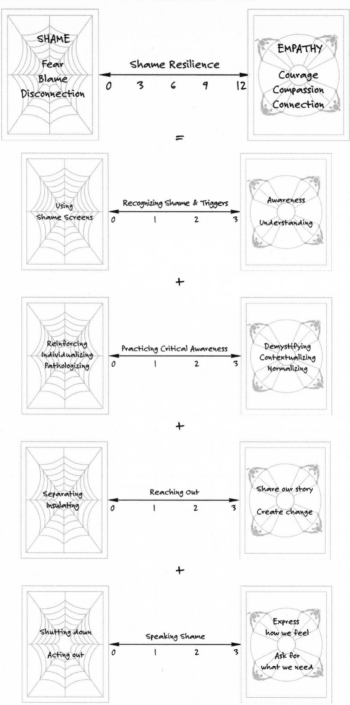

TEN

Creating a Culture of Connection

In April 2006, I attended an awards dinner hosted by the Feminist Majority Foundation. The celebration was in honor of four women who had won the prestigious Nobel Peace Prize: Shirin Ebadi (Iran, 2004), Rigoberta Manchú Tum (Guatemala, 1992), Betty Williams (Ireland, 1975) and Jody Williams (USA, 1997). At the end of the evening, women's rights activist Mavis Leno took the stage to close the event. She looked out at the enthusiastic audience and said, "We can all make a difference." I took a deep breath and waited to hear what would come next.

Unless you want to sound like a bumper sticker, how can you inspire people to change the world in one or two sentences? How do you help people believe they really can make a difference without overwhelming them with responsibility or patronizing them with clichés? Most of us haven't dedicated our lives to world peace. We aren't convinced that we have what it takes to change the world. In fact, sometimes it takes every ounce of our energy just to unload the dishwasher.

Well, I have to say that on this particular night, I was moved.

Mavis Leno nailed it. She looked at the audience and simply said, "If you want to make a difference, the next time you see someone being cruel to another human being, take it personally. Take it personally because it *is* personal!" It was the single most inspiring call to change I've heard.

We all know how to take it personally. In fact, when we witness cruelty, it's human nature to take it personally. If we choose not to get involved or pretend it's not happening, we're going against the very sense of connection that makes us human.

If we want to transform our culture of shame into a culture of connection—we need to take what we see, hear, witness and do *personally*. Shaming is cruel. When our children are watching reality TV shows that rely on shame and degradation as entertainment, we turn them off and explain why. When someone uses hurtful and demeaning stereotypes, we find the courage to explain why we're not comfortable with the conversation. When someone shares her shaming experience with us, we make the choice to practice compassion—we work to hear what she is saying and to connect to what she is feeling.

Taking it personally means changing the culture by owning our experiences and holding ourselves and others accountable. Too often, when we experience shame we stay quiet. If we do find the courage to tell our story, we are often told that we are "too sensitive" or that we are taking it "too personally." I've never understood that. Should we be insensitive and detached? The culture of shame feeds on insensitivity and detachment.

Caroline is a great example of the power of taking it personally. In the Introduction, I shared this snippet of her story:

> One day I was driving down the street in our neighborhood and I stopped next to a car full of young men at a light. They were looking over and smiling. I smiled back and even blushed a bit. Then out of nowhere, my fifteen-year-old daughter, who was sitting in the backseat with her best friend, snapped, "Geez Mom,

stop looking at them. What do you think—they're flirting with you? Get real!" I could barely hold the tears back. How could I have been so stupid?

Caroline was in her early fifties when we first met in 2003. She told me this story in 2005, when I interviewed her for a second time. She explained that her handling of this shaming moment was a turning point for her. Here's Caroline's story of ordinary courage and resilience.

It's not this experience that changed the way I feel about myself, it was how I handled it with my daughter. Rather than yelling at her or sulking, I decided to use what I knew about shame resilience. I dropped the girls off, came home and called my neighbor. We've been friends for a long time. I told her what happened and how ashamed I was. I told her that I was ashamed for smiling at the young men and I was ashamed of how my daughter treated me in front of her friend. When my friend asked me why I was ashamed for smiling at the men, I told her that I had actually thought, for one split second, that they were smiling at me. I explained that I forgot that I'm old and that doesn't happen anymore. She understood my shame. She didn't try to make it better. She just listened. Finally she said, "It hurts when they don't see us—the boys in the cars . . . our kids . . . they just stop seeing us." She understood.

My husband picked up my daughter from her friend's house and my other daughter from softball practice. When they got home I was in my room. I came out right away and asked my daughter if I could talk to her. She responded by saying, "Oh, God—are you menopausal again?" The rest of the family laughed. This time, rather than laughing with them or pretending not to care, I said, "No. You really hurt my feelings today and we need to talk about it." On that note, my husband and younger daughter flew out of the room.

I sat down with my daughter and explained how ashamed I felt when she made that comment and why. I even explained how hard it was for me as a woman, not as a mother, but as a woman. I told her that I understood that it was very important for her to be cool and have her friends like her. However, it was unacceptable for her to be hurtful to others in order to make that happen.

The entire time I was talking she was making faces and rolling her eyes. I finally reached out and took both of her hands and said, "What you said made me feel very ashamed and hurt. I'm telling you this because I know you love me and our relationship is important. I'm also telling you this so you know that you should not let people shame you or put you down so they look cool or popular. I won't let you do that to me and I hope you don't let anyone do that to you."

As Caroline told me her story, I waited anxiously to hear about her daughter's heartfelt apology and the tender mother-daughter embrace. Of course, it never happened. Caroline said that her daughter responded with a resounding "Oh, my God, can I please go now?" Caroline told her daughter that she needed to apologize, and she did. Then she went to her room, shut the door and turned on her radio. We will never know what impact this conversation had on Caroline's daughter; however, based on my professional and personal experience, I believe these conversations can be life-changing.

Caroline took it personally, and if all parents lived by these beliefs and had talks like this with their children, we would start to see the culture change. If the children who heard these talks expected more from themselves and their friends, we'd see a cultural shift. It doesn't take momentous events—it takes critical mass. If enough of us make small changes in our lives, we will see big changes.

To create real cultural change, I think it's equally important that we understand how men and children are affected by shame. I think it makes sense for shame resilience to start with women—we are often the primary caregivers of children, and women are more likely to be the psychological and cultural change agents for our families.

Resilience can start with us; however, it can't stop with us. We need to understand how and why men struggle with shame and how they build resilience. We need to understand how we can support and connect with our partners, sons, fathers, brothers, friends and colleagues. We also need to understand more about shame and children—for most of us, our experiences with parents and teachers shaped our current struggles with shame. In fact eighty percent of the people I interviewed could remember a specific shaming incident in elementary school or junior high that changed how they felt about themselves as learners.

In the following two sections, I'll share an overview of my new research on men and shame and my study on how shame is in parenting and in classrooms. These are both works in progress, but what I've learned so far speaks to how inextricably connected we all are.

Men and Shame

My initial decision to study only women was based on the current academic literature on shame. Many researchers believe that men and women's experiences of shame are different. Because I wanted to conduct an in-depth study of resilience, I chose to look at women only. I was concerned that if I combined the data from men and women I'd miss some of the important nuances of their experiences. I did actually interview some young men in the beginning of my study. I'll share that experience with you because it proved to be very profound.

Several years ago, when the shame categories (appearance and body image, motherhood, family, parenting, money and work, mental and physical health, addiction, sex, aging, religion, being stereotyped and labeled, speaking out and surviving trauma) first started emerging from the research, I interviewed groups of older teens to find out how the categories fit for this age group. My intention was to interview young women only. Well, as it turned out, the clinicians who ran the groups scheduled time for me to meet with several groups of young men.

I had never worked with older teenage boys before and I was a little nervous. I remember writing the categories on a chalkboard, sitting down, looking at this group of young men and thinking, "They aren't going to say anything."

I started with a question about appearance: "OK, guys, what about appearance? Are there expectations about how you're supposed to look?" They looked at one another and one young man said, "Yeah, miss. I gotta look like I can kick your ass." The rest of the boys laughed and agreed.

I moved on. "OK. What about health?" Again, they laughed. Another boy said, "Yeah, miss. It's the same thing. You can't be too sick to kick someone's ass."

Many of these boys were already fathers, so I thought I'd move away from the easy ones to something more complex like fatherhood. "OK, tell me about fatherhood." Again, they laughed, but a little less this time. One boy said, "Look. You talk about my baby or my baby's mother, I'm gonna kick your ass."

Well . . . call me a researcher, but I was starting to see a theme. The more we talked, the more I realized that these young men meant business. It didn't matter what they did or what they looked like as long as they maintained their image of being able to kick someone's ass.

I wrote up my "ass-kicking" field notes and filed them away. It wasn't until I started interviewing men last year that I realized how honest, poignant and truthful these young men had been. In their own language they told me almost everything I needed to know.

A Stranger, a Penis and a Feminist

In 2005, three separate incidents convinced me to commit more time to studying shame and men: a stranger, a penis and a feminist.

We'll start with the stranger. He was a tall, thin man who I'd guess was in his early sixties. He was attending one of my lectures with his wife. After the lecture, he followed his wife to the front of the room to talk to me. I spoke with her for a few minutes, and as she started to walk away, he turned to her and said, "I'll be right there—give me a minute." His wife looked concerned. I don't think she wanted him to stay and talk to me. She finally walked toward the back of the room and he turned to face me.

He said, "I like what you have to say about shame. It's interesting." I thanked him and waited—I could tell there was more coming. He said, "I'm curious. What about men and shame? What have you learned about us?" I felt instant relief. This wasn't going to take long, because I didn't know much. I explained, "I haven't done many interviews with men, just women." He nodded and said, "Well. That's convenient."

I was curious what he meant. I smiled and asked him, "Why convenient?" He replied by asking me if I really wanted to know. I told him yes and I meant it.

His eyes welled up with tears. He said, "We have shame. Deep shame. But when we reach out and share our stories, we get the emotional shit beat out of us." I struggled to maintain my eye contact with him. I felt like crying. He continued, "And it's not just by other guys. Of course, they beat it out of us. But so do the women. You say you want us to be vulnerable and real, but c'mon. You can't stand it. It makes you sick to see us like that."

By this point tears were streaming down my face. I had this very visceral reaction to what he was saying. He let out a long sigh, and as quickly as he had begun, he said, "That's all I wanted to say. Thanks for listening." Then he just walked away.

I was still processing that conversation when, a few days later, I was lying on a table as a woman glided a little receiver back and forth over my big pregnant belly. She looked at Ellen and said, "What do you want—a brother or a sister?" Ellen shouted, "A brother. I want a brother." The woman smiled and said, "It's your lucky day. Mommy is having a boy." I smiled at Ellen and put my hand on my stomach. "Are you sure?" I asked. She smiled, "I see the penis!" I managed to smile again at Ellen as she jumped up and down. On the inside I was screaming, "A boy! No. Not a boy! They get the emotional shit beat out of them. How will I protect him? I don't know anything about the boy world."

Fast forward to a few weeks after Charlie, my beautiful baby boy, was born. Charlie and I were having lunch with some of my favorite feminist friends when we started talking about the challenges of raising boys. As we were all doting on Charlie, my friend Debbie Okrina, a social worker and domestic violence activist, said, "You know, if we aren't helping boys and men, we're really not helping girls and women. We need to do more." Her statement led to a long and important conversation about gender and masculinity. Our conversation helped me put words to my strong belief that feminism is not just about equality for women, but also about the fight to liberate both men and women from our gender straitjackets. Until both men and women are allowed to be *who we are* rather than *who we are supposed to be*, it will be impossible to achieve freedom and equality.

A stranger, a penis and a feminist—it might sound like the start to a bad joke, but these three events changed my mind and my life. The next week I starting reading the literature and lining up interviews. It was overwhelming. At some level, I think my resistance was based on an intuitive sense that I would be stumbling into a new and strange world—a world of hurt.

Describing Shame

Before I even started interviewing, I had presented my theory to thousands of helping professionals and lay people. Over the years, I've e-mailed and spoke with many men about my work—some of them strangers, others friends and colleagues. Almost all of them would say something like "Your work fits for us, but there's something different about our experiences. Our world is different. The expectations are different."

As a researcher, the big question for me was this: Does shame resilience theory fit for men? If I interviewed men about their shame experiences and the various strategies they use to combat shame, would I find that, like women, they experience fear, blame and disconnection when they are in shame? Would they move out of shame using the same elements of shame resilience? Or, because the expectations that drive shame for both men and women are very gender-specific, would I need to develop an entirely new theory—one especially for men?

The conclusion I've drawn from my research is this: When we experience shame, we respond to it with our entire being. It affects the way we feel, think, and act; and, often, we have a strong physical response to shame. In other words, shame is a core emotion—it strikes us at our center and radiates through every part of us. While there are certainly significant differences between men and women's experiences, we are very much the same at our core.

As I wrote in the Introduction, we are wired for connection. All of us, men and women alike, have the basic need to feel accepted and to believe that we belong and are valued. The definition that I developed from my interviews with women fits equally well with men. Just like us, they experience shame as *the intensely painful feeling or experience of believing they are flawed and therefore unworthy of acceptance and belonging*. And, just as women described it, shame leaves men with overwhelming feelings of fear, blame and disconnection. In fact, if you look at the shame resilience model on page 270, it all fits. After interviewing fifty-one men, I feel confident that their experiences of shame and the strategies they use to build shame resilience are, again, at the core, the same basic process that women experience.

But there are tremendous differences when it comes to the social-community expectations that drive shame and the messages that reinforce those expectations. For men, the expectations and messages center around masculinity and what it means to "be a man." In other words—the "*how* we experience shame" might be the same, but the "*why* we experience shame" is very different.

In Chapter 2, I introduced the shame web and how women most often experience shame as a web of layered, conflicting and competing social-community expectations that dictate who we should be, what we should be and how we should be. When I spoke with men, I didn't hear about layered, conflicting and competing social-community expectations. The expectation, clear and simple: ***Do not let people see anything that can be perceived as weakness.***

- Who should men be? Anyone, as long as you're not perceived as weak.
- What should men be? Anything, as long as you're not perceived as weak.
- How should men be? Any way, as long as you're not perceived as weak.

And, to better understand what constitutes weakness, we can start by looking at the definitions of shame I heard from some of the men I interviewed:

- "Shame is failure. At work. On the football field. In your marriage. In bed. With money. With your children. It doesn't matter—shame is failure."
- "Shame is being wrong. Not doing it wrong, but being wrong."
- "Shame is a sense of being defective."
- "Shame happens when people think you're soft. It's degrading and shaming to be seen as anything but tough."
- "Revealing any weakness is shaming. Basically, shame is weakness."
- "Showing fear is shameful. You can't show fear. You can't be afraid. No matter what."

- "Shame is being seen as 'the guy you can shove up against the lockers.'"
- "Our worst fear is being criticized or ridiculed—either one of these is extremely shaming."

It is a major oversimplification, but if you think back to my story about the teenage boys and their "kick your ass" approach to avoiding shame, they seem to be right on target.

Men are under tremendous pressure to appear tough, strong, stoic, powerful, successful, fearless, in-control and able. These are the social-community expectations that form their valued identities. While women have the impossible task of balancing, negotiating and traversing expectations that are unattainable and often conflicting, men are suffocating under the tremendous pressure of always appearing "strong, fearless and powerful"—which is equally unattainable.

The metaphor I use to explain the phenomenon for women is the shame web. For men, I see something different. As men described their shame experiences to me, I started seeing a very small box. A box that is hammered closed by expectations of always appearing tough, strong, powerful, successful, fearless, in-control and capable.

As the mother of a one-year-old son, I've have learned and already witnessed that we place men in these small, cramped boxes very early—basically at birth. We keep them trapped by rewarding, reinforcing and punishing. We reward their willingness to stay in the box by celebrating their "toughness" and reinforce and punish by labeling any demonstration of vulnerability or emotion (especially fear, grief and sadness) as weakness. At first, when boys are little, they have some wiggle room in the box. Parents, peers and our society at large are more willing to tolerate vulnerability and emotion.

However, as boys grow older and bigger, there is less room in the box. We quash their efforts to escape by shaming boys and men for being weak, soft, fearful, inadequate, powerless, and incapable. And, based on the participants' stories, it seems that fathers and male peers can be especially wounding to boys and men who stray from the norms of masculinity. Certainly women—mothers, sisters, partners, girlfriends, daughters—also shame men about their masculinity and power; however, across the interviews they seem to have more of a "reinforcing role," whereas men, especially fathers, brothers, peers and coaches tend to do more punishing.

Paul's story is a powerful example of how shame and the fear of shame are used to reward, reinforce and punish men. Both Paul and his younger brother grew up playing competitive baseball—they even played in college. Paul said that he remembers his father saying things like "Don't be a pussy" and "Stay tough" as early as first or second grade. Paul described his life growing up as equal parts "stressful" and "awesome." The stress was due to the constant pressure to perform and succeed. But he also said, "I was always very popular and had lots of hot girlfriends." He also explained that he received many special allowances from teachers and school administrators due to his athletic abilities and popularity.

After college, Paul went to work for a dot-com owned by a friend and married Meg, a young woman he had dated in college. About one year into their marriage, Paul's company folded. He had received such an inflated salary at the dot-com that he struggled to find a comparable salary right away. After two months, he told Meg that he was going to take a sales job and that his salary would be about half of what it had been. He suggested to her that they sell their cars and buy less expensive cars and cut down on other shopping expenses. He told me, "Meg lost it. She said that it was totally unfair for her to have to give up her lifestyle because I couldn't find a job. She went on and on until she finally asked, 'Aren't you embarrassed that you can't support me?'"

Paul said he was devastated. He felt tremendous shame about not being able to make enough money and he was deeply hurt by Meg's lack of concern for him. Unsure what to do, he called his father for advice. In the middle of the story, Paul started to cry a bit. He told me that it was the first time he ever remembered crying in front of his father.

After listening to the story, Paul's father told him that he needed to "set Meg straight" and "get in their face at work about a better salary." When Paul asked what that meant, his father said, "Don't be so weak—you don't need to put up with that shit. Meg doesn't want to be married to someone who lets her talk that way. You're a bigger loser for letting her get away with that. And those guys at work want someone who has the balls to demand a better salary. What's wrong with you?"

Paul described the two days in which these conversations with his wife and father took place as "the beginning of the end." He went into what he called a "dark spot." He started hanging out with his friends and drinking almost every night. Meg and Paul got divorced and Paul's parents are now separated after twenty-five years of marriage. The good news is that, at the time of our interview, Paul's mother and brother had started visiting Paul more often and the three of them are trying to build a new, stronger relationship. He also told me that recognized that the drinking was "getting out of hand" and had decided to "slow down."

In Paul's story, we can see how his masculinity—his athleticism, winning and toughness—was rewarded. He was popular, he dated many attractive young women, he was given special privileges at school and he was offered an extremely high-paying job by a former teammate. We can also see how Meg reinforced the social-community expectations of men as providers by ridiculing him about his lower salary and his career struggles. Lastly, Paul's father's behavior is a clear example of how name-calling and shaming is often used to punish men when they don't meet the social-community expectations set before them.

I plan to continue interviewing men, possibly with the help of a male researcher. I think there are important conversations about shame and vulnerability that need to happen between men and women. Men are certainly socialized to hide their vulnerabilities and fears, but it seems that women play an important role in that socialization. One man told me, "Women would rather see us die on top of that white horse than to be forced to watch us fall off it." I think this captures a lot of what I heard in the interviews with both men and women. However, I don't think it's what we really want.

When men and women shame each other and reinforce unattainable gender expectations, we kill intimacy. If we can't be authentic, we can't connect in a meaningful way. Our relationships move from compassion and connection to fear, blame and disconnection. I don't think any of us want this for ourselves or for our children.

Shame, Parenting and Education

Shame starts at home. Fortunately, so does shame resilience. As parents, we have the opportunity to raise children who are courageous, compassionate and connected. We can choose to learn the tools we need to parent without using shame. We can even teach our children empathy skills. But as you might guess, before we can teach or model these skills, we must understand the role shame plays in our own lives and practice resilience in our relationships.

Parenting is a shame minefield. Not only do we hang our self-worth on how we are perceived as parents, but we hang a big part of it on how our children are perceived. We have to contend with our list of unwanted identities and an entirely new list for our children. We don't want to be perceived as bad parents and we don't want our children to be perceived as bad kids. Developing shame resilience is twice as difficult, but well worth the reward.

Once we begin practicing courage, compassion and connection as parents, we can start to help our children navigate their increasingly complex worlds. We might not be able to control what happens at our children's schools or in their peer groups, but when we teach them shame resilience, we help them recognize shame, move through it constructively and grow from their experiences.

It's important to understand that parents also have the power to teach and model fear, blame and disconnection. Sometimes our children learn fear, blame and disconnection because we use shame to parent them. Rather than focusing on their behaviors, we attack who they are or belittle them. We threaten them with disconnection or ridicule them in front of others.

Sometimes, even if parents aren't shaming their children, the children still experience fear, blame and disconnection simply because we haven't taught them the skills of shame resilience. So, even if we're not shaming them, we've left them very vulnerable to shame from teachers, coaches and peers.

I'm not singling out teachers and coaches—like the rest of us, most are doing the best they can with the information they have. I'm a teacher and I'm proud to say that both of my sisters are elementary school teachers. Teachers and coaches are also negotiating the culture of shame in their own professions. At the same time education spending is being cut and classrooms are overcrowded, teachers are under tremendous pressure to raise standardized test scores. Coaches who push too hard are criticized and parents who want their kids to be "winners" harass coaches who emphasize fun and health over winning. As I continue to interview parents, teachers, coaches and child-development experts, I hope to learn more about what we can do to change our own parenting approaches and build a stronger culture of connection for our children.

I think it's important that this book ends where it began—with connection. We are wired for connection. It's in our biology. As infants, our need for connection is about survival. As we grow older, connection means thriving—emotionally, physically, spiritually and intellectually. Connection is critical because we all have the basic need to feel accepted and to believe that we belong and are valued for who we are. Although it might seem overly optimistic that we can create a culture of connection simply by making different choices, I think it is possible. Change doesn't require heroics. Change begins when we practice ordinary courage.

RECOMMENDATIONS, RESOURCES AND REFERENCES

Recommendations and Resources

To see a complete list of recommended books and to access resources from the book, please visit www.brenebrown.com.

References

ONE

xix "... now a growing number of researchers and practitioners are examining shame and its role in a wide range of mental and public health issues ..."

The following articles/books explore the relationships between shame and various issues:

Balcom, D., Lee, R., and Tager, J. (1995). The systematic treatment of shame in couples. *Journal of Marital and Family Therapy, 21*, 55–65.

Dearing, R., Stuewig, J., and Tangney, J. (2005). On the importance of distinguishing shame from guilt: Relations to problematic alcohol and drug use. *Addictive Behaviors, 30*, 1392–1404.

Ferguson, T. J., Eyre, H. L., and Ashbaker, M. (2000). Unwanted identities: A key variable in shame-anger links and gender differences in shame. *Sex Roles, 42,* 133–157.

Hartling, L., Rosen, W., Walker, M., and Jordan, J. (2000). *Shame and humiliation: From isolation to relational transformation* (Work in Progress No. 88). Wellesley, MA: The Stone Center, Wellesley College.

Jordan, J. (1989). *Relational development: Therapeutic implications of empathy and shame* (Work in Progress No. 39). Wellesley, MA: The Stone Center, Wellesley College.

Lester, D. (1997). The role of shame in suicide. *Suicide and Life-Threatening Behavior, 27,* 352–361.

Lewis, H. B. (1971). *Shame and guilt in neurosis.* New York: International Universities Press.

Mason, M. (1991). Women and shame: Kin and culture. In C. Bepko (ed.), *Feminism and addiction* (pp. 175–194). Binghamton, NY: Haworth.

Nathanson, D. (1997). Affect theory and the compass of shame. In M. Lansky and A. Morrison (Eds.), *The widening scope of shame.* Hillsdale, NJ: Analytic.

Sabatino, C. (1999). Men facing their vulnerabilities: Group processes for men who have sexually offended. *Journal of Men's Studies, 8,* 83–90.

Scheff, T. (2000). Shame and the social bond: A sociological theory. *Sociological Theory, 18,* 84–99.

———. (2003). Shame in self and society. *Symbolic Interaction, 26,* 239–262.

Talbot, N. (1995). Unearthing shame is the supervisory experience. *American Journal of Psychotherapy, 49,* 338–349.

Tangney, J. P. (1992). Situational determinants of shame and guilt in young adulthood. *Personality and Social Psychology Bulletin, 18,* 199–206.

Tangney, J. P., and Dearing, R. (2002). *Shame and guilt.* New York: Guilford.

xxiv **"I'm not sure where the term *ordinary courage* first appeared, but I discovered it in an article on women and girls by researcher Annie Rogers."**

Rogers, A. G. (1993). Voice, play, and a practice of ordinary courage in girls' and women's lives. *Harvard Educational Review, 63,* 265–294.

3 **"Of course, there are some researchers and practitioners doing very important work on women and shame—June Tangney and Ronda Dearing, researchers and clinicians at the Stone Center at Wellesley; Harriet Lerner; and Claudia Black, to name just a few."**

June Tangney and Ronda Dearing are the authors of *Shame and Guilt* by Guilford Press.

Harriet Lerner is the author of several books, including *The Dance of Anger, The Dance of Connection* and *The Dance of Fear.*

Claudia Black is the author of several books, including *It Will Never Happen to Me* and *Changing Course.*

To learn more about the Stone Center and the Wellesley Centers for Women, visit www.wcwonline.org.

13 **"The majority of shame researchers agree that the difference between shame and guilt . . ."**

I believe the best review of the current literature on shame and guilt can be found in *Shame and Guilt* by June Tangney and Ronda Dearning (Guilford Press).

15 **"Donald Klein captures the differences between shame and humiliation when he writes . . ."**

Klein, D. C. (1991). The humiliation dynamic. An overview. *The Journal of Primary Prevention, 12*(2), 93–122.

21 **"For example, research show that overweight and obese women have lower incomes . . ."**

For information on size discrimination, visit http://loveyour-body.nowfoundation.org. The study is from Schwartz, John (1993). "Obesity Affects Economic, Social Status: Women Far Worse, 7-Year Study Shows." *Washington Post*, September 30, 1993, p. A1.

22 **". . . the average American is exposed to more than three thousand advertisements a day . . .":**

Kilbourne, J. (1999). *Can't buy my love: How advertising changes the way we think and feel.* New York: Touchstone.

"Marilyn Frye defines a double bind as a situation . . ."

Frye, M. (2001). Oppression. In M. Anderson and P. Collins (Eds.), *Race, class and gender: An anthology.* New York: Wadsworth.

29 **"We believe that the most terrifying and destructive feeling . . ."**

Miller, J. B., and Stiver, I. P. (1997). *The healing connection: How women form relationships in both therapy and in life.* Boston: Beacon Press.

TWO

33 **"Another definition I like comes from a counseling textbook by writers Arn Ivey, Paul Pederson and Mary Ivey. They describe . . ."**

Ivey, A., Pederson, P., and Ivey, M. (2001). *Intentional group counseling: A microskills approach.* Belmont, CA: Brooks/Cole.

37   **"In the growing body of empathy research . . ."**

Read more about the importance of empathy in Daniel Goleman's work on emotional intelligence:

Goleman, D. (2005). *Emotional intelligence: Why it can matter more than I.Q.* New York: Bantam.

"Teresa Wiseman, a nursing scholar in England . . ."

Wiseman, T. (1996). A concept analysis of empathy. *Journal of Advanced Nursing, 23,* 1162–1167.

39   **"According to research conducted by Sidney Shrauger and Marion Pattersen . . ."**

Shrauger, S., and Patterson, M. (1974). Self evaluation and the selection of dimensions for evaluating others. *Journal of Personality, 42,* 569–585.

43   **"In her article on ordinary courage in girls' and women's lives, Annie Rogers . . ."**

Black, C. (1999). *Changing course: healing from loss, abandonment and fear.* Bainbridge Island, WA: MAC Publishing.

Rogers, A. G. (1993). Voice, play, and a practice of ordinary courage in girls' and women's lives. *Harvard Educational Review, 63,* 265–294.

44   Chödrön, P. (2002). *The places that scare you: A guide to fearlessness in difficult times.* Boston: Shambhala Classics.

49   **". . . Lorraine Gutiérrez and Edith Anne Lewis's concept of connection . . ."**

Gutiérrez, L., and Lewis, E. (1999). *Empowering women of color.* New York: Columbia University Press.

57   **"On missing the opportunity to be empathic . . ."**

Miller, J. B., and Stiver, I. P. (1997). *The healing connection: How women form relationships in both therapy and in life*. Boston: Beacon Press.

62   **"There is a small group of researchers, especially those working from an evolutionary or biological perspective . . ."**

If you are interested in reading alternative perspectives on shame, I recommend the following book. It is fairly academic, so the reading can be a bit heavy: Lansky, M., and Morrison, A. (Eds.) (1997). *The Widening Scope of Shame*. Hillsdale, NJ: The Analytic Press.

66   **"In an editorial piece written by Poe . . ."**

Poe, T. (1997, September 17). Shame is missing ingredient in criminal justice today [Op/Ed]. The *Houston Chronicle*, p. A27.

Lerner, H. (2001) *The dance of connection: How to talk to someone when you're mad, hurt, scared, frustrated, insulted, betrayed or desperate*. New York: Harper Collins.

THREE

74   **"Researchers Tamara Ferguson, Heidi Eyre and Michael Ashbaker argue that 'unwanted identity' is . . ."**

Ferguson, T. J., Eyre, H. L., and Ashbaker, M. (2000). Unwanted identities: A key variable in shame-anger links and gender differences in shame. *Sex Roles, 42*, 133–157.

80   **"From the field of health psychology . . ."**

Aiken, L., Gerend, M., and Jackson, K. (2001). Subjective risk and health protective behavior: Cancer screening and cancer prevention. In A. Baum, T. Revenson and J. Singer (Eds.),

Handbook of health psychology (pp. 727–746). Mahwah, NJ: Erlbaum.

Apanovitch, A., Salovey, P., and Merson, M. (1998). The Yale-MTV study of attitudes of American youth. Manuscript in preparation.

"From the field of social psychology, personal vulnerability . . ."

Sagarin, B., Cialdini, R., Rice, W., and Serna, S. (2002). Dispelling the illusion of invulnerability: The motivations and mechanisms of resistance to persuasion. *Journal of Personality and Social Psychology, 83*, 3, 536–541.

"Judith Jordan, a Relational-Cultural theorist from the Stone Center . . ."

Jordan, J. (1992). Relational resilience (Work in Progress No, 1992). Wellesley, MA: The Stone Center, Wellesley College.

I also recommend reading the working papers written by the researchers and clinicians at the Stone Center and the Wellesley Centers for Women. You can purchase and download these papers at www.wcwonline.org.

88   **"Dr. Shelley Uram, a Harvard-trained psychiatrist . . ."**

This information was taken from a workshop on women and addiction sponsored by The Meadows, a multidisorder facility specializing in the treatment of trauma and addictions. The Meadows Web site is www.themeadows.org. The information was also published in the following article:

Uram, S. (2006). Traveling through trauma to the journey home. *Addiction Today, 17, 99.*

89 **"Dr. Linda Hartling, a Relational-Cultural theorist, uses Karen Horney's work . . ."**

Hartling, L., Rosen, W., Walker, M., and Jordan, J. (2000). Shame and humiliation: From isolation to relational transformation (Work in Progress No. 88). Wellesley, MA: The Stone Center, Wellesley College.

FOUR

95 **"What is the impact of these expectations? Well, let's see . . ."**

The information on dieting and obesity was taken from U.S. Government statistics; Jean Kilborne's 1999 book *Can't buy my love: How advertising changes the way we think and feel;* and the Love Your Body Web site (retrieved in 2006 from http://loveyourbody.nowfoundation.org).

The information on plastic surgery was taken from the American Society for Aesthetic Plastic Surgery (retrieved in 2006 from www.surgery.org/press/procedurefacts.php).

96 **"Who benefits from the appearance expectations?"**

These industry estimates were taken from Wikipedia Encyclopedia.

110 **"What political, social and economic realities do divorced women face?"**

Bogolub, E. (1994). Child support: Help to women and children or government revenue? *Social Work, 39,* 5, 487–490.

McKeever, M., and Wolfinger, N. (2001). Reexamining the economic costs of marital disruption for women. *Social Science Quarterly, 82,* 1, 202–218.

FIVE

130   **"I once heard her describe laughter as a 'bubbly, effervescent form of holiness.'"**

I heard this quote while watching one of Anne Lamott's book readings on BookTV on C-SPAN 2.

133   **"Marketing research shows that women are the decision makers . . ."**

Quinlan, M. L. (2003). *Just ask a woman: Cracking the code of what women want and how they buy.* Hoboken, NJ: Wiley.

134   Lerner, H. (1990). *The dance of intimacy: A woman's guide to courageous acts of change in key relationships.* New York: Harper Collins.

143–   ***Shame* by Vern Rutsala**
44   This poem was first published in *The American Scholar* (Autumn 1988, Vol. 57 Issue 4, p. 574). The poem also appears in Vern Rutsala's book, *The Moment's Equation* (2004, Ashland Poetry Press). *The Moment's Equation* was a 2005 National Book Award Finalist.

Special thanks to Professor Rutsala for allowing us to reprint the poem.

SIX

156   **"Narrative therapists Jill Friedman and Gene Combs, write . . ."**

Friedman, J., and Combs, G. (1996). *Narrative therapy: The social construction of preferred realities.* New York: Norton.

SEVEN

204   Pipher, M. (1997). *In the shelter of each other: Rebuilding our families.* New York: Ballantine Books.

206 **"Harriet Lerner offers some wonderful advice . . ."**

Lerner, H. (2001). *The dance of connection: How to talk to someone when you're mad, hurt, scared, frustrated, insulted, betrayed or desperate.* New York: Harper Collins.

EIGHT

214 **"Shame researchers June Tangney and Ronda Dearing . . ."**

Tangney, J. P., and Dearing, R. (2002). *Shame and guilt.* New York: Guilford.

217 **"A stereotype is an overgeneralized and rigid definition . . ."**

Robbins, S. P., Chatterjee, P., and Canda, E. R. (2006). *Contemporary human behavior theory: A critical perspective for social work.* (2nd ed.). Boston: Allyn and Bacon.

219 **"According to researchers, positive stereotypes produce . . ."**

Miller, P., Miller, D., McKibbin, E., and Pettys, G. (1999). Stereotypes of the elderly in magazine advertisements 1956-1996. *International Journal of Aging and Human Development, 49, 4,* 319–337.

"Here's what Michelle Hunt, an organizational development and diversity expert, writes . . ."

Senge, P., Kleiner, A., Roberts, C., Ross, R., and Smith, B. (1994). *The fifth discipline fieldbook: Strategies and tools for building a learning organization.* New York: Doubleday.

224–225 **Research on negative and positive aging stereotypes:**

Hummert, M. L. (1990). Multiple stereotypes of elderly and young adults: A comparison of structure and evaluation. *Psychology and Aging, 5,* 182–193.

Hummert, M. L. (1993). Age and typicality judgements of stereotypes of the elderly: Perceptions of elderly vs. young adults. *International Journal of Aging and Human Development*, 37, 217–227.

Hummert, M. L., Garstka, T. A., Shaner, J. L., and Strahm, S. (1994). Steretotypes of the elderly held by young, middle-aged, and elderly adults. *Journal of Gerontology*, 49, 240–249.

Hummert, M. L., Garstka, T. A., Shaner, J. L., and Strahm, S. (1995). Judgements about stereotypes of the elderly. *Research on Aging*, 17, 168–189.

Ingersoll-Dayton, B., & Talbott, M. M. (1992). Assessments of social support exchanges: cognitions of the old-old. *International Journal of Aging and Human Development*, 35, 125–143.

Schmidt, D. F., & Boland, S. M. (1986). Structure of perceptions of older adults: Evidence for multiple stereotypes. *Psychology and Aging*, 1, 255–260.

239 **". . . a problem-posing dialogue developed by researcher and educator Mary Bricker-Jenkins."**

Bricker-Jenkins, M. (1991). The propositions and assumptions of feminist social work practice. In M. Bricker-Jenkins, N. Hooyman and N. Gottlieb (Eds.), *Feminist social work practice in clinical settings* (pp. 271–303). Newbury Park, CA: Sage Publications.

NINE

242 **"Social work educators Dean H. Hepworth, Ronald H. Rooney and Jane Lawson . . ."**

Hepworth, D. H., Rooney, R. H., and Lawson, J. A. (1997). *Direct social work practice: Theory and skills.* Pacific Grove: Brooks/Cole Publishing Co.

253   **"Many of the most recent alcohol and drug studies . . ."**

Studies cited in *Newsweek*/MSNBC—"Gender Equality":
Young women are catching up with their male counterparts
when it comes to alcohol—often to disastrous effect. Retrieved 4/26/06 from www.msnbc.msn.com. Article cites
studies from the National Center on Addiction and Substance Abuse at Columbia University.

254   **"Ronda Dearing, who led the study . . ."**

Dearing, R., Stuewig, J., and Tangney, J. (2005). On the
importance of distinguishing shame from guilt: Relations to
problematic alcohol and drug use. *Addictive Behaviors, 30*,
1392–1404.

259   **"Psychologist and activist Charlotte Sophia Kasl . . ."**

Kasl, Charlotte (1992). *Many roads one journey: Moving beyond
the 12 steps.* New York: Harper Paperbacks.

261   **"There is a beautiful quote . . ."**

Williamson, Marianne. (1992). *A return to love: reflecting on the
principles of a course in miracles.* New York: HarperCollins.

264   **"According to social work educator Dennis Saleebey, the
strengths perspective . . ."**

Saleebey, D. (1996). The strengths perspective in social work
practice: Extensions and cautions. *Social Work, 41,* 3,
296–306.

267   **"I really like the definition of *theory* found in *The Fifth
Discipline Fieldbook* . . ."**

Senge, P., Kleiner, A., Roberts, C., Ross, R., and Smith, B.
(1994). *The fifth discipline fieldbook: Strategies and tools for building a learning organization.* New York: Doubleday.

Brené Brown, Ph.D., L.M.S.W., is an educator, writer, and nationally renowned lecturer, as well as a member of the research faculty at the University of Houston Graduate School of Social Work, where she recently completed a six-year study of shame and its impact on women. She lives in Houston, Texas, with her husband and two children.